STRUCTURAL FUNCTIONS

OF HARMONY

STRUCTURAL FUNCTIONS OF HARMONY

By

ARNOLD SCHOENBERG

Revised Edition with Corrections

Edited by LEONARD STEIN

W · W · NORTON & COMPANY · INC · NEW YORK

ISBN 0 393 00478 3 Paper Edition
ISBN 0 393 02089 4 Cloth Edition

Library of Congress Catalog Card No. 74-81181

PRINTED IN THE UNITED STATES OF AMERICA
7 8 9 0

CONTENTS

ACKNOWLEDGEMENT

I HAD been constantly dissatisfied with the knowledge of harmony of my students of composition at the University of California, Los Angeles. To remedy this shortcoming I instituted a new class to which the conventional harmony teaching should be the prerequisite: STRUCTURAL FUNCTIONS OF HARMONY. At this time (1939) a young former student of mine, Leonard Stein, had already become my assistant and remained in this capacity for the next three years. Thus naturally when I started to write the present book I could not select one better to help me express my ideas. He had observed the development of these ideas from the very beginning and had watched me struggling with their formulation.

I was not wrong in this selection. While perhaps a perfectionist might have tortured me with corrections of my English, upsetting the flow of ideas, he had the patience to let me pronounce my sentences in their rudest forms if only they expressed the idea clearly. Of course the gravest grammatical errors had to be eliminated, but the polishing of the style could be postponed.

In spite of the preliminary work done in classes and Mr. Stein's collection of notes and examples at this time, the real writing and frequent rewriting of the book demanded nearly two years. The extreme number of examples necessary for illustrating and clarifying every problem, the application of the theories in the analysis of the examples from literature and the inevitable work of writing and copying are indications of Mr. Stein's share in the production of this book.

I use with pleasure this opportunity to thank him for his intelligent, careful, assiduous and discriminating assistance.

ARNOLD SCHOENBERG

28 *March* 1948

PREFACE TO
THE REVISED EDITION

THE REISSUANCE OF *Structural Functions of Harmony* some fifteen years after its first publication is an important event for a number of reasons: not only does it permit the correction of numerous errors and the inclusion of a much-needed index for accessibility of material, but, more importantly, it offers again the definitive statement of a central musical problem by one of the great creative minds of our time. Appropriately this new edition arrives at a time—eighteen years after its author's death—when Schoenberg's towering influence and authority as composer and theorist have become widely accepted. In fact, his words have greater pertinence today, and for a wider public, than they ever had during his lifetime.

Structural Functions can be studied not only as a practical guide in harmonic technique and analysis but, at the same time, as a document of the evolution of Schoenberg's own musical philosophy. In the course of this work one can trace the basic presentation of harmonic principles, their enlargement into a unified system of *monotonality* which, in turn, is applied to the examination of various kinds of musical forms from the eighteenth century to the twentieth, leading, logically and inevitably, to a consideration of their relevance to twelve-tone composition. Schoenberg's statement in the last chapter ("Apollonian Evaluation of a Dionysian Epoch"):

One day there will be a theory which abstracts rules from these [twelve-tone] compositions. Certainly, the structural evaluation of these sounds will again be based on their functional potentialities.

not only has a prophetic ring in our contemporary theory and practice, but also emphasizes his evolutionary concept of musical composition.[1]

As has been noted elsewhere, this work is the result of Schoenberg's teaching in an American university. It includes

[1] Although Schoenberg himself originally wanted to have this last chapter appear first and was overruled by the first publisher to whom he submitted the manuscript, the present order does not materially alter the inherent consequences leading from the study of harmony to its ultimate goal.

material collected by his students in class, much of which he improvised on the spot. Discovering then (1936–43) that his students were poorly prepared, he compiled a number of basic texts in harmony, counterpoint, and composition in an attempt to correct their deficiency.[2] These texts, therefore, strongly emphasize training in fundamentals and can be used by beginners in musical theory; but they also pose new concepts and interpretations which challenge musicians at any stage of their development.

Structural Functions stands in direct lineal descent from Schoenberg's first great text, his *Harmonielehre*.[3] Acquaintance with this earlier book is of inestimable value for a thorough understanding of the later text, although Schoenberg, realizing that a complete translation of *Harmonielehre* was not available, undertook a condensation of some of its basic principles in Chapter II of the present work. Among these principles the most important is the concept of *root progressions*. This is the foundation of Schoenberg's explanation of all harmony progressions, involving altered chords as well as simple triads. Starting with this basic assumption, it is applied at first to diatonic harmony, then to chords constructed with substitute tones (Chapter III), to transformations (Chapter V), and finally to vagrant harmonies (Chapter VI). It is recommended that one studies alterations of chords in this order before proceeding to the study of regions. The regions in minor, particularly (see Chapter IV), involve the use of altered chords before their elaboration in succeeding chapters. The other main derivation of altered chords, that of tonic minor and subdominant minor, which plays an important part in the *Harmonielehre,* is now incorporated into the discussion of "Interchangeability of Major and Minor" (Chapter VII).

It is this very change of interpretation, from chord derivation to *region,* which distinguishes *Structural Functions* from the *Harmonielehre* and is its main point of departure. What

[2] Besides *Structural Functions of Harmony* these works include *Models for Beginners in Composition* (G. Schirmer, 1942), *Preliminary Exercises in Counterpoint* (Faber and Faber, 1963), and *Fundamentals of Musical Composition* (Faber and Faber, 1967).
[3] Originally published in 1911, subsequently revised in 1922 and reprinted in 1966 (Universal Edition, Vienna), it has been partially translated into English under the title, *Theory of Harmony* (Philosophical Library, New York, 1948).

appeared as modulation in the *Harmonielehre* (and in most other treatises on harmony as well) now becomes part of a unified concept of monotonality (see p. 19 for a complete explanation), so that instead of measuring distances from key to key (by their relationship within the circle of fifths) a single tonality (tonic) is accepted as the center of all harmonic movement to and from its various regions. Although Schoenberg had for many years employed terms associated with regions, he did not apply them consistently until his *Models for Beginners in Composition* in 1942: in its Glossary there is a definition of regions which is essentially the one found in *Structural Functions*. However, it is only in the latter work that Schoenberg provides a thorough explanation of their relationships, principally in the "Chart of the Regions" (pp. 20 and 30) and in "Classification of Relationship" (Chapter IX). Admittedly, the theory is not complete; Schoenberg, as was his usual custom, postulated certain hypotheses regarding the main problem of key relationships within a composition — how, in fact, harmony functions in determining the structure of a piece. Of the relationships between the regions many, but not all, are explored, at first in four-part harmony. Moreover, when the regions are later applied to the analysis of examples from literature, many instances occur where other explanations of regions could be given. An examination of the classification of regions (Chapter IX) shows the difficulty of finding simple analyses for indirect and remote relationships. This results from a number of causes — the effect of enharmonic changes, the approach to regions from "flats or sharps," the interchangeability of major and minor, etc. — so that more than one region at a time may be valid. Further ambiguities may be brought about by the multiple meanings of transformations, vagrant harmonies, and other altered chords. It is suggested that theorists and students search for other solutions to these problems of regions.

In cases where the relationships move very rapidly, as in the *Durchführung* [Development section] or among the so-called "free forms" (see Chapter XI), only the concept of *roving harmony* is applicable (see p. 164). Although he seemingly avoids the issue of regions, Schoenberg does not claim

that this theory will explain every relationship (see his statement on p. xii). Instead, as he had done in his other theoretical
writings, he advances certain concepts which can be absorbed
by anyone who is able to master the basic ideas of musical
relationships and is not merely satisfied with superficial defini-
tions or attracted by the ephemeral qualities of music. It may
be true, as some critics claim, that Schoenberg is essentially a
preserver of traditional values rather than the revolutionary
he is popularly supposed to be. Unlike most preservers of
the past, however, who only seek, by historical or stylistic
references, to codify theory within a closed system, his concepts, though rooted in tradition, are vital to our time because
they derive from the resources of an ever-enquiring and
constantly growing musical intellect. Thus, above all, *Structural Functions* should be approached as a challenge to the
musician who wishes to deepen and enrich the understanding
and practice of his craft.

LEONARD STEIN

Los Angeles, California, 1969

EDITOR'S PREFACE TO
THE FIRST EDITION

WRITTEN in the last years of Schoenberg's life, *Structural Functions of Harmony* represents the master's final thoughts on "traditional" harmony, and sums up all his conclusions on the subject subsequent to the *Harmonielehre*. There is no need for me to stress the value and importance of this work; the reader will be able to appreciate this for himself. Having been entrusted by Mrs. Schoenberg with the task of preparing the book for publication, I need only explain the extent of such "editing" as has been done. This has mainly consisted of purely grammatical alterations designed to make easier reading here and there, without altering Schoenberg's thought in any way. In addition some explanatory phrases have been interpolated; these are enclosed in square brackets. Schoenberg's prose style was always extremely compressed, even elliptical; and these interpolations are merely designed to bring out the meaning more easily.

The remaining problem is that of the technical terms used. Many of these were devised by Schoenberg himself, and do not correspond to the normal American or English usages; as Mrs. Schoenberg says: "He was striving sometimes for days to find the right expression if he felt that many of the usual terms were misleading and erroneous and did not correspond to the meaning". In these circumstances, and also in view of the fact that the book is designed for both American and English readers, whose musical nomenclature often varies considerably from each other's, clearly the right course is to leave Schoenberg's musical terms without alteration, and to provide an explanatory glossary of those terms which differ from either American or English usage. This will be found on p. 197.

In conclusion, I would draw the reader's special attention to the Chart of the Regions (p. 20); thorough mastery of the symbols contained in this chart is essential for the understanding of the analyses in the latter part of the book. In particular, it is important to remember Schoenberg's practice, following the normal German usage, of writing the names of major keys in capitals and of minor keys in small letters, without any explanatory "major" or "minor"—thus **F**= F major; **f**=F minor; **SD**=subdominant major; **sd**= subdominant minor.

My grateful thanks are due to Mr. Leonard Stein of Los Angeles, who helped Schoenberg in the preparation of the book, particularly with regard to the musical examples. His practical assistance and advice have been invaluable.

Many thanks are also due to the following publishers for permission to print quotations from copyright works.

Strauss. Salome	Boosey & Hawkes Ltd.
Grieg. Cello Sonata ⎱	Hinrichsen Edition Ltd., the proprie-
Reger. Violin Concerto ⎰	tors of Peters Edition.
Schoenberg. Der Wanderer ⎫ Lockung ⎪ 1st Chamber Symphony ⎬ Pelleas & Melisande ⎭	By arrangement with Universal Edition (Alfred A. Kalmus, London)
Dvorak. New World Symphony	Alfred Lengnick & Co., Ltd.
Debussy. Images	Edition Jean Jobert and United Music Publishers Limited

HUMPHREY SEARLE

London

THE USE OF THIS BOOK FOR TEACHING
AND SELF-INSTRUCTION

THIS book contains in condensed form the methods of teaching harmony as presented in my *Harmonielehre*. Those whose training is based on these methods will easily be able to follow the more remote conclusions on the evaluation of structural functions. Unfortunately the understanding of harmony by many students is superficial, and foreign to the procedures of great composers. This is caused by the general use of two obsolete teaching methods. One, consisting of writing parts above a figured bass, is much too easy a task; the other, harmonizing a given melody, is too difficult. Both are basically wrong.

Practising part-writing is the only achievement of the figured-bass method. The expectation that becoming familiar with correct harmonic progressions will train the ear is not justified. If such were the case, familiarity with good music would make further teaching superfluous. Besides, playing from figured bass is no longer customary. I suppose that my generation was the last to know it. Today even good organists prefer written-out harmonies to the obsolete shorthand notation.

Harmonizing given melodies is in contradiction to the process of composition; a composer invents melody and harmony simultaneously. Subsequent correction may sometimes be necessary; improvements anticipating later developments and adaptations for changed purposes may challenge the composer's technique. One might also be obliged to harmonize a melody—a folksong, or one by a "one-finger composer". Again, this can be done only by one who has been born with or has acquired the sense for the evaluation of harmony.

More than forty years of experience have proved to me that it is not difficult to study harmony according to the method of my *Harmonielehre*—that is, to compose harmony progressions from the very beginning. It is also the intention of this book to provide students who have been taught in other ways with a full insight into this technique. Basic advice for this purpose is given in Chapter II; additional recommendations appear in the following chapters.

Of course, part-leading must not be allowed to be a handicap to one who attempts these advanced studies. One who cannot control four parts with a certain ability either has not worked seriously or is entirely untalented and should give up music at once.

Knowing the *treatment of dissonances*, obeying the advice for the use of root progressions, and understanding the process of " neutralization "[1] will provide the background for further conclusions. It is important to relate " substitutes "[2] and " transformations "[3] to degrees[4], and to understand that they do not alter the structural functions of the progressions. They intensify the affinity between tones and promote melodically convincing part-leading.

It should not be overlooked that harmonies with multiple meaning—the " vagrants "[5]—may occasionally proceed in conflict with the theory of root progressions. This is one of the short-comings of every theory—and this theory cannot claim to be an exception; no theory can exclude everything that is wrong, poor, or even detestable, or include everything that is right, good, or beautiful.

The best I can aim at is to recommend such procedures as will seldom be wrong, to draw the attention of the student to the fact that there are distinctions to be made, and to give some advice as to how the evaluation of harmonic progressions will help him to recognize his own shortcomings.

[1] See p. 18 and p. 24.

[2] cf. Chapter III.

[3] cf. Chapter V.

[4] "Degree" means the *root* and the *chord* constructed on a degree of the scale. " The tones of the scale, each of which is the root or lowest tone of a triad, are called *degrees* " (Schoenberg, *Harmonielehre*, p. 35; *Theory of Harmony*, p. 11.)

[5] See Chapter VI.

STRUCTURAL FUNCTIONS
OF HARMONY

PUBLISHER'S NOTE

CERTAIN CORRECTIONS that could not be accommodated in the body of the text have been placed in an Appendix (p. 198). An asterisk in the margin of the text indicates that additional material will be found in the Appendix.

CHAPTER I

STRUCTURAL FUNCTIONS OF HARMONY

A TRIAD standing alone is entirely indefinite in its harmonic meaning; it may be the tonic of one tonality or one degree of several others. The addition of one or more other triads can restrict its meaning to a lesser number of tonalities. A certain order promotes such a *succession* of chords to the function of a *progression*.

A *succession* is aimless; a *progression* aims for a definite goal. Whether such a goal may be reached depends on the continuation. It might promote this aim; it might counteract it.

A *progression* has the function of establishing or contradicting a tonality. The combination of harmonies of which a progression consists depends on its purpose—whether it is establishment, modulation, transition, contrast, or reaffirmation.

A *succession* of chords may be *functionless*, neither expressing an unmistakable tonality nor requiring a definite continuation. Such successions are frequently used in descriptive music (see Ex. 1).

The harmony of popular music often consists only of a *mere interchange* of tonic and dominant (Ex. 2), in higher forms concluded by a cadence. Though a mere interchange is primitive, it still has the function of expressing a tonality. Ex. 3 illustrates beginnings with mere interchange of I—IV, I—II, and even I—IV of the submediant region.[1]

*See CHART OF THE REGIONS, p. 20

The centripetal function of progressions is exerted by stopping centrifugal tendencies, i.e., by establishing a tonality through the conquest of its contradictory elements.

Modulation promotes centrifugal tendencies by loosening the bonds of affirmative elements.[2] If a modulation leads to

[1] For the *regions*, see Chapter III.
[[2] i.e. Elements which affirm one definite tonality.]

another region or tonality, cadential progressions may establish this region. This occurs in subsections, preliminary endings, contrasting additions of subordinate themes, connecting passages with the purpose of co-ordination and subordination, transitions, and in modulatory sections of scherzos, sonatas, symphonies, etc.

Roving harmony is often to be observed in modulatory sections—for example, in fantasies, recitatives, etc.[1] The difference between a modulation and roving harmony is illustrated in Ex. 4. Evidently in Ex. 4b, c, d, no succession of three chords can unmistakably express a region or a tonality.

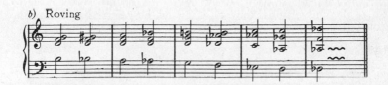

[1] See The So-called "Free Forms", p. 165 f.

CHAPTER II

PRINCIPLES OF HARMONY
(A Brief Recapitulation)

HARMONY teaches:

Firstly, the constitution of chords, that is, which tones and how many of them can be sounded simultaneously in order to produce consonances and the traditional dissonances: triads, seventh chords, ninth chords, etc., and their inversions.

Secondly, the manner in which chords should be used in succession: to accompany melodies and themes; to control the relation between main and subordinate voices; to establish a tonality at the beginning and at the end (cadence); or, on the other hand, to abandon a tonality (modulation and remodulation).

Whether the chords built on the seven tones of the major scale appear as triads, seventh chords, ninth chords, etc., or as their inversions, they will always be referred to according to their *root*, i.e., as first *degree* (I), second *degree* (II), third *degree* (III), etc.

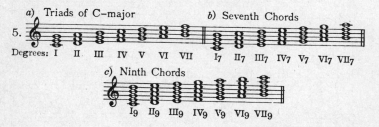

PART LEADING

When connecting chords it is advisable that each of the four voices (soprano, alto, tenor and bass, generally used to present harmonic successions) should move no more than necessary.[1] Accordingly large leaps are avoided, and if two chords have a tone in common it should, if possible, be held over in the same voice.

[1] " Sie gehorchen dem *Gesetz* des nächsten Weges " (They obey the *law* of the shortest way), Anton Bruckner taught his class at the Vienna University.

This advice is sufficient to avoid the greatest mistakes in part leading, though special precautions are necessary to avoid open or hidden parallel octaves or fifths. Contrary rather than parallel motion is recommended.

DISSONANCES AND THEIR TREATMENT

While consonances such as simple triads, if faulty parallels are avoided, can be connected unrestrictedly, dissonances require special treatment. In a seventh chord the dissonance usually descends one step to become the third or fifth of the following harmony, or is held over to become its octave.

Treatment of Dissonances

If ninth chords are used, a similar treatment of both seventh and ninth is necessary.

OUTER VOICES

Of greatest importance is the construction of the two outer voices, soprano and bass. Leaps and successions of leaps which tradition calls unmelodic should be avoided; both voices need not become melodies, but should possess as much variety as possible without violating the rules of part-leading. In the bass, which one might rightfully call the " second melody ", 6-chords, $^6_4$-chords, $^6_5$-chords, $^4_3$-chords and 2-chords should frequently be used in place of root positions of triads and seventh chords. But the $^6_4$-chord, when not a mere passing harmony, should be reserved for the " $^6_4$-chord of the cadence ".

Passing $^6_4$-Chords $^6_4$-Chord of the Cadence

Remember: in a 2-chord the dissonance is in the bass, and must accordingly descend to a $^6_3$-chord.

ROOT PROGRESSIONS

Note: there is a difference between the bass of a chord and its root. In a 6-chord the third is in the bass; in a $\frac{4}{3}$-chord the fifth is in the bass, etc.

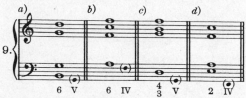

The structural meaning of a harmony depends exclusively upon the degree of the scale. The appearance of the third, fifth or seventh in the bass serves only for greater variety in the " second melody ". Structural functions are exerted by *root progressions*.

There are three kinds of root progressions:

(1) *Strong* or *ascending* progressions:[1]

(a) A fourth up, identical with a fifth down:

Ascending Progressions: 4th Up

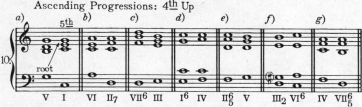

[1] The term *strong* is used because great changes in the constitution of the chord are produced. When the root progresses a fourth up the root note of the first chord is degraded, becoming only the fifth of the second chord. In the case of the root progression a third down, the root note of the first chord is degraded even further, becoming the third of the second chord. The term *ascending* is used in order to avoid the term *weak* progressions in contrast to *strong*. *Weak* qualities have no place in an artistic structure. This is why the second category of root progressions is not called *weak* but *descending*. For more on this subject see Arnold Schoenberg: *Harmonielehre*. p. 140. *Theory of Harmony*, p. 69 ff.

(b) A third down:

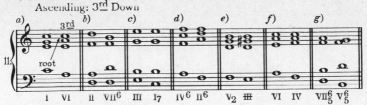

(2) *Descending* progressions:[1]

(a) A fourth down:

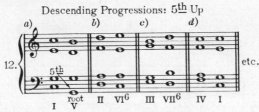

(b) A third up:

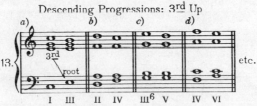

(3) *Superstrong* progressions:[2]

(a) One step up:

---

[1] They do not possess the conquering power of the *ascending* progressions. On the contrary, they promote the advancement of inferior tones. In I–V, II–VI, III–VII, etc., the fifth of the first chord always advances to become the root of the second. And in I–III, II–IV, III–V, etc., a tone of inferior importance, the third, advances to become the root.

[2] In both cases all the tones of the first chord are " conquered ", i.e. eliminated entirely.

(b) One step down:

" Ascending " progressions can be used without restriction, but the danger of monotony, as, for example, in the circle of consecutive fifths, must be kept under control.

" Descending " progressions, while sometimes appearing as a mere interchange (I–V–V–I, I–IV–IV–I), are better used in combinations of three chords which, like **I–V–VI** or **I–III–VI**, result in a strong progression (see especially Ex. 17 e).

Superstrong progressions often appear as *deceptive*[1] [i.e. false] progressions, generally when the first chord is a dominant (or an " artificial dominant," etc.; see Chapter III), in the

---

[1] The term " deceptive cadence " should be replaced by deceptive *progression*, since there is no cadence: the superstrong progression avoids a cadence.

progressions V–VI, V–IV (III–IV, III–II).[1] Traditionally, in the progression V–IV, IV appears as a 6-chord, and the progression V–VI is seldom used otherwise than from one root position to another.

Superstrong progressions may be considered too strong for continuous use.

THE MINOR TONALITY

Our two main tonalities, major and minor, derive historically from the church modes. The contents of the three major-like modes—Ionian, Lydian and Mixolydian—are concentrated in the one major tonality, and the contents of the three minor-like modes—Dorian, Phrygian and Aeolian—in the same manner, are concentrated in the minor.

Because of this origin, the minor tonality consists of two scale forms. The tones of the descending form do not differ from those of the relative major scale. The ascending form substitutes for its natural seventh tone a leading tone a half-step higher. Often, to lead more smoothly to the substitute

---

[1] Crossed Roman numerals—VI, V, III, II, etc., indicate that the chords are altered through the use of substitute tones.

seventh tone, the natural sixth tone is also replaced by a tone a half-step higher.[1]

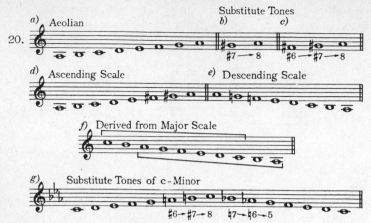

Ascending and descending scale forms (sixth and seventh tones) should not be intermixed, but kept apart to avoid cross-relations.

The inclusion of substitute tones in the minor tonality produces thirteen different triads, while there are only seven in the major. When advice has been given for " *neutralization* " of cross-related tones, it will become apparent that some of these chords endanger the tonality.[2]

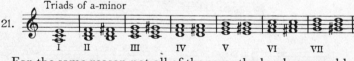

For the same reason not all of the seventh chords are usable.

The treatment of *dissonances* in the minor is often obstructed by the necessity of keeping a substitute tone apart from its natural tone. The discrepancy between the *treatment of the*

---

[1] J. S. Bach frequently uses the substitute seventh and sixth tones when descending for melodic reasons.

[2] For more about the process of *neutralization* see p. 18 and Arnold Schoenberg: *Hamonielehre*, p. 116. *Theory of Harmony*, p. 49.

dissonance (i.e. its necessity either to be held over or to fall) and the necessity of the leading tone to rise is the cause of some problems.

Augmented and diminished steps are traditionally considered unmelodic.

In Ex. 23 a number of progressions are illustrated.

a) Ascending Progressions

I   IV   I   VI   I   VI₇   II⁶   V   II   V

IIIᵇ   VI   III   VI   III   I   III   I   etc.

b) Descending Progressions

I ⟶ V   IV⁶   I ⟶ V ⟶ VI   III   I ⟶ VI

c) Superstrong Progressions

V   VI   III   IV⁶   III⁶   IV⁶   etc.

ESTABLISHMENT OF TONALITY

THE CADENCE I

A tonality is expressed by the exclusive use of all its tones. A scale (or part of one) and a certain order of the harmonies affirm it more definitely. In classical and popular music, a mere interchange of I and V is sufficient if not contradicted by extra-tonal harmonies. In most cases, for sharper

definition, a *cadence* is added at the end of an entire piece
or of its sections, segments, and even smaller units.

Distinguishing a tonality from those tonalities which
resemble it most is the first step towards its unmistakable
establishment. **C** major differs from **G** major (Dominant) and
F major (Subdominant) by only one tone in each case, **f♯** and
b♭ respectively. But it also has many tones and triads in common with **a** minor (submediant), **e** minor (mediant), and
even **d** minor (dorian). Thus, Ex. 24a illustrates that the
first three triads admit the establishment of **C** major as well
as **G** major or **e** minor. Similarly, in 24b such "neutral" triads
can be in **C** major, **a** minor or **F** major; and three neutrals
in 24c can be continued in **C** major or **d** minor. A succession
of neutral triads fail to establish a tonality.

[In the following examples the various tonalities—from **C**
major—are expressed in terms of regions: **T**, **D**, **m**, **sm**, **SD**,
and **dor**. See CHART OF THE REGIONS, p. 20.]

The chords which express a tonality unmistakably are the three main triads: I, IV and V. IV, by contradicting the **f♯**, excludes the dominant of **G** major; the **b♮** of V excludes the subdominant's **b♭**. In the cadence the traditional order is IV–V–I, consisting of the superstrong progression IV–V and the ascending V–I.

V in the cadence is never replaced by another degree and appears exclusively in root position. But IV is often replaced by II (ascending to V) or by VI (superstrong to V).

THE $\frac{6}{4}$–CHORD OF THE CADENCE

The $\frac{6}{4}$–chord of the cadence is often considered as a prepared or unprepared dissonance to be resolved into V (see Ex. 27 a, b). By convention this function of the $\frac{6}{4}$–chord has acquired such prominence that it is often misleading if a $\frac{6}{4}$–chord, especially on a degree other than I, appears in another context (see Ex. 27 c, d).

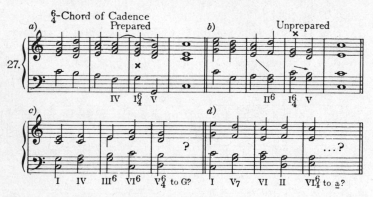

THE HALF CADENCE: OTHER CADENCES

Half cadences bring forth all degrees belonging to a full cadence, but, instead of proceeding to I, stop on V: e.g. IV–V, II–V or VI–V.

Plagal cadences, IV–I or II–I, and the phrygian cadence, II–III (or ~~III~~), are only a means of stylistic expression and are structurally of no importance.

CHAPTER III

SUBSTITUTES AND REGIONS

DERIVATION OF THE SUBSTITUTES[1]

Just as the substitute tones in the minor scale are derived from the Aeolian mode, several other substitutes are derived from the remaining modes. They may belong to an ascending scale—like the artificial leading (seventh) tones of Dorian, Mixolydian, Aeolian and occasionally also Phrygian—or to a descending scale—like the minor sixth in Dorian and the perfect fourth in Lydian.

[1 i.e. "Borrowed" tones or notes.]

In Ex. 29 the modes and their substitutes are shown in reference to a C major scale, and in transpositions to B♭ and A major, and are classified as ascending or descending substitutes. By substituting for [altering] the third in minor triads, they produce " artificial " major triads and " artificial " dominant seventh chords (Ex. 30 a, b). Substituting for [altering] the fifth changes minor triads to " artificial " diminished triads (30c), commonly used with an added seventh as in (30f), and changes major triads to augmented (30d). Note also the diminished seventh chords[1] (30e) and the artificial minor triad on V.[2](30g).

Artificial dominants, artificial dominant seventh chords, and artificial diminished seventh chords are normally used in progressions according to the models V–I, V–VI and V–IV, i.e. the authentic leap a fourth up and the two superstrong progressions, a second up and down. This is because their thirds are leading tones.

---

[1] The seventh of a diminished seventh chord will be treated here as the ninth of a ninth chord whose root is omitted (see Chapter V, Transformations).

[2] A dominant is a major triad. If a minor third replaces the natural third this triad must be called *five-minor* (v). [i.e. $\frac{5}{3}$♭].

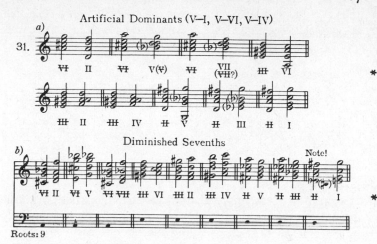

Artificial Dominants (V–I, V–VI, V–IV)

Diminished Sevenths

Roots: 9

The artificial minor chord on V preferably follows the model of IV—V in minor. But V–I (Ex. 32c) or V–IV (32d) will also be found.

Diminished triads, in the 19th century, appear more frequently with the added minor seventh. The same is true of the artificial diminished triads on III, which forms successions resembling II–V, II–I and II–III of minor.

The artificial dominant on II is the first of the *transformations* of this degree (see Chapter V) which are much in use, especially in cadences, where they introduce either I_4^6 or V_7.

INTRODUCTION OF SUBSTITUTES

Tones foreign to the scale can be introduced either quasi-diatonically or chromatically. Both procedures are melodic improvements of the part-leading and seldom involve a change of the degree.

Quasi-diatonic introduction is best carried out in a way similar to the introduction of the seventh and sixth tones in the minor. The substitute seventh tone is a leading tone and must ascend to the eighth tone [octave]. A substitute sixth tone should not lead to a natural sixth or seventh tone, nor should a natural sixth or seventh tone be followed by a substitute sixth or seventh tone. Substitute tones are "neutralized" by ascending, natural tones by descending (35c). However, the natural sixth tone is combined with the substitute seventh in a diminished seventh chord (36e).

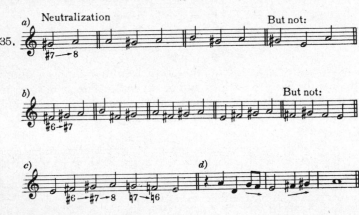

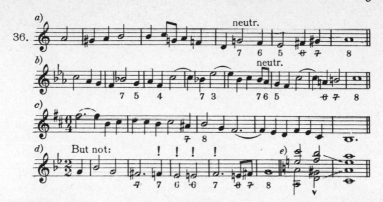

REGIONS I

Only four ascending and one descending leading tones were used in the modes (cf. p.15). These and other substitutes are derived from the relation of a tonality to segments of it which are carried out like independent tonalities: the *regions*. This consideration serves to provide a more profound understanding of the unity in the harmony of a piece.

Intermixing of substitute tones and chords with otherwise diatonic progressions, even in non-cadential segments, was considered by former theorists as modulation. This is a narrow and, therefore, obsolete concept of tonality. One should not speak of modulation unless a tonality has been abandoned definitely and for a considerable time, and another tonality has been established harmonically as well as thematically.

The concept of regions is a logical consequence of the principle of *monotonality*. According to this principle, every digression from the tonic is considered to be still within the tonality, whether directly or indirectly, closely or remotely related. In other words, there is only *one tonality* in a piece, and every segment formerly considered as another tonality is only a region, a harmonic contrast within that tonality.

Monotonality includes modulation—movement towards another *mode* and even establishment of that mode. But it considers these deviations as regions of the tonality, subordinate to the central power of a tonic. Thus comprehension of the harmonic unity within a piece is achieved.

In the following chart the regions are presented by symbols in an order which indicates their relationship.

CHART OF THE REGIONS

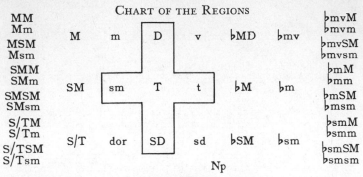

MM							♭mvM
Mm							♭mvm
MSM	M	m	D	v	♭MD	♭mv	♭mvSM
Msm							♭mvsm
SMM							♭mM
SMm	SM	sm	T	t	♭M	♭m	♭mm
SMSM							♭mSM
SMsm							♭msm
S/TM							♭smM
S/Tm	S/T	dor	SD	sd	♭SM	♭sm	♭smm
S/TSM							♭smSM
S/Tsm					Np		♭smsm

ABBREVIATIONS

T	means	tonic	Np	means	Neapolitan
D	,,	dominant	dor	,,	Dorian
SD	,,	subdominant	S/T	,,	supertonic
t	,,	tonic minor	♭M	,,	flat mediant major
sd	,,	subdominant minor	♭SM	,,	flat submediant major
v	,,	five-minor	♭MD	,,	flat mediant major's dominant
sm	,,	submediant minor	♭m	,,	flat mediant minor
m	,,	mediant minor	♭sm	,,	flat submediant minor
SM	,,	submediant major	♭mv	,,	flat mediant minor's five
M	,,	mediant major			

[*N.B.* All symbols in capitals refer to major keys; those in small letters to minor keys.]

The first symbol always indicates the relation to the tonic. The second symbol shows the relation to the region indicated by the first symbol. Thus: **Mm** reads "mediant major's mediant minor"(in **C,** a minor region on **g♯**); **SMsm** reads "submediant major's submediant minor"(in **C,** a minor region on **f♯**); ♭**smSM** reads "flat submediant minor's submediant major" (in **C** a major region on **F♭**), etc.

The tonics of the regions of **C** major are presented below, corresponding to the relations shown in the preceding chart.

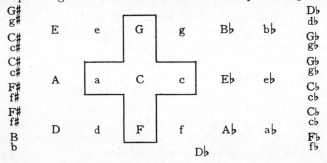

G♯							D♭
g♯							d♭
C♯	E	e	G	g	B♭	b♭	G♭
c♯							g♭
C♯							G♭
c♯	A	a	C	c	E♭	e♭	g♭
F♯							C♭
f♯							c♭
F♯							C♭
f♯	D	d	F	f	A♭	a♭	c♭
B							F♭
b				D♭			f♭

The regions closest related to a tonic are those in the centre of the chart: dominant region (**D**), subdominant region (**SD**), submediant region (**sm**) and tonic minor region (**t**). In Chapter IX the regions are classified as: I. Close and Direct; II. Indirect but Close; III. Indirect; IV. Indirect and Remote; V. Distant.

INTRODUCTION OF REGIONS

Among the regions which resemble the modes, three are major-like (**T, D, SD**) and three minor-like (**dor, m, sm**). The minor-like regions substitute [alter] those tones which make them similar to relative minor (**sm**).

Similarly, the major-like regions replace natural tones with substitutes, in order to simulate major tonalities.

Modulation from one region to another—after neutralization of cross-related tones has been carried out—is based on *at least one harmony [chord] common to both regions.* Whether a region has to be established by a cadence depends on its compositorial purpose. Substitute tones alone, however, will seldom suffice to establish it distinctly. Three or more of the characteristics of a region should be present. In every other respect the advice given for the quasi-diatonic introduction of substitutes (cf. p. 18) applies here also.

In Ex. 41 substitutes are used without the establishment of a region. Here, they merely produce enrichment by enhancing the part-leading. Ex. 41f, which consists of the same root progressions as 41e, does not use any substitutes, and thus illustrates how effective substitutes are in enriching the harmony. In these examples (at ×) chromatic progressions are used occasionally, especially in order to facilitate melodic part-leading.

CHROMATIC PROCEDURE

Chromatic ascent produces upward leading tones; chromatic descent produces downward leading tones.

In **C** major, the ascending leading tones from **f** to **g**, **g** to **a** and **c** to **d** should be written respectively **f♯**, **g♯** and **c♯**, and not **g♭**, **a♭** and **d♭**. Similarly, the descending leading tones should be written **b♭** between **b** and **a**, **e♭** between **e** and **d**, **a♭** between **a** and **g** and **d♭** between **d** and **c**. But between **g** and **f** the notation should preferably be accommodated to the tonality and key signature; the **f♯** of Ex. 43b is preferable to the **g♭** of 43a.

If remote transformations[1] of a seventh chord are used, as in 43c and 43d, **e♯** might be written instead of **f**. But in tonalities with many sharps or flats the notation is often simplified rather illogically, irrespective of the harmonic meaning. In 42b at ×, the **c♯** in the bass is evidently the third of IV of **m** and it would be senseless to spoil the recognizability of the chord by pedantically writing **d♭**. It is advisable not to contradict the key-signature, and in more remote regions chromatic substitutes should be written as if the key-signature were changed. Note the changing notation of the same pitch at + (Ex. 44).

---

[1] See Chapter V, Transformations.

Chromatic procedure, if it does not alter the harmonic progression, is, like substitution, a purely melodic matter arising out of the part-leading. It is useless if it does not render the progressions smooth.

In Ex. 46 chromatic procedures, though in the form of *enriched cadences*, express nothing else than the tonic region.

In Ex. 47 introduction of various regions and modulation back to the tonic is illustrated.

Alternatives to 47b (see p.29)
Half Cadences

Full Cadences

In Ex. 47a, IV of **T** is identical with VI of **sm**; accordingly V of **sm** (at ✕) can follow, as the **g** of the beginning has been neutralized. After this the harmonies are *registered*[1] in **sm**, until I of **sm** (at *L*) is considered as VI of **T**. The return to **T** is then carried out through **H**. The cadence in this case is rather rich because of the long extension of **sm**; it uses successively **HI**7, **VI**2, II and **H**.

In 47b the problem of moving from **SD** to **D** is carried out indirectly in order to introduce one harmony common to both; III of **SD**=II of **D** (at ✕).

Dor to **m**, as in 47i, is a longer way than one might suspect because there are not many characteristic harmonies in common. The same is true of all regions whose tonics are only one step apart: **SD** to **D, D** to **sm,** etc. (See Remotely Related Intermediate Regions, p. 65f.).

Those harmonies in which one or more natural or substitute tones can be employed as ascending or descending leading tones are considered most characteristic. For this reason, in 47i, I of **T** must at once be considered as VII of **dor.**

Examples which end in the tonality with which they began can be considered as *enriched cadences*, even if several regions

[1 i.e. The music is considered as being temporarily in that region.]

have been passed through. Examples which do not return to
the tonality of the beginning are *modulations*.

FUNCTIONAL LIMITATIONS OF ARTIFICIAL DOMINANTS

A dominant with the function of V–I must be a major triad
whose third is either natural or introduced quasi-diatonically
(cf. p. 18). Accordingly the quasi-diatonically introduced
artificial dominants on II, III, VI and VII ("substituting"
a major third and, in the case of VII, a perfect fifth also),
and on I (adding a minor seventh) can function like V–I
(or V–VI) within their regions (at x in Ex. 48a). In contrast to
this, an artificial dominant whose major third is chromatically
introduced is functionally not a dominant, and the degree a
fourth above it is not the tonic of any region (at x in Ex. 48b).

48.

In every other respect artificial dominants, provided their
" substitute " tones follow their natural tendency, can progress as if no alteration had occurred, i.e. according to the
models V–I, V–VI, V–IV. Other progressions may appear in
free composition in order to express some formal or emotional
purpose; thus, one may find in masterworks a chromatically
produced V leading to a final I as if the former were a real
dominant. But such deviations cannot be tolerated in bare
harmonic examples.

THE CADENCE II (ENRICHED)

Ex. 46b, 46d and 47c, d, e are alternative endings producing half cadences to V of **T**, V of **sm**, V of **m** and V of **dor**. They contain many substitute harmonies. In Ex. 47f, g and h, full cadences to the same regions are carried out, i.e. to I of **sm**, I of **m** and I of **dor**. In some cases *transformations* have been used (marked + in Exs. 46–48) which will be discussed later (p. 35).

CHAPTER IV

REGIONS IN MINOR

REGIONS II

In establishing the relationships among the regions in minor,[1] it must be kept in mind that the minor tonality is a residue of one of the modes, the Aeolian. As such, it uses the seven tones of the diatonic (Ionian) scale, and produces all its characteristic differences by means of substitutes. As a mere stylistic convention, it had acquired the emotional quality of sadness in the vocabulary of the classical composers, in spite of the many gay folk-songs in minor-like modes.

From the standpoint of structural functions, a minor tonic does not maintain as direct a control over its regions as a major tonic. Thus the number of directly related regions is small, and modulation to indirectly related regions through its relative major (**M**), tonic major (**T**), dominant (**D**), etc., is definitely more remote.

CHART OF THE REGIONS IN MINOR[2]

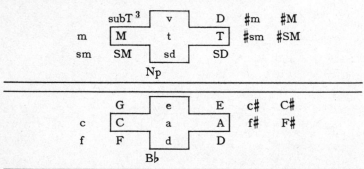

While a major tonality, i.e. the tonic, has at least the power of a dominant over its subdominant, such a power is denied to the tonic of a minor tonality; a dominant must be a major triad (see p. 16).

[1] See Classification of Regions in Minor, p. 75.
[2] See abbreviations, p. 20.
[3] The term " supertonic " (**S/T**) indicates that the root of this region lies two fifths *above* the tonic. Correspondingly, the term " subtonic " (**subT**) is introduced here, indicating that the root of this region lies two fifths *below* the tonic of a minor tonality.

The order of the regions in the chart of minor is the reverse of the order in major (see p. 20). In spite of the close relations, the change of *gender* (i.e. from minor to major keys) requires caution and careful neutralization.

Again the regions in the centre of the chart must be considered as the closest related. Nevertheless in masterworks the first part of binary or ternary forms will just as often end on dominant (**D**) as on **v** [a minor triad on the fifth degree], especially if a repetition is demanded to whose tonic a dominant leads more powerfully. Obviously the regions on the right side of the chart are even more distantly related than those in major on the same side.

The examples, 49 a—e, demonstrate passing through the following regions: **M, v, sd, D, SM** and **T**.   *

In Ex. 49a I of **v** is avoided through the deceptive progression to VI of **v** (at ×, ms. 4), thus facilitating the turn to **M**. " Registration " of harmonies in two or more regions (cf. p. 27) explains their relationship. In 49b the diminished 7th chord (× in ms. 2) is repeated in a different notation in ms. 3 with a different meaning, a procedure very often used in this and following examples, not only for instructional but also for structural purposes; the multiple use of such harmonies has a smoother effect.

In 49d the diminished 7th chord in ms. 5 (×) is " registered " in three regions; this is not uncommon for a diminished 7th chord.

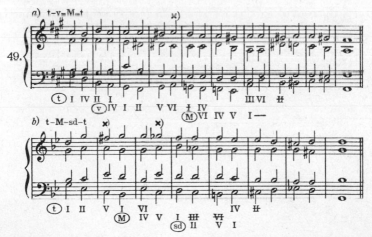

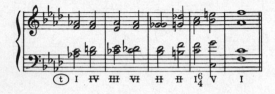

CHAPTER V

TRANSFORMATIONS

RICHNESS and greater variety of harmony are based on the relationship between a tonality and its regions, on the substitutions which are produced in the harmonies through the influence of this relationship, and on the possibility of using harmonies in a manner different from their original derivations. Many such chords deserve the name *vagrant* harmonies because they seem to wander nomadically between regions, if not tonalities, without ever settling down. Nevertheless, every " transformation " [altered chord] must be registered as a degree belonging to one of the regions; thus, even seemingly unusual progressions will prove to be normal.

TRANSFORMATIONS OF THE SECOND DEGREE (II)

" Transformations " of the second degree result from the influence of **D**, **SD** and **sd** (for *subdominant minor* see Chapter VII). Under the influence of **D**, the [minor] third of II is substituted for, as discussed under *Artificial Dominants* (p. 28), by a major third. Substituting for the fifth of II a tone from **sd** or **t** produces a diminished triad. Most of these transformations are employed as seventh and ninth chords.

50.

In Ex. 50c both **D** and **sd** are operative. The same is the case in d, e and f, while g, the Neapolitan sixth chord, is borrowed unchanged from **sd** where it is a natural VI. All the forms in d, e and f are basically ninth chords, though in their normal use the root is omitted. Diminished seventh chords, as 50d, were formerly considered seventh chords on natural or artificial leading tones. Accordingly a diminished seventh chord in **c** minor (b–d–f–a♭) would be considered to be on VII and, worse, 50d would be considered as based on a " substituted " root (f♯), an assumption which must be rejected as nonsensical. Besides the progressions VII–I and IV–V then look like *deceptive* progressions, while their function as V–I and II–V is truly *authentic*. Registering every diminished

seventh chord as a ninth chord on II (or V, or any other
degree), root omitted, prevents it being used as a "Jack-of-
all-trades" and enforces consciousness of the structural
functions of the root progressions.[1]

Foreign tones can again be introduced either quasi-diatonically or chromatically as in the following examples.

Several forms of these transformations can be used in succession; chromatic progressions are helpful here. Change
of notation is sometimes advisable but should not obscure
the reference to the degree of the scale.

The tones of the Neapolitan sixth chord appear occasionally
in root position. It will then be called the *Neapolitan triad*
(at *).

[1] For more on this subject see Arnold Schoenberg: *Harmonielehre*, p. 234; *Theory
of Harmony*, p. 144.

On account of their functional similarity to the dominant and to artificial dominants, transformations appear most frequently in progressions after the models of V–I, V–VI, V–IV; i.e. II–V, II–I, II–III.

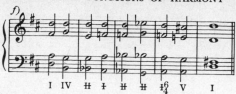

I IV ♯♯ ♯ ♯♯ ♯ ♯⁶₄ V I

In 54a (*) observe the progression e♭ to e♮. As e♭ is the ninth of II, it should either descend or be sustained like 54e (*), where it prepares the third of a minor tonic. But if a major tonic follows it is necessary to use a *silent* enharmonic change treating the e♭ as if it were d♯.

In 54b (*) the succession from ♯ (Neapolitan sixth) to III of the tonic minor obscures the tonic major, but might be usable in long examples.

In 54c (at *) a ♯ derived from **sd** is followed by a natural III,—a very harsh progression, because III, as I of the *mediant* region, is very foreign to **sd** (see CHART OF THE REGIONS, p.20).

TRANSFORMATIONS OF OTHER DEGREES IN THE TONIC REGION

In Ex. 55 the transformations applied to II are now applied to I, III, IV, V, VI, and VII. Some forms are unusable, at first glance. Others which also endanger the tonality might be usable under certain compositional assumptions. Here are examined only the most important progressions, according to the models of V–I, V–VI, and V–IV.

55.
a) ♯
(62a)
b) ♯♯♯
c) ♯V
(62b)
d) V
(62c)
e) VI
f) VII

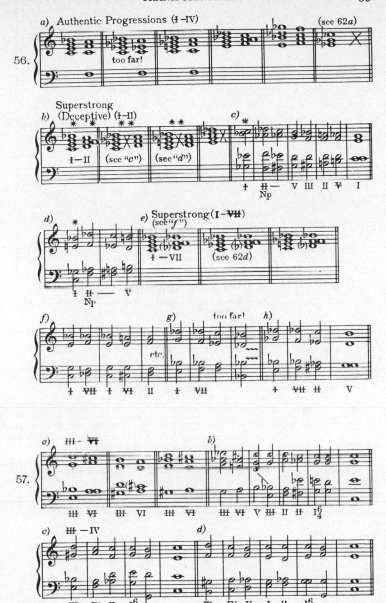

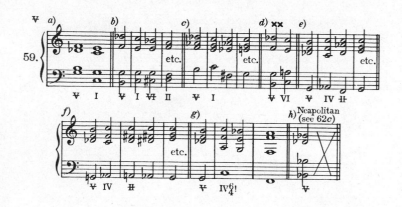

Restrictions (see below)

In order to evaluate the methods of using these transformations, the following restrictions must be followed.

RESTRICTIONS

Transformation does not change the degree, but some products of it do seem *irreconcilably remote*. The most decisive reason against the introduction of such chords is generally that they are not "borrowed" from closely related regions, as, for instance, the Neapolitan of II. There is no close region containing a **c♭** which justifies a Neapolitan on I like Ex. 55a (at *). The Neapolitans in 55c and d, (at *), on IV and V, may be similarly evaluated.

Because they are so remote, it is also difficult to introduce and resolve the Neapolitans on I, IV and V (Ex. 62a, b, c).

The same applies to all transformations of I, IV and V which substitute a diminished fifth for a perfect fifth, (see Ex. 62d at *). It is, of course, not impossible to reconcile the remoteness of such harmonies by an appropriate continuation, as in 62d, 58a, b, etc. Ex. 56c and d show that the Neapolitan sixth on II can follow, which is entirely acceptable. Traditionally, however, transformations which substitute the diminished fifth for the perfect fifth, tend to be followed by a major triad, according to the model of II–V in minor (62e).

To sum up, the following advice may be given. A succession of two harmonies which appear in remotely and indirectly related regions often produces the effect of intolerable harshness (see Remotely Related Intermediate Regions, p. 65), as, for instance, Ex. 56b (✻ ✻) and 59d (✕ ✕). The transformation of I in 56b first appears in the natural triads of the *Neapolitan* region (**D♭**), while the minor triad on **d** might be understood as I of **dor**. The other case (59d) can be similarly judged.

Neapolitan sixths on VI and VII (Ex. 60, 61) lead to $^6_4$-chords of V and VI respectively (or to the dominants on to which they resolve). This can be misleading, on account of the traditional meaning of a $^6_4$-chord. But Ex. 60d, e, f and 61e, f, g, show that it is not too difficult to counteract this tendency.

A I of any region introduced by a transformation of V (Ex. 58b) will not function as a tonic and requires a continuation which will reaffirm it.

In cases like Ex. 57e, an enharmonic change in notation, (**a♭** instead of g♯ at *), disregarding the derivation, is advisable.

Transformations like the preceding can be built on all degrees of all regions. Many of these forms might duplicate forms of less remote regions. Even so the number of cases would be immense. This excludes a thorough evaluation of them; some progressions might be impossible, others might be " dangerous but passable ".

In Ex. 63 transformations in minor are illustrated and one example of their application is added (63h). The principles of their evaluation and the restrictions to be followed do not differ from those of the major key.

Transformations in Minor

63.

CHAPTER VI

VAGRANT HARMONIES

MANY of the transformations are vagrant harmonies because of their constitution (diminished sevenths, augmented triads, augmented $\frac{6}{5}$-chords and $\frac{4}{3}$-chords, etc.), and also because of their *multiple meaning*.

There exist only three diminished seventh chords and four augmented triads. Accordingly every diminished seventh chord belongs to at least eight tonalities or regions, and every augmented triad belongs, in the same manner, to six tonalities or regions.

By an enharmonic change in their notation, augmented $\frac{6}{5}$- and $\frac{4}{3}$-chords can become dominant seventh chords , and vice versa (see Ex. 64c and Ex. 65a at ×).

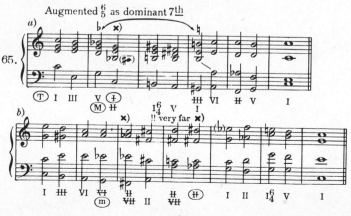

44

Adding minor sevenths, and minor or major ninths to augmented triads, with or without the root, produces another series of chords which are vagrants by constitution (Ex. 66 and 67; also Ex. 69, marked *L*).

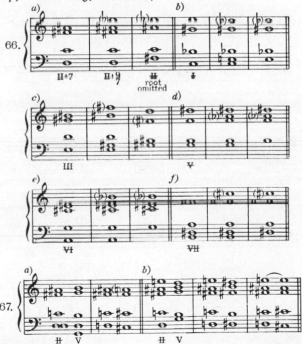

Change of interpretation—whether or not based on the chord constitution—means change of the degree. From the standpoint of structural functions only the *root* of the progression is decisive. But emotional or compositional conditions often require strong contrasts, friction or sudden change.

An example of a surprise modulation can be seen in Ex. 68, from Beethoven's Eighth Symphony. The tone **d♭**, first derived from **sd**, is later interpreted as **c♯**, V of **f♯** minor.

To base a modulation or a change of region solely on the altered interpretation of one single chord is sometimes harsh, sometimes unconvincing, as, for instance, at ✕ in Ex. 65a, b, c.

The Neapolitan sixth chord is, in fact, the first inversion of a major triad. Its progressions, ₦-V and ₦-I, can be imitated on every sixth chord of a natural or artificial major triad (at x in Ex. 69).

---

[1] This interpretation has been systematically worked out by Max Reger in a little pamphlet, *Beiträge zur Modulationslehre*, 1903.

Progressions like those in Ex. 70 can be as valuable as the previously discussed vagrant harmonies in preparing for a transition to another region. But, again, one extra-diatonic chord does not establish a region, nor will it result in the definite abandonment of a region. The " registration " (cf. p. 27) of such chords depends on their interpretation.

Some of these progressions are used in a two-fold manner in Ex. 71. Ex. 71 a, c and e prove that the tonic region need not be abandoned, while 71b, d and f prove such progressions to be adequate preparations for modulatory movements to **sm, ι,** and **m** respectively.

CHAPTER VII

INTERCHANGEABILITY OF MAJOR AND MINOR

(Tonic Minor, Subdominant Minor and v-Minor Regions)

REGIONS III (MAJOR)

A dominant can introduce a major or a minor triad, and can be the dominant of a major or of a minor region. Upon the potency of the dominant is based the interchangeability of major and minor. This power makes the following regions close relatives of a major tonality: tonic minor (**t**), subdominant minor (**sd**), and v-minor (**v**) (cf. p. 56). Because of the principle of interchangeability, the following regions are also closely related: the major forms of mediant (**M**) and submediant (**SM**) and (derived from tonic minor) the major and minor forms of flat mediant (♭**M**, ♭**m**) and flat submediant (♭**SM**, ♭**sm**), which will be discussed as *indirectly related* in the next chapter. Through this relationship numerous substitute chords become available (see Ex. 72).

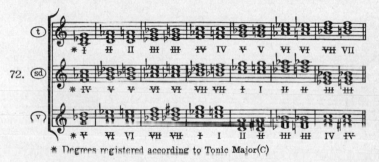

72.

* Degrees registered according to Tonic Major(C)

TONIC MINOR REGION

In Ex. 73 substitute harmonies derived from **t** are introduced in various ways. In 73a I of **T** (**₮** of **t**) introduces IV of **t**. VI of **t** is followed by a transformation of II of both **I** and **t**. Ex. 73b and c demonstrate that even a longer sojourn in **t** is no obstacle to the re-establishment of **T**. In 73d the deceptive progression V–VI of **t** is followed by a frequent interchange of major and minor. Chromaticism supports the change to **T** in 73e (at ✕).

In classical music, major and minor are often exchanged without much ado; a passage in minor follows a passage in major without any harmonic connective, and vice versa.

a) Beethoven: Symphony No. 2, Larghetto

b) Schubert: A minor Quartet, Op. 29, 1st Movement (Recapitulation)

SUBDOMINANT MINOR REGION

The successive use of too many harmonies derived from **sd** can obscure the tonality. In mss. 2–3 of 75a not only is the tonality obscured, but **sd** could even be mistaken for ♭**SM** because of an accumulation of harmonies drawn from the descending minor scale. In such a case one might balance the sub-regions [flat keys] by elements of the super-regions, e.g. dorian and mediant, as in this example. Introducing such much more remote regions as ♭**SM** prolongs the examples and requires stronger means to counteract it.

Structurally the Neapolitan sixth is certainly a remote relation of a tonality, though convention has admitted the use of this popular mannerism. But of course the Neapolitan of **sd** (Ex. 75b) is extremely remote. This chord is the cause of all the subsequent shortcomings of 75b. For instance, in ms. 4, iv/iv [i.e. iv of iv] is one of the most remote harmonies. Strong means are required to counterbalance it—vagrant harmonies, diminished seventh chords and chromatic progressions. Unfortunately some of the harmonies cannot be " registered " in two regions; this, at least theoretically, would justify their exclusion [from an example which does not modulate]. The alternative, 75c shows that an early return to **T** is not impossible.

In 75d the change from major to minor is supported by the chromatic progression (ms. 2) in the bass. The Neapolitan sixth, here a natural VI of **sd**, is introduced by an augmented $^6_5$ on **Ĥ**. This is enharmonically presented (**g**♭ instead of f♯)

as a 2-chord on III of **sd** (ms. 3). In the following measure
the return to **SD** is prepared through the chromatic step in the
tenor, **d♭** to **d♮**.

Alternative to "*b*"

FIVE-MINOR REGION (v)

The function of a dominant can only be exerted, as previously stated (p. 16), by a major triad. The term "sub*dominant*" is illogical and "sub*dominant minor*" is wrong. If V dominates I, then I dominates IV, not the reverse. The term "dominant minor" would be mere nonsense; therefore this region will here be called "five-minor" (**v**).[1]

The **v**-region is very well suited to prepare the appearance of **dor** and **SD**. In 76b III of **t** (ms. 4), introduced by a deceptive progression, requires special treatment. In 76c the **v**-region appears through interchange with its major (V).

---

[1] For more on this subject see Arnold Schoenberg: *Harmonielehre*, p. 232; *Theory of Harmony*, p. 139.

CHAPTER VIII

INDIRECT BUT CLOSE RELATIONS

(Mediant Major, Submediant Major, Flat Mediant Major
and Minor, Flat Submediant Major and Minor)   *

REGIONS IV

MAJOR

IN BACH'S time all movements of a cyclic work generally
stayed in one tonality, and even the interchange of major and
minor was not too frequent. In the masterworks of the Classical
and Romantic eras one or both middle movements are to be
found in closely related contrasting tonalities such as **t**, **D**, **SD**,
sm, **sd**, **m** and **v**, and also in the more indirectly related
M, **SM**, ♭**M**, ♭**SM**. Most of these relationships, as regions of
Class 1 and 2 (see p. 68), and even of Class 3, appear as
contrasts within a movement. A few such cases of contrasts
between movements or within a movement illustrate this
point:

M: Beethoven Trio Op. 97 in B♭ (3rd movement in D
major); Beethoven Piano Sonata Op. 53 in C (1st movement,
subordinate theme in E major); Brahms 3rd Symphony in F
(1st movement, subordinate theme in A major).

SM: Schumann Symphony in E♭ (2nd movement, C major).

♭**M**: Schubert C major Quintet (1st movement, subordinate
theme in E♭ major).

♭**SM**: Beethoven and Brahms Violin Sonatas in A major
(middle movements in F major); Beethoven Piano Sonata
Op. 7 in E♭ (Largo movement in C major, subordinate theme
in A♭ major).

These masters observed such relationships almost as strictly
as if they were rules. This proves the validity of the concept
of monotonality. Nevertheless there exist exceptions—violations
—such as the second movement of Beethoven's C♯ minor
String Quartet, Op. 131, in D major, the F♯ major movement
of Brahms' Second Cello Sonata in F major, etc.

Submediant major (**SM**) and mediant major (**M**) are
related to **sm** and **m** respectively on the basis of the interchangeability of major and minor. This is an indirect but
very close relation. Presenting this relation as an equation:

57

$$\left.\begin{array}{l}\textbf{M:m}\\ \textbf{SM:sm}\end{array}\right\} \ = \ \textbf{T:t}$$

The relation of flat submediant (♭**SM**) and flat mediant major (♭**M**) is indirect, based on the relationship of **t** to **T** and **sd** to **SD**:

$$\left.\begin{array}{ll}\textbf{t} \ (c): & \flat\textbf{M} \ (E\flat)\\ \textbf{sd} \ (f): & \flat\textbf{SM} \ (A\flat)\end{array}\right\} \ = \ \textbf{sm} \ (a): \textbf{T} \ (C)$$

The movement into these regions applies the inter-change-ability of minor and major to the intermediate regions, thereby taking advantage of common harmonies as before. In **M** and **SM** the introduction of a common dominant will promote the change. A minor chord on IV (i.e. iv) will function as the bridge to ♭**M** and ♭**SM**. Transformations and vagrant harmonies assist in producing smooth transitions.

Interchangeability of major and minor also includes ♮**sm**, because of ♮**SM**, and ♮**m**, because of ♮**M**.

* MINOR

In minor, interchangeability furnishes **m** and **sm**, derived from the descending (natural) scale, and also **♯m** and **♯M**, **♯sm** and **♯SM**, derived from the ascending scale (containing the substitutes).[1] Thus, in an **A**-minor tonality,

m, **sm**, **♯m** and **♯sm** would be minor regions on
c, f,   c♯ and f♯;

and

♯M and **♯SM** would be major regions on
C♯ and F♯.

[1 See also Ex. 49 for **D** and **SM** regions.]

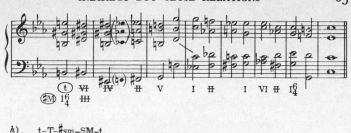

REMOTELY RELATED INTERMEDIATE REGIONS

The connection of regions which have no common harmonies, such as **v** (in C major, g) and **SM** (A) or ♭**SM** (A♭), **dor** (d) and **M** (E) or ♭**M** (E♭), and **m** (e) or **M** (E) and **SD** (F) or **sd** (f) offers difficulties. Their relation to the main tonality might be indirect but not remote, in spite of which their relation to one another can be as irreconcilably remote as, for instance, that of ♭**M** or ♭**m** with **sm** or **SM**.

The preceding statement may be generalized as follows:

Regions, and even tonalities, whose tonics differ a major or minor second or augmented fourth (diminished fifth) have so little in common that it would seem justifiable to consider them as " irreconcilably remote ", were it not that the imagination of a real artist is capable of overcoming even this obstacle. On the other hand, one should not forget that the progressions of the Neapolitan sixth chord to the tonic chord, II—I [or i], and to the dominant chord, II—V [i.e. progressions of a minor second or augmented fourth] are common.

Much in these examples is imperfect. Trying to improve some of their shortcomings might be an interesting exercise. It is, however, doubtful whether the natural cause of their defects can be eliminated; they are only exercises in harmonic progressions for which there is no compositional stimulation. Good part leading will always be of great assistance. This refers especially to the main voices, the outer voices—soprano and bass; difficult and even unmelodious progressions will better be hidden in the middle voices—chromatic and quasi-diatonic progressions can soften many a harsh connection by their melodious qualities. The outer voices are also helpful in introducing substitutes—transformations and vagrant chords—if their directional tendencies are carefully observed. The final cadence must not be too short, especially if it has been preceded by remote deviations. Common natural chords are most effective for transitions, but in the examples even Neapolitan sixth chords, augmented triads and $^6_5$-chords, and diminished 7th chords have been treated like common chords.

CHAPTER IX

ACCORDING to the practice of composers of the tonal period up to and including most of the 19th century, the relationships between tonalities can be classified as follows:

MAJOR

1. Direct and Close: [as related to T],
   SD, D, sm, m (Chapter III, p. 26 ff, Ex. 47).
2. Indirect but Close:
   A. Through Common Dominant:
      (1) t, sd, v (Chapter VII, p. 51 ff, Exs. 72–76).
      (2) SM, M (Chapter VIII, p. 58, Ex. 77).
   B. Through Proportional Transposition:
      ♭M, ♭SM (Chapter VIII, p. 60, Ex. 77).
3. Indirect:
   ♭m, ♭sm, MM, Mm, ♭smSM, ♭smsm (Chapter VIII, p. 61, Ex. 78).
4. Indirect and Remote:
   Np, dor, S/T, ♭MD, ♭mv (Chapters VIII and IX, p. 66 ff, Exs. 80–83).
5. Distant:
   MSM, Msm, SMM, SMm, SMSM, SMsm, S/TM, S/Tm, S/TSM, S/Tsm, ♭mvM, ♭mvm, ♭mvSM, ♭mvsm, ♭mM, ♭mm, ♭mSM, ♭msm, ♭smM, ♭smm (Chapter IX).

Class 1 is called DIRECT AND CLOSE because all these regions have five (or six) tones in common with **T.**

Class 2 is called INDIRECT BUT CLOSE because all these regions are closely related to the regions of Class 1 or to tonic minor, and have three or four tones in common with **T.**

Class 3 is called INDIRECT because all these regions are more distant than Class 2, upon which their relationship is based, and the number of tones in common with **T** is negligible.

MM and **Mm,** **♭smSM** and **♭smsm** are very distant on the chart,[1] but if enharmonically changed they sound like

_____
[1] See p. 20.

68

more closely related regions. **MM** and **Mm** sound like ♭**SM** and ♭**sm** (in terms of their tonics in **C** major, like **G♯** and **g♯**= **A♭** and **a♭**); similarly, ♭**smSM** (**F♭**) and ♭**smsm** (**f♭**) sound like **M** (**E**) and **m** (**e**).

Structurally this means that these rather distant regions may be reached either by way of the flats or by way of the sharps, respectively—or, so to speak, either clockwise or counter-clockwise in the circle of fifths. Thereafter they can be enharmonically changed (see the second and third endings to Ex. 77e, pp. 59–60).

Class 4 is called INDIRECT AND REMOTE because these five regions are connected in the following manner:

Dorian (**dor**) is subdominant's submediant minor (**SDsm**);
Supertonic (**S/T**) is subdominant's submediant major (**SDSM**);
Neapolitan (**Np**) is subdominant minor's submediant major (**sdSM**);
Flat major mediant's dominant (♭**MD**) is subdominant's subdominant (**SDSD**);
Flat minor mediant's " five-minor " (♭**mv**) is subdominant minor's subdominant minor (**sdsd**).

In 19th century music, these extremely remote regions, and most of the regions of Class 5 (DISTANT) customarily appear in the *Durchführungen* (developments or elaborations)[1]. But ♭**MD** (A♭ in the tonality of B♭ major) appears in the contrasting middle section of the cavatina, " Voi che sapete ", from *The Marriage of Figaro*[2] (Ex. 81a). This same region is also employed within the first statement of the main theme (in substitution for the usual II) in Beethoven's Sonata, Op. 53 (Ex. 81b). See also in his Sonata, Op. 31/1, the relation F to G major (Ex. 81c).

---

[1] Schoenberg's reasons for using the term *Durchführung*, rather than " development ", " elaboration " or " working out ", will be found on p. 145.]

[2] The difficulty of finding a second illustration of this kind, coupled with some other circumstances (for instance, the long roundabout return to the tonic), suggests the following hypothesis: the page, Cherubino, accompanies himself and is also the author of the poem. Has he not also composed the music? Did not Mozart by such extravagant features hint at Cherubino's professional imperfections?

a) Mozart: Marriage of Figaro (Voi, che sapete)

b) Beethoven: Sonata, Op. 53

c) Beethoven: Sonata, 31/1

An example of **S/T** is to be found in the *Durchführung*[1] of Beethoven's Sonata, Op. 2/3, in C major (Ex. 82).

Np is usually approached through **sd** or through the augmented ⁶₅ of II̶. Though this region is fairly distant, an extended episode often takes place within it. Examples of this kind are frequent, as, for instance, the two following cases from Beethoven Piano Sonatas.

[1] cf. p. 69.

b) Beethoven: Sonata, Op. 7, Rondo

Tonalities or regions whose tonics are a major or minor second, a diminished fifth or an augmented fourth distant from the tonic are less frequently considered as related by the composers of the period mentioned above.[1]

The relation **Msm** (mediant major's submediant minor)— c♯ in C major or e in E♭ major—takes place in the Eroica, ms. 284, in the *Durchführung* (see Ex. 149, p. 155).

Even more interesting cases can be found in the works of Brahms, for instance in the F minor Piano Quintet. In the recapitulation, the first subordinate theme (ms. 201), which in the first division stood on **sm** (c♯), ms. 35, should have been transposed to tonic minor (f). Instead it is transposed to **Msm** (f♯). In the 'Cello Sonata in F major, Op. 99, one is surprised to find the second movement in F♯ major, only to discover later that F major and f minor are contrastingly connected with F♯ (G♭) major and f♯ minor in all four movements. What makes these Brahms examples so striking is that most of them do not occur in *Durchführungen* but in place where " establishing " conditions exist—in regions, that is.

MINOR

The evaluation of the regions in the minor requires a different yardstick, because a natural dominant is lacking, and the two substitute tones of the ascending scale increase the number of possible harmonies.

Relations derived from the natural tones of the descending scale differ from those of the major in that the fifth degree (v) is not a dominant, while the mediant (**M**, relative major) exerts an influence similar to a dominant. Besides, there is no Dorian region on II (because of its diminished triad) comparable to that in the major; but the region on VII (**subT**) often functions like a dominant to **M**.

Relations derived from the ascending scale contain a functional dominant (**D**), but the subdominant, though here a major chord, seems a greater departure from the tonic region than the subdominant in major.

[1] See p. 65.

The indirectly related regions:

m, sm, ♯m, ♯M, ♯sm, ♯SM, Np, Dsm, DSM, subT, SD

derive from

M, SM, D,   D,   T,   T,   SM, D,   D,   M,   sd.

Two remarkable, if not exceptional, examples from Beethoven's String Quartets, Op. 59/2 in E minor (3rd movement) and Op. 132 in A minor (4th movement), can be understood as a cadence and half cadence, respectively, to V of **M**.

a) Beethoven: Quartet, Op. 59/2, 3rd Movement

b) Beethoven: Quartet, Op. 132, 4th Movement

The evaluation of the more remote regions will best be based on mediant (relative major). (Compare Ex. 79 and later examples, especially analyses of *Durchführungen*—see p. 145 ff.).

Should a modulation have to pass through two regions which have no common natural chords (such as **v** and **♯M**). it is best to interpolate a few chords of an intermediate region (in this case, **D**).

CLASSIFICATION OF REGIONS IN MINOR

1. Close: M, T, v, sd (Chapter IV, p. 31 ff., Ex. 49).
2. Indirect but Close: D, SM (Chapter IV, p. 32 ff., Ex. 49).
3. Indirect: m, sm, SD (Chapter VIII, p. 63, Ex. 79).
4. Indirect and Remote: ♯sm, ♯SM, ♯m, ♯M, subT, subt, Np (Chapter VIII, p. 64, Ex. 79).
5. Distant: All other regions.

CHAPTER X

EXTENDED TONALITY

THE COMPOSERS of the Romantic period believed that music should " express " something. As so often in preceding periods, extramusical tendencies, such as poetic and dramatic subjects, emotions, actions, and even philosophical problems of *Weltanschauung* (philosophy of life) had become influential. These tendencies caused changes in every feature of the musical substance. Alterations in the constitution of chords decisively changed the intervals of the melodies and also resulted in richer modulations; the rhythms and dynamics of the accompaniment, and even of the melody, symbolized their extramusical objects instead of deriving from purely musical stimuli. The origin of these new features may be debatable aesthetically, if not psychologically; however, whatever the source of the musical inspiration may have been, it resulted in great developments.

In descriptive music the background, the action, the mood and the other features of the drama, poem or story become incorporated as constituent and formative factors in the musical structure. Their union thereafter is inseparable. Neither the text nor the music conveys its full significance if detached from its companion. Their union is an amalgamation comparable to an alloy whose components can be separated only by complicated processes.

Drama and poetry are greatly inspiring to a composer. But much of what they evoke on the one hand, they revoke on the other. A melody, if it followed the dictates of its musical structure alone, might develop in a direction different from that in which a text forces it. It might become shorter or longer, produce its climax earlier or later—or dispense with it entirely —require less striking contrasts, much less emphasis, or much less accentuation. Besides, the text is frequently so overwhelming in itself as to conceal the absence of value in a melody.

These extramusical influences produced the concept of extended tonality. Remote transformations and successions of harmonies were understood as remaining within the tonality. Such progressions might or might not bring about modula-

tions or the establishment of various regions. They function
chiefly as enrichments of the harmony and, accordingly, often
appear in a very small space, even in a single measure. Though
referring them to regions may sometimes facilitate analysis,
their functional effect is, in many cases, only passing, and
temporary.

In the beginning of the Prelude to *Tristan*, V of **a** minor is
followed by two modulating sequences (see Ex. 85a), the last
of which prepares for the recurrence of the opening V (ms. 16).
In 85b, from Strauss' *Salome*, ms. 3 (at +) a harmony appears
which seems difficult to explain. But if one considers the **e♮**
as a mere passing note, connecting the **f** with the **d♯ (e♭)**, it
becomes clear that it is a diminished seventh chord of **♯**,
sounding much more remote here.

However, far-reaching deviations, resulting from remote progressions, occur frequently in Brahms. In the C minor String Quartet, Op. 51, first movement, the contrasting middle section ends on the tone **f♯** (ms. 21), which must undoubtedly be analyzed as V of dominant's mediant minor (Dm), an extremely remote point scarcely appropriate to reintroduce I of **c** minor. A little unaccompanied fragment then serves as a retransition to **t** (Ex. 86a).

If Brahms were not a profound thinker and a great virtuoso in the treatment of harmonic problems, he would simply have repeated this procedure in the recapitulation. But in order eventually to recapitulate the subordinate theme in **t** he shifts the a¹ section[1], ms. 23, to **sd**, a fifth below (86b). Accordingly the tone which precedes the little fragment of ms. 22 should have been transposed similarly, i.e. to **B**. But instead of that he arrives at **E**, the V of **♯sm**, and requires two more modulatory measures for the introduction of **sd**.

Brahms gave similar advice to young composers. Thus, in Ex. 87a, ms. 2, he recommended, instead of a simple repetition, the replacement of the last chord by a minor triad which could be employed in the *Durchführung* to change to the flat keys (" zu den B-Tonarten ", he said).

<hr>

[1] Cf. p. 98 n.

In the works of earlier composers many passages of extended
tonality are to be found. Ex. 88 and Ex. 89 from Bach's G
minor Organ Fantasy and from the Chromatic Fantasy are
composed of such remotely related transformations.

a)   Bach: Organ Fantasy in G minor

Bach: Chromatic Fantasy (D minor)

Deviation into remote regions often occurs in descriptive music, even in " establishing " [expository] sections. Songs, operas, choral works and symphonic poems take advantage of the emotional expressiveness of extravagant modulations. See, for instance, the two examples, 90 and 91—" Auf dem Flusse " by Schubert and " Der Tod, das ist die kuhle Nacht " by Brahms—and the little recitative from the St. Matthew Passion, Ex. 92, to the words " Ach, Golgotha ".

mich schläfert der Tag hat mich müd' ge-macht.

Bach: St. Matthew Passion
Ach Golgotha!

The inclusion of the Neapolitan sixth within the main themes of the Beethoven String Quartets Op. 59/2 in E minor and Op. 95 in F minor (Exs. 93, 94) certainly should be regarded as extended tonality. Even richer in the inclusion of regions within a main theme are the first movement of the String

Quintet in G major, Op. 111 (Ex. 95) and the main theme of
the Piano Concerto in D minor (Ex. 96), both by Brahms.

Brahms: Concerto in D minor, Op.15

Enriched harmony makes for variety, especially when repetitions threaten to produce monotony. One of the most interesting examples of this kind can be found in Schubert's song, " Sei mir gegrüsst " (Ex. 97). In his songs Schubert always expresses and intensively illustrates the mood and character of the poem. In " Der Lindenbaum ", " Die Krähe ", " Letzte Hoffnung ", Erlkönig ", " Gretchen am Spinnrad ", for instance, the piano illustrates, respectively, the sound of the wind, the flight of the crow, the falling of leaves, the galloping horse, and the sound of the spinning wheel. He achieves even more through strange harmonic progressions, as in "Der Wegweiser" (Ex. 98), or abrupt modulations, as ms. 18 of "In der Ferne" (Ex. 99) and in "Erlkönig" (Ex. 100).

Schubert: Erlkonig (ms. 77—81, 102—108)

But in " Sei mir gegrüsst " (Ex. 97) the procedure is very different. Here the piano style, unchanged in general throughout the whole piece, does not illustrate at all, but closely resembles a guitar accompaniment. The refrain, " sei mir gegrüsst ", appears at the end of each strophe, a total of six times in only 100 measures. This would be extremely monotonous were it not that far-reaching changes in the harmony make every repetition an interesting variation.

" Variation is that kind of repetition which changes some

of the features of a unit, etc., but preserves others."[1] Obviously whole sets of variations, which often repeat their model ten times or more, would annoy instead of please if they merely applied changes of piano style, as is the case in some of Handel's variations. But variations by Haydn, as, for example, Op. 76/3 (Emperor Quartet), 2nd movement, are based in many instances on enrichment of the harmony.[2]

Haydn: Quartet, Op.76/3, 2nd Movement

[1] Arnold Schoenberg: *Models for Beginners in Composition*, G. Schirmer, Inc.
[2] In *Models* instruction is given for enriching the harmony by inserted additions (p. 13–14).

Beethoven, in his three large sets of variations for piano; the
15 Variations, Op. 35 (Eroica), the 32 Variations in C minor,
and the 33 Diabelli Variations, Op. 120, similarly, but much
more far-reachingly, varies his harmony by using substitutions
and transformations (sometimes remote ones) and passing
through various regions. This is most significant in the
Diabelli Variations, which, in respect of its harmony,
deserves to be called the most adventurous work of Beethoven.

Some of the progressions in this work are difficult to analyse
in terms of regions, for instance, mss. 9 12 in Var. 15 (Ex.
102a)—substituting for the original sequence (Ex. 103a)—
and the corresponding units, mss. 9–12 and 25 28, in Var. 20
(Ex. 102b and 102c). The treatment of diminished 7th
chords in Var. 20 (at +) corresponds to the viewpoint of former
theorists who simply said: "a diminished 7th chord can
precede and follow every harmony." It must not be overlooked that the harmony, besides providing structural advantages, is also capable of producing stimulating means of
expression. Under such uncontrollable circumstances analysis
has to resign in favour of faithful confidence in the thinking
of a great composer.

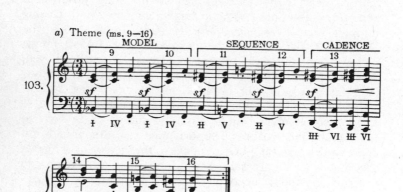

n) Var. V   MODEL   "SEQUENCE"

o) Var. V

In this work one result of extended tonality is illustrated by the numerous harmonic variations of a segment of four measures. It is the aforementioned segment of mss. 9–12 in the theme, consisting of the progression ~~I~~-IV (9), its repetition (10), and their sequence ~~II~~-V, ~~II~~-V (11-12) (see Ex. 103a). These progressions in the " a " section[1] lead through ~~III~~-VI, etc., to V (16). Curiously, in the " a¹ " section—mss. 25–28 (Ex. 103b)—the same progressions by way of V end on the tonic.

In some of the variations (1, 2, 3, 8, etc.) the initial progression of mss. 9–10 is preserved in both " a " and " a¹ "; but instead of the sequence II–V of mss. 11–12 there appears in " a " of Var. 1, IV–♭VII (Ex. 103c), and in " a¹ " of Var. 1, ~~VI~~-II (Ex. 103d); in Var. 2, ~~VII~~-III (Ex. 103e); in Var. 3, IV–V (103f). The progressions of mss. 25–26 are always repeated here (without much change) in mss. 27–28, with the exception of Var. 3, where mss. 27–28 substitute ~~II~~-V for IV–V, and Var. 8 (Ex. 103g), where ~~VII~~-III is followed by ~~II~~-I. Similar deviations occur in other variations, e.g., Vars. 11 and 12.

In Vars 1–3 the cadence to the dominant in " a " starts on III (ms. 13), and the cadence to the tonic in " a¹ " starts on V (ms. 29) [see Ex. 103d, e, f]. The connection between the ending of the sequential segment (ms. 12) and the beginning of the cadence is often surprising, as, for instance, in Var. 1 (Ex. 103c)—♭VII–~~III~~ (dim. 7th). In other cases ms. 9 is replaced by ~~III~~-VI (Vars. 4 and 7) [Ex. 103l, m].

The cadence to V in Var. 4 starts on a chromatic passing ~~IV~~ (Ex. 103l). Var. 5 deviates extensively from the original progressions in that mss. 9–10, with incomplete chords, builds a two-measure model (III–~~VII~~) freely sequenced (ms. 11–12) by ~~VII~~-~~III~~ (Ex. 103n). In the same variation the sequence in ms. 27–28 proceeds through ♭VI to the Neapolitan triad on ~~II~~ (Ex. 103*o*).

Another remote variation occurs in ms. 9–12 of Var. 7 (Ex. 103m), where mss. 10 and 12 are only free melodic repetitions of mss. 9 and 11 respectively; ~~III~~-VI is followed by IV–~~IV~~₆, and ~~VII~~ (dim. 7th)–~~VII~~ (art. dom.) by III–~~VII~~.

Now follow some examples from contemporaries and

[1 " a "=expository section; " a¹ "=recapitulatory section.]

successors of Wagner. The motto-like introduction to the second movement of Dvorak's Symphony, " From the New World ", can easily be understood as remaining within the tonic region.

Dvorak: E minor Symphony, Largo

Ex. 105, from the second movement of Grieg's 'Cello Sonata, includes, among its many passing harmonies, a number of transformations, passing notes and suspensions, some of them unresolved (at +). But it is definitely in the tonic region.

Grieg: 'Cello Sonata, 2nd Movement

Ex. 106, the Adagio from Bruckner's 7th Symphony, also in the tonic region, likewise contains passing harmonies, passing notes and suspensions.

Bruckner: Symphony No.7, Adagio

Ex. 107, a quotation from *Karwoche* (Holy Week) by Hugo
Wolf—who was one of the most prominent followers of Wagner's achievements in expression, musical illustration and
harmony—is similar in style to many other songs by this
composer. The progressions in this example are better understood if analysed partly in the submediant region. The **f♭** in
ms. 1(+) is a free suspension and does not constitute a harmony
different from that of I. Such "non-constitutional" tones
are characteristic of this period.

Ex. 108 is from Bizet's *Carmen*. Bizet is one of those composers whose rich harmony does not derive from a precon-
ceived scheme of modulation. It is, in other words, not an
embellishment, but it is conditioned by the nature of his
melodies. It can be analysed in the tonic region (**t**), but some
of the progressions are more convincingly presented in mediant
(**M**). Curiously, the tonic harmony does not come before
ms. 13, and, more unusually, it comes here in root position,
as a result of the doubling of the voice melody in the accompaniment (mss. 8–12). Normally, after the Neapolitan (ms. 11)
the $^6_4$-chord can be expected, followed by a dominant on the
same bass tone. Here the voice, leaping up to the **f♯**, forms,
together with the **d**, a kind of inverted pedal on **d–f♯**, below
which the bass proceeds as the true continuation of the melody
toward a pseudo-cadence to I.

The example from César Franck's Symphony (109) is characteristic of the time in which it was written. It is a typical case of chromatic ascent or descent based less on the relations of the main harmonies than on the multiple meaning of diminished 7th chords and other vagrants. Still, an analysis according to **sm** and **m** presents the relation to **t.** The tones marked (+) are best considered as passing melody tones.

In Ex. 110, the first four measures express I in mss. 1 and 2 and VI in mss. 3 and 4, through the combination of two melody lines without the addition of complete harmonies. In ms. 5 II is incomplete and becomes complete only in ms. 6, also by melodic progression.

Similarly, Ex. 111, though without complete harmonies, distinctly passes through two (or three) regions. The music of Max Reger, like that of Bruckner and Mahler, is little known outside Germany. But his music is rich and new, through his application to " absolute " music of Wagner's achievements in the realm of harmony. Because these were invented for dramatic expression, the application of these procedures in this way provoked an almost " revolutionary " movement among Wagner's successors.

Nine examples from Wagner's operas—probably not the most characteristic ones—illustrate non-modulatory procedures within a tonality. While in classical music many essential changes seldom occur in one measure, Ex. 112a shows the novelty of this procedure by the use of numerous transformed degrees. In 112b, leading to **D**, the essential change occurs at + in ms. 10.

Even richer is Ex. 113; this almost suggests a modulation and remodulation,[1] when in ms. 4 it arrives at ♭**mM**, which must be classified as ⑤, i.e. Distant.[2]

[1 i.e. modulation back.]
[2 See Classification of Relationship, Chapter IX.]

In Ex. 114 this modulatory contrasting middle section contains two sequences; the same degree numbers appear in every phrase. This modulation is also classified as ⑤.

[*N.B.* **t/T** means tonic minor *or* tonic major.]

The first 24 measures of Ex. 115a remain, in spite of some transformed degrees, close to **T** (or **t**). But the closing segment (115b) modulates very fast to **SMsm**, V–I, Class 5, which, perforce, one could register as **SM** (III–VI).

It is advantageous to register Ex. 116 in several regions because the progression in mss. 1–2 is in **S/T**: II (Neap.)–V, similar to **T**: II (Neap.) –V at the end.

Even in a melody with popular appeal, Ex. 117, the tonality is fairly far extended. Such deviations from simplicity were obstacles for Wagner's contemporaries.

Ex. 118, from " *Die Meistersinger* ", is based on a change between **T** and **sm**. So much of it refers to **sm** that one would be inclined to consider it in **g** minor, were the ending in ms. 11 not distinctly on V of **B**♭.

Ex. 119, from *Tristan*, is one of those Wagnerian melodies which are built by quasi-sequential repetitions of a short phrase. It is analysed as being in B minor in spite of the F minor-like progression ♮ (Neap.)–V, because this method offers the opportunity of analysing the last phrase (mss. 7–8) as an ending on **v**, substituting for an ending on V. The progressions in the second (mss. 3–4) and third (mss. 5–6) phrases are better called " quasi-Neapolitan " (♮–V) because the harmonies in mss. 3 and 5 are not major chords.

Analysis of Ex. 120a reveals that it is less modulatory than
it seems at first glance. It is only the section mss. 6–17 which,
deviating from **t,** moves through **sm** to **♯m** and (mss. 11–14)
to **♯M.** The progressions in mss. 11 and 12 are explained in
120b as sequences of two transformations of II, also transposed
to III (120c) and VI (120d). If mss. 13 were also a sequence,
it would appear like 120e; instead, two chromatically gliding
diminished 7th chords (used melodically rather than functionally) are connected with I of **♯M,** equivalent to **♯III** of **t** in
ms. 14. This measure, despite the melodic changes, is analysed
as two forms of one and the same degree, i.e., the 9th of the
diminished 7th chord (f♭) descends and the 7th (d♭) ascends
(through d♮) to the octave (e♭) (Ex. 120f). (Such a procedure
is not infrequent in Wagner, as illustrated in 120g, a form of the
Rheintöchter-Motiv (Rhinemaidens' motive) from *Siegfried*.) The
eighth-note figure in mss. 17–24 (120a) is played in unison by
the strings without harmonic accompaniment. Evidently
such a passage would not be logical in Wagner's style without
an intelligible relation to a tonality. Here a rather convincing
attempt has been made to reveal this relation as two transformations of **Ħ** (mss. 18–22) followed by a cadence (mss. 23–
25).

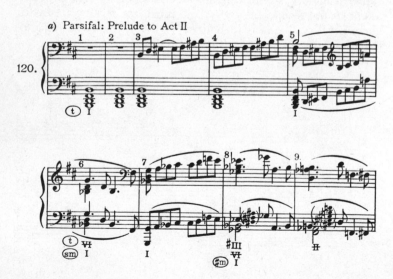

a) Parsifal: Prelude to Act II

120.

Extended tonality is also characteristic of my first period (1896–1906); fragments of two songs from Op. 6 are analysed here. At first glance Ex. 121 looks as if it were extremely modulatory. But analysis shows that changes of regions occur only in ms. 3 (♭**SM**), 5 (♭**M**), 6 (♭**m**) and 9—back to ♭**SM**, on whose tonic this section later ends. The apparently free passing notes and suspensions (marked +) are merely melodic but not harmonic. The harmony at " a " (ms. 1) is to be understood as an imperfect form of a 9th chord on V (Ex. 121a). It reappears similarly in ms. 7. Ex. 121b explains the progression IV–Ⅱ of ♭**SM** as changing the roots of one diminished 7th chord, a procedure which is discussed in my *Harmonielehre*, Ex. 304[1]. Similarly, the main theme of my *Kammersymphonie* is introduced by multiple root reference of a diminished 7th chord (121c).

Schoenberg: Der Wanderer, Op. 6, No. 8

+) passing notes or free suspensions.

121.

---

[1] Used without acknowledgement by A. E. Hull.

Ex. 122 is characterized by a number of far-reaching transformations with multiple meanings. The examples, a, b, c and
d explain mss. 11–12, 13, 20 and 21 respectively as transformations and substitutions of 9th chords on **b♭**. The enharmonization of many of these notes somewhat obscures this fact. The
5th (f) is often replaced by f♯, but in ms. 20 by f♭ (e♮) and in
21 by both f♯ and f♭. In ms. 22, Ex. 122d, the root is omitted
and the 7th is in the bass.

Perhaps the most interesting feature of this song, as mentioned
in my *Harmonielehre*, is that the tonic, E♭, does not appear
throughout the whole piece; I call this " schwebende Tonali-
tät " (suspended tonality). Many parts of the song must be
analysed in **sm**. The contrasting modulatory section, mss. 32–
41, uses for a retransition [i.e. modulation back], the segment
mss. 5–10 in mss. 42–47. This is analysed in 122e in **sm** and
subT. It begins (in ms. 42) and ends (45–46) at the same
chords as mss. 5 and 8–9 respectively. The fine point is that
this similarity is produced in spite of the transposition of the
melody a half-step higher (mss. 42–44). Accordingly all
degrees are one step higher.

Schoenberg: Lockung, Op.6, No.7

122.

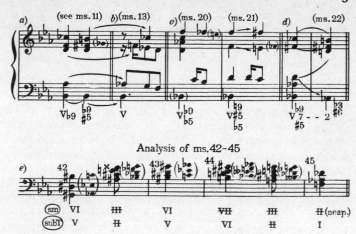

Analysis of ms. 42-45

The ear of the contemporary musician and music lover is no longer disturbed by far-reaching deviations from diatonic harmonies. This was an obstacle to the contemporaries of Mozart, who called his C major String Quartet the " Dissonance " Quartet. It was again an obstacle to the contemporaries of Wagner, Mahler and Strauss and will remain so for some time to come. But time heals all wounds—even those inflicted by dissonant harmonies.

CHAPTER XI

PROGRESSIONS FOR VARIOUS COMPOSITIONAL PURPOSES

THE FORMS for which harmony progressions are recommended in the following chapter are described in Arnold Schoenberg: *Models for Beginners in Composition* (G. Schirmer, N.Y.). Thus all the advice given here refers to the school-forms constructed for the sake of practice. A school-form is an abstraction which differs, often considerably, from reality. For this reason these studies must be complemented by analysis of masterworks. The progressions recommended here will provide for the following forms or formal requirements: sentence, period, codetta, contrasting middle section, transition, sequence, *Durchführung* (elaboration or development), introduction and other so-called " free " forms.

SENTENCE

The school-form for the sentence (eight measures) begins with a two-measure unit, followed by a repetition (mss. 3–4) which can be a sequence or else a more or less contrasting repetition. The sixth measure will be a sequence of the fifth, and mss. 7 and 8 will be cadences to various degrees.

The first unit (mss. 1–2) may consist of two harmonies: I–V, I–IV, I–VI, I–III, I–II; or of three harmonies:
I–IV–V, I–VI–V, I–II–V, I–V–I, etc.

Similarly I–IV, etc., can be extended; e.g. I–III–IV, I–VI–IV; or I–III–VI, I–V–VI; or I–VII–III (III), I–II–III; or I–VI–II, I–IV–II, etc.

There may also be four or more harmonies in this unit.

The second unit (mss. 3–4) may be a mere interchange of the harmonies of the first, by reversing their order. This method is seldom applicable if there are more than two harmonies.

A few examples of mss. 1–4 follow:

	First unit	*Second unit*
(a)	I–V	V–I
(b)		II–VI
(c)		III–VII
(d)		VI–III, etc.
(e)	I–IV	IV–I
(f)		II–V
(g)		III–VI

	First unit	*Second unit*
(h)		VII–III, etc.
(i)	I–VI	II–VII
(j)		III–I
(k)		IV–II, etc.
(l)	I–III	IV–VI, etc.
(m)	I–II	IV–V
(n)		V–VI
(o)		II–III, etc.
(p)	I–V–I	V–I–V, etc.

The third unit (ms. 5) and its sequence (ms. 6) will, for the sake of practice, preferably avoid repetition of a preceding progression.

An eight-measure sentence might be based on progressions like the following:

ms.	1–2	3–4	5	6	7	8
(a)	I–V	V–I	VI–II	VII–III	VI–IV	I⁶₄–V–I
(b)	Alternative				I–VI–IV–II	I⁶₄–V–I
(c)	Same 6 ms. cadencing to **D**:			**T** VI–II	V
				D II–V	I
(d)	Alternative:			**T** VI–III–VI–II	V
				D II–VI–II–V	I
(e)	Same 6 ms. cadencing to **m**:			mVI–II	I⁶₄–V–I

Here follow harmonic excerpts of sentences from Beethoven's Piano Sonatas:

	ms.	1–2	3–4	5	6	7	8
Op. 2/1 1st mvmt., f minor:		I	V	I	V	I–II	V(D)
Op. 2/3, 1st mvmt., C major:		I–V	V–I	I–V	I–V	I–II	V–I
Op. 7, 2nd mvmt., C major:							

ms.	1	2	3	4	5	6	7	8
	I–V	V–I	I–II	II–V	I–V–I	II	V	I

PERIOD

The school-form for the period consists of two segments of four measures each. The first, the antecedent, may end on V, either through mere interchange (e.g. I–V–I–V) or in a more elaborate manner, or through a half cadence with or without substitutes (Ex. 123a). In the minor, the procedure is similar (124a).

The second segment, the consequent (mss. 5–8), may repeat part of the antecedent, and usually concludes with a perfect cadence to I, V, or III in major (123b), or I, III, V or v in minor (124b).

PERIODS
Antecedents

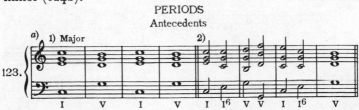

123.	I	V	I	V	I	I⁶	V	V	I	I⁶	V

Consequents

123.

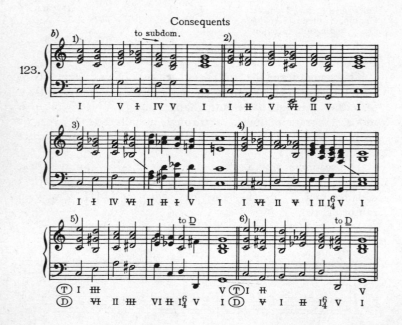

PERIODS: minor
Antecedents

Here are a few illustrations of periods from Beethoven's Piano Sonatas:

ms.	1	2	3	4	5	6	7	8
		Antecedent				*Consequent*		
Op. 2/1, 2nd mvmt., F maj.:	I	V	I–V–I	V,	I	IV–V–I	IV–I–V	I
Op. 2/2, 4th mvmt., A maj.:	I	V	I–V–IV	I–V,	I			
					D: IV–I	II	I–V	I
Op. 7, 4th mvmt. E♭ maj.:	V–(I)	V	I–V–I	V,	V–(I)	V	I–II–I–V	I

CODETTA

A codetta, as regard its structural functions, is merely a cadence, whatever its motival or thematic implications may be. In classical music its harmonic range comprises all forms from the mere interchange of I–V, etc., to the most remotely enriched

cadences. See, for instance, mss. 113–144 in the 1st movement
of the Eroica (Ex. 125).

Beethoven: 3rd Symphony, 1st Movement, Codetta

* This is Ⓓ with reference to Ⓣ = E♭

CONTRASTING MIDDLE SECTION

As the middle part of forms which consist of more than two parts, i.e. simple ternary forms—minuets, scherzos, etc.—and other forms consisting of three divisions—sonatas, symphonies, concertos, etc.,—the middle section is supposed to form a contrast to the preceding and the succeeding sections. The harmony plays a decisive role in the production of this contrast. In simple cases a change of region is enough. Thus, as the " a " section presents **T** or **t**, whether it ends on I or on another degree of the scale, the regions of either **D, m** or **SD** in major, or **D, M** and **v** in minor, are a sufficient contrast. For the region of **D** see Beethoven's Piano Sonata, Op. 2/2, 2nd movement; for **SM**, his Sonata op. 14/1, 2nd movement.

Ex. 126 illustrates progressions for simple as well as more elaborate cases. 126a is a mere interchange of V–I on a pedal (for pedal see p. 137). 126b (I–V, I–V) and c (I–IV–V, I–IV–V) begin on I. Generally the contrasting middle section will begin on a degree other than that used to begin or end the " a " section. Therefore the following progressions (126d–m) begin on V, III, VI, II, IV, and on I–minor, v–minor, IV-minor, flat III and flat VI.

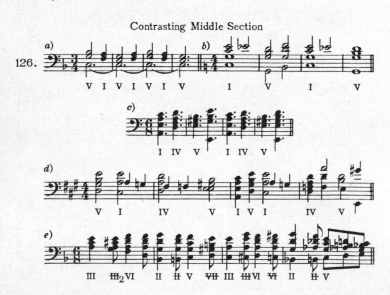

Contrasting Middle Section

In many of these examples mss. 3–4 repeat 1–2 with a slight change required for the introduction of the upbeat harmony, V.[1]

[1 Schoenberg used "upbeat harmony" to describe the penultimate chord leading to the returning tonic, i.e., the "downbeat".]

The harmony is richer in the following examples taken at random from musical literature. In Schubert's *Morgengruss* (Ex. 127), the movement from **v** to **V** is carried out with substitutes. An example from Chopin's Prelude in Db (Ex.128) passes through **v** to **sm** which finally, as VI of **T**, is followed by V. In Ex. 129 from Brahms' G minor Piano Quartet, Op. 25, the contrasting middle section starts on V and soon moves to **m**, on whose V a little episode is built, repeated with a slight variation on I of **M** which is HI of **T**. The middle part of the Bridal Chorus from Wagner's *Lohengrin* (Ex. 130) after an interchange of IV and V, returns to **SM**, passes again through **T** and, in its last segment, proceeds to **M/m**. Ex. 131, from my *Kammersymphonie* (middle part of the Adagio section) offers some difficulty because of the double meaning of the tones marked +. The tones on the third quarters of mss. 2 and 3 and the B♮ on the fourth quarter of ms. 2 are anticipations of the harmony on the following beats. The whole segment is based on the frequent interchange of **D** and **v**.

Brahms: Piano Quartet in G minor, Op. 25 (3rd Movement: Eb maj.)

(harmonic excerpt)

Wagner: Bridal Chorus, Lohengrin

Schoenberg: Kammersymphonie, Adagio

SEQUENCE

A sequence is an exact repetition of a segment transposed to another degree. A true transposition to another degree will express another region, thus producing a modulation. So-called tonal sequences, using only the diatonic tones, are imperfect sequences because they necessarily replace major chords by minor and vice-versa (Ex. 132).

The sequence offers the technical advantage of being a repetition and yet producing a slight contrast by the use of another region. For this reason it has been used abundantly by almost all the great composers. It was especially the sequential transposition within the structure of a theme, from a tonic to a Dorian region,—used sometimes even by great composers (see, for example, Beethoven's C major Symphony, Schubert's Trio in Bb and C major Quintet, Ex. 133),—which seemed hackneyed to later composers. Composers of Brahms'

school avoided not only this kind of sequence but every unchanged repetition, no matter in what region.

The progressions for contrasting middle sections in Ex. 134
consist of sequential (or quasi-sequential) repetition. The
ending of the original segment, or MODEL, should introduce
or lead to the harmony which begins the sequence. Accordingly, part of the modulation will often occur within the model,
as, for instance, in 134d, e, f, g, etc.

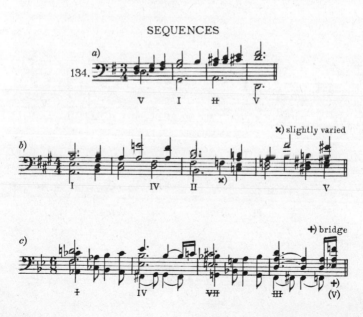

For compositional purposes it is often necessary to arrive at the end of a sequence on a definite degree of the scale, for example, in a transition (see p. 139) or for an up-beat harmony before a recapitulation, etc. Hence it is necessary to build the model in a certain manner and to start the sequence on a definite degree. If the model, for example,

begins on					the sequence will be
I (T/t) and ends on				II(2nd up),	IV to V
I	,,	,,	,,	♭II(–2nd up),	♯IV to V (enhar-monic)
I	,,	,,	,,	III(3rd up),	♭III to V
I	,,	,,	,,	♭III(—3rd up),	III to V
I	,,	,,	,,	IV(4th up),	II to V
I	,,	,,	,,	VI(3rd down),	♭VII to V
I	,,	,,	,,	♭VI(+3rd down),	VII to V
I	,,	,,	,,	VII(2nd down),	♭VI to V
I	,,	,,	,,	♭VII(+2nd down)	VI to V

In Ex. 135 three of the more difficult problems regarding regions are carried out. In 135a the model should end on II, i.e. **dor**, a minor region. If the sequence must really end on **D** this could be an exact sequence except for the last chord. Ex. 135b is remarkable because of the ending on ♭III (I of ♭**M**). The sequence then begins on I of (♮) **M** as Neapolitan of ♭**M**. Ex. 135c begins with an artificial dominant 7th chord on I.

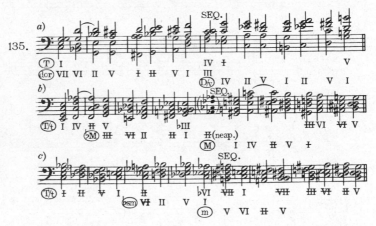

In Ex. 136 sequences on various degrees are shown: major 2nd up (136d and h,) major 2nd down (136g), minor 3rd up (136e and f), minor 3rd down (136a and c), 5th up (136b). The sequence is introduced by a V in 136b, led in as a I to ₶

progression in 136c, as a IV–V–VI progression in 136a, by a repetition of the same harmony in 136d, and by interchanging **m** for **M** in minor in 136e. The sequence in 136g becomes more understandable if, eliminating some subordinate tones, one substitutes the roots on which the progressions are based (136h). In 136f the $^6_4$-chords at the beginnings of model and sequence obscure the progressions slightly, but the roots mark them as a deceptive progression, V–VI, in **D**. In 136i the beginning of the sequence does not suggest deviation from **T**; only at the second measure does the change to **S/T** become evident.

a) Bach: Brandenburg Concerto No. 2 (F major)

b) Beethoven: Sonata Op. 2/3 (C major)

c) Beethoven: Sonata Op. 10/1 (C minor)

d) Beethoven: Sonata Op. 2/2, Scherzo (A major)

e) Tschaikovsky: Symphony No. 6 (B minor)

VARIATION OF THE SEQUENCE

Of higher value æsthetically are sequences in which variations produce an even stronger effect without endangering the
memorability of the model. Slight changes in the part leading,
passing notes, chromaticism, suspensions, etc., produce more
vital variants of the original. Substitutes and transformations,
and especially interpolated chords, are further means to this
end. Substitutes and transformations will best be used to
make the part leading more effective or convincing.

In Ex. 137, sequences in almost every region have been
added to a model I–V. They preserve the I–V of these regions
but insert one or more intermediate harmonies. Similarly,
other models can be enriched—for instance, I–III, I–IV, I–VI,
and I–II; one may also use models consisting of more than
two harmonies—for instance, I–IV–V, I–II–V, I–VI–V,
I–VI–IV, I–VI–II, etc., or, like the model in 137l, I–V̶–V̶I̶–I̶I̶.
Evidently a model in the middle of a piece can also begin with
a degree other than I, as in Ex. 138a and c. In 138b and d
these sequences are enriched in the part leading through passing chromatic notes and even through passing transformations. In the examples of 139 the part leading is more elabor-
ately varied. The relation between model and sequence in
140a is closer than the notation reveals.

Sequences to a Model, I–V, with Insertions

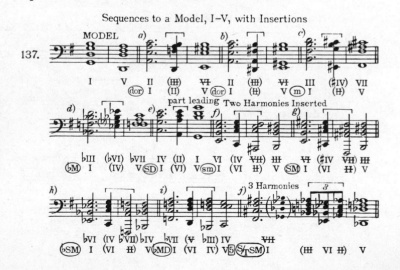

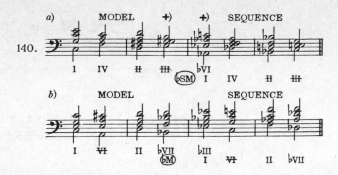

In Ex. 141 are a few illustrations from musical literature in which the structural advantages of the sequence—namely repetition, harmonic progress and slow development—are achieved without strict sequential treatment of the model. Evidently such deviations can only be used if the substituting progressions are not weaker than those of the original—which is not easy to determine.

c) Brahms: Piano Quintet

PEDAL

A pedal point, a retarding or restraining device of compositional technique, appears in various places. The restraint is produced by one or two voices, which sustain one or two tones, usually root and fifth, while other voices move freely through various harmonies. The conventional rule demands that the sustained voice should begin and end as a consonance; between these consonances, even harmonies which are dissonant to the pedal tone may occur. Generally the sustained note is in the bass. If in another voice, it is called an " inverted " pedal. The general belief that " every " harmony can appear in these circumstances requires a correction. No other harmonies should appear than those consistent with the structural and stylistic conditions of the environment—in other words, only harmonies which would be usable if there were no sustained voices.

Accordingly, from the standpoint of structural functions there is not much interest in pedal points.

If it occurs at the beginning of a piece, the sustained note is usually a pedal on I or V. Here it assists establishment of the tonality by retarding an early modulatory movement. Such pedals can be seen in the following masterpieces: Beethoven's Sonata, Op. 28, 1st and 4th movements; String Quartet, Op. 74, 1st movement; Mozart's E♭ String Quartet, Trio of Minuet; D major Quartet No. 7, Minuet; D major Quartet No. 8, 1st movement; Schubert's A minor String Quartet, Op. 29, 1st movement; Brahms' C minor Quartet, Op. 51, 1st movement.

Here one seldom finds more than an interchange of I–I̶–IV– V–I; sometimes II, I̶I̶, VI and I̶V̶ also appear. I̶I̶ is then generally a diminished 7th chord or an artificial dominant.

In contrasting middle sections (see Beethoven's Sonatas, Op. 2/1, Adagio, and Op. 2/2, Rondo, etc.) before the recapitulation, in transitions (Beethoven's Sonata, Op. 53, 1st movement; Op. 7, 1st movement, etc.) and in *Durchführungen* (cf. p. 145) (Beethoven's Eroica, 1st movement; String Quartet, Op. 74, etc.), the pedal marks the end of the modulatory process. Dwelling on the pedal enhances the expectation of the tonality or region to follow by delaying its appearance. The harmonies here do not differ much from those found over pedals at beginnings of movements, except that they generally begin on a V of a tonality or region and end on a I (or deceptively on VI, IV or II).

In addition, pedals may be found in codettas, episodes and even subordinate themes. Certain exceptional cases should be mentioned: the Prelude to *Das Rheingold*, which is based unchangingly on an E♭ triad; the Fugue of Brahms' *Deutsches Requiem*, and the entire *Durchführung* and Coda of his D minor Violin Sonata, Op. 108, 1st movement, both written over a pedal bass throughout.

But the use of a pedal point to conceal the poverty of the harmony or the absence of a good bass line is not justified. Unfortunately most of the pedal points of mediocre composers are of this kind. This is the poorest form of homophony.

TRANSITION

In larger forms themes in different regions are often connected by means of a transition. In classical music subordinate themes are seldom to be found in a region more remote than Class 2 (see p. 68). Transitions therefore are not very complicated harmonically. They are either new themes beginning at the end of a main theme (Ex. 142) or modulatory transformations in lieu of an ending. (Ex. 143).

In Ex. 142 the procedure with such new themes is illustrated by one example of Beethoven and three of Brahms. Sequences and liquidations[1] make the procedure a gradual one. The Beethoven example (142a) is quite simple. In two of the Brahms examples (142b and c) the final turn occurs only after the sequence of an extraordinarily long model (142b) or after a partial modulatory repetition (142c). Here the final goal is analysed as **sm**, which is an enharmonization comparable to that discussed on p. 162. That this analysis is correct, i.e. that it need not be registered **♯Mm**, is proved in the continuation and at the end of this division of the movement, where **SM** is presented in flats. The third Brahms example (142d) takes a detour before arriving at **M**; this, perhaps, accounts for the deviation into mediant major's Neapolitan, which enharmonizes to sharp mediant major (**♯M**).

a) Beethoven: Sonata, Op. 10/1, Transition

142.

[1] See Arnold Schoenberg, *Models for Beginners*, p. 11.

b) Brahms: Symphony No. 3, F major: Transition

c) Brahms: Piano Quintet in F minor, Op. 34

d) Brahms: Quartet Op.51/2, A minor

Modulatory transformations of the main theme, on the other hand, move without so many intermediate steps directly toward the goal.

d) Sonata Op. 7

Other transitions function as connecting links between codettas (with which a division of a movement ends) and the repetition demanded by repetition marks (first endings of expositions)—see, for instance, Beethoven Sonatas Op. 31/2, Op. 53 and String Quartet Op. 59/3, all 1st movements—or (second endings of expositions) as introductory transitions to the *Durchführung*, or as transitions from the end of the *Durchführung* back to the recapitulation.

As in the recapitulation all the subordinate themes are supposed to appear in the tonic region, a transition would seem superfluous, were it not that the composer knows that the listener likes to hear again valuable material of the first division [exposition]. In most cases there is a turn to the subdominant, followed by a simple transposition leading to V. In other cases, like Beethoven's Quartet Op. 18/6, the Piano Sonata Op. 106, etc., an extended roundabout way is taken to produce a contrast between tonic and tonic. One of the most interesting instances in this respect is illustrated in Ex. 144 from Mozart's G minor Symphony.

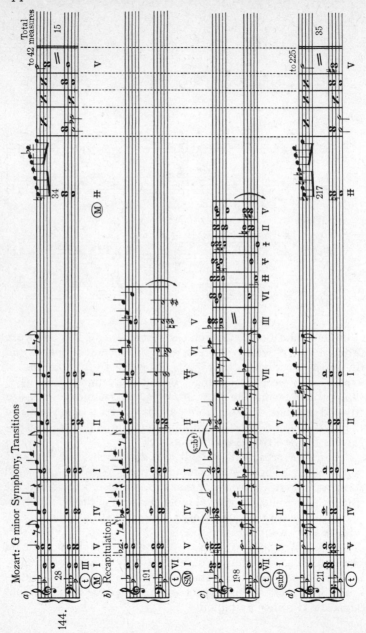

144.

Mozart: G minor Symphony, Transitions

DURCHFÜHRUNG (ELABORATION)

Almost every larger composition contains one or more divisions which are of modulatory construction. In medium-sized compositions (minuets, scherzos, etc.) this part is best called a *modulatory contrasting (middle) section*. In larger forms, in accommodation to the more complex construction of the first division and its recapitulation—the third division—a more elaborate and more compound contrasting second division is required. This second division is usually called "development", "elaboration", "working-out", etc. There is development everywhere in a piece of music, especially in the first division, where a number of themes are developed from a basic motive. Nothing can remain without being elaborated or worked out. What happens in this second division is something different. Themes of the first division and their derivatives are found in a constant modulatory movement through many and even through remote regions.

This movement through the regions is much better characterized by the term *Durchführung*, which means that the themes which have not modulated in the first division are now *geführt durch*, (led through) contrasting regions in a modulatory procedure.

Bach's modulatory contrasting sections in his larger forms—for instance, Preludes, Toccatas, Gigues, even Fugues, etc.—certainly lead a phrase, a theme, or some other segment of the first section through a number of regions (Ex. 145).

a) Bach: Prelude, English Suite II (A minor)

b) Bach: Gigue, Partita VI (E minor)

In comparison, Haydn passes through more regions and more remote ones in the G major (Surprise) Symphony. He includes here even a region which is classified as indirect and remote (**subT**).[1]

[1] Equivalent to ♭**mv**, Class 4.

Haydn: G major Symphony: Durchführung

Even richer than the preceding *Durchführung* is the compass
of modulation in the first movement of Mozart's G minor
Symphony (Ex. 147). It passes successively through regions
classified as close and direct [1], indirect but close [2], indirect
[3] and distant [5]. The compass of the last movement is even
more remote (Ex. 148).

Mozart: G minor Symphony: Durchführung

Mozart: G minor Symphony 4th Movement

148.

Beethoven's *Durchführungen*, with their dramatic inclinations, often aim for even greater contrasts than structural considerations require. In the Eroica this can best be seen (Ex. 149) in the succession of **sm** (ms. 178), **♯sm** (ms. 181), **mv** (ms. 185) which are classed respectively as 1, 5 and 5. Moreover, these regions are very distantly related among themselves. If, for instance, the beginning of this segment were the tonic, the sequence in ms. 181 would be a 5 relation and, similarly, the same relation would exist in the following sequence. One of the most extravagant ventures occurs when a new theme is placed in **SMm** (ms. 284), followed by a partial repetition in **SMsm** (ms. 292), which are the most distant relations. These same segments are later repeated (mss. 322 and 330) in **t** and **♭M**. The relation between this segment and its repetition is also a very distant one.

Beethoven: Symphony No.3, Durchführung

The richness of Schubert's harmony perhaps marks the actual transition to Wagnerian and post-Wagnerian composers' procedures. In a relatively short *Durchführung* of a String Quartet (!) (Ex. 150) he stays, for longer or shorter periods, in the following regions: **sd**, **sm**, **m**, **sd**, **smsm**, the relations of which are classed respectively ⓵, ⓶, ⓶, ⓵ and ⓹. The **smsm** region (ms. 150) seems more distant because of the somewhat roving modulations in the preceding measures, which define it as derived from **sm**. But an enharmonic change would make it tonic major's mediant (db=c♯).

Schubert: String Quartet in A minor, Op. 29 Durchführung

The *Durchführung* of Mendelssohn's Third Symphony in A minor (Ex. 151) is richer in modulation and passes through more remote regions than the first movement of the Fourth Symphony in A major. It starts by considering the tone " e " of the first ending on **v** as the third of I of **♯m** (evaluated as ④) in the second ending. A further modulation to **dor** ④ leads over **subt** ④ to **m** ③, again to **subt** and **sd** ① followed by **SM** ②, then **subt** and, with roving harmony, to **t**.

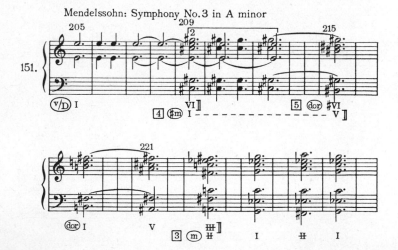

Mendelssohn: Symphony No. 3 in A minor

Schumann resembles Mendelssohn in that his modulation is tamer than one would expect from his rich and fluent harmony. Ex. 152 shows that he includes regions of classes ①, ②, and ③, that is **t, sd, v, dor** (all minor), also ♭**M**, ♭**m** and **t**.

Schumann Piano Quintet in E♭

In order to connect the *Durchführung* proper (ms. 77) of the 1st movement of Brahms' 3rd Symphony in F major (Ex. 153) with the second ending of the first division (on **m**), an introductory transition is inserted. The beginning of the *Durchführung* (written as a c♯ minor region in the strings and woodwind) is, as the analysis reveals, an enharmonization of a d♭ minor region (so written in the brass); thus the region is in fact ♭**sm**, not **Mm**, which is rather remote from the **m** of the second ending. For a real understanding of the modulatory procedure it is necessary to " register " the regions according to the way they are introduced. This region (♭**sm**) was introduced by way of the flat regions. This ♭**sm** (ms. 77) and later **subT** (ms. 101) are the only points at which the *Durchführung* settles down for a longish time. Between these two points the harmony is roving, in a circle of fifths, mss. 92–97, or along a chromatic bass line, mss. 98–99. The section from mss. 110 to 112 is analysed as **subT** followed by **subt** to ms. 117, in spite of some incidental deviations (mss. 106–109). The reason for analysing it in this way is the fact that in ms. 120 Brahms introduces a major triad on F, not as a tonic but as a dominant. Accordingly, ms. 117 is considered the turning point to **sd**, of which ms. 120 would be V. This V is now changed in an interesting manner to function as a I in ms. 124, in correspondence to his " motto " motive.

Brahms: Symphony No.3 in F major: Durchführung

The preceding analyses indicate that while the actual modulation may be either audacious and roving or simple and gradual, regions may be approached whose distance from the tonic region is not always what might be expected. For instance, long segments of a Haydn theme may be based on one or two harmonies only, while the first theme of Schumann's Piano Quintet requires a rich succession of harmonies. Nevertheless, the analyses above show that the distance of regions reached in Haydn's Symphony is greater than that of those in the Schumann example.

The method of evaluation established here can be applied to do justice to composers whose compass of modulation has been underrated, on the one hand, and to those who have been overrated in this respect, on the other hand. The findings might prove in many cases the contrary of what one expected. Thus, for instance, analysis of the Prelude to *Tristan* proves that, on the basis of the interchangeability of **t** and **T**, ♭**M** and ♭**SM** (of **T**) comprise the furthest compass of the modulation, —if one recognizes that those sections which seem to go farther are only roving on the basis of the multiple meaning of a vagrant harmony. Of course this is not a criticism of the beauty of this music.

Roving Harmony

Roving harmony was discussed in Chapter I (p. 3). In our analyses of *Durchfuhrüngen* some segments have been defined as roving. Extended tonality may contain roving segments, though, on the other hand, various regions may occasionally be firmly established.

Roving harmony need not contain extravagant chords. Even simple triads and dominant 7th chords may fail to express a tonality. See Ex. 154 and the following examples selected from musical literature (Ex. 155 ff.) which are discussed in the following chapter under other considerations.

Beethoven: Sonata Op. 2/2 (C major), 1st movement, 97–109

154.

Roving harmony is based on multiple meaning. Accordingly chords which are vagrants because of their constitution are very effective for this purpose: diminished 7th chords, augmented triads, augmented $\frac{6}{5}$- and $\frac{4}{3}$-chords, Neapolitan triads, other transformations and fourth chords [chords composed of fourths].

THE SO-CALLED "FREE FORMS"

Introduction, Prelude, Fantasy, Rhapsody, Recitative and others are types of musical organization which previous theorists did not describe but simply called "free", adding, "no special form is adhered to" and "free from formal restrictions". Form to them was not organization but restriction; thus, "free" forms would seem amorphous and unorganized. The cause of this failure of the theorists may be that no two of their "free" forms have a similar structure. But even among forms which are *not* free from formal restrictions—scherzos, rondos, first movements of sonatas and symphonies—it is difficult to find two movements which resemble each other in more than the most primordial outline. It is these differences that make one a work of Beethoven, but another only a work of XY—just as other differences make one creature a man, but another an ape. If composers did not eagerly try to name their works correctly, theorists might also consider those " restricted " forms as unorganized.

Fortunately a composer knows when it is not advisable to begin a piece directly with the subject matter, and when he needs preliminaries. It does not matter whether or not a theorist finds such preparatory sections to be justified. In most cases they are imponderables, and one could scarcely contend that the introduction to Beethoven's Fourth Symphony or Sonata Pathétique could be omitted. Of course, even such things as the first two measures of the Eroica or the first two phrases of the Fifth Symphony would be, strictly speaking, superfluous, were there not such imponderables as a composer's sense of form and expression.

As far as I know, only one scholar has charged himself with the task of investigating the formal conditions for a Prelude: Wilhelm Werker, in his *Studien über die Symmetrie im Bau der Fugen* and *Die Motivische Zusammengehörigkeit der Präludien und Fugen des Wohltemperierten Klaviers von Johann Sebastian Bach* (Breitkopf & Härtel, Leipzig, 1922). Among the problems which he discusses is that of the relationship between a prelude and a fugue; in particular, he reveals that those preludes which he analyses are preparations for the succeeding fugues in the same tonality. The preludes develop out of little germs—motives or phrases—the main features of the themes of their fugues. Though some of Werker's methods may be questionable, there is great merit in his book. Musicology is here what it should be: research into the profundities of musical language.

From the standpoint of structural functions Bach's preludes do not differ essentially from the fugues. It is clear that all the deviations from the respective diatonic scales of each piece should not be considered as modulations. According to the previously given definition of modulation, only a definite departure from a region, together with the appearance of the cadential elements of a new region, constitute a modulation. Substitute tones producing substitute harmonies are to be found in great numbers; real modulations are few. If every tone foreign to the scale were to mean a modulation, how many modulations would there be in the 24th fugue in the first volume (B minor)?

Analysis of other " free " forms offers a different aspect. In all of them a tendency to avoid the predominance of a tonality gives them a certain resemblance to a *Durchführung*. In some of them, Fantasies and Rhapsodies for instance, a tonal centre may be absent in spite of the establishment of certain regions, because in its tonality the harmony is modulatory or even roving.

Introductions, on the other hand, approach the tonic region, at least at their ends. This is definitely true in the Andante, Adagio, etc., introductions to the Allegro, Presto, etc., first movements in Haydn's and Mozart's symphonies. Their modulations, seldom going beyond the regions of classes 1 and 2, are, frequently carried out by sequences, even in roving sections. Whether or not they begin in the tonic region, they certainly end on an " upbeat " harmony [i.e. preparatory dominant].

Haydn: G major Symphony (6): Introduction

Mozart: String Quartet in C major, Introduction

156.

Beethoven's introductions, like everything this great tone-poet created, immediately express part of the drama to follow. The introduction to the Leonora Overture No. 3 (Ex. 157) starts with a descending scale, passing in unison through all the tones of C major. In spite of this, every one of the four measures exhibits a multiple harmonic meaning comparable to that produced by roving vagrants; therefore, the dominant 7th chord on F♯ (mss. 5–6) can introduce the minor triad on B. The following triad on G (ms. 8) is the first distinct expression of C major, but does not introduce the tonic; instead it turns to ♭**SM** (ms. 9), in which there is an episode of six measures, A roving segment leads to a short segment in **m** (ms. 17) which is then followed by **t** (ms. 24). The harmony on A♭ in ms. 27, though introduced by a dominant, is best considered here as VI of **t**, which in ms. 31 is changed to **T**.

Beethoven: Leonora Overture No.3: Introduction

The introduction to the First Symphony is noteworthy because of its beginning on the subdominant. This and also the introduction to the Second Symphony (Ex. 158) do not go very far afield. The introduction to the Fourth Symphony (Ex. 159), after an introduction of 17 measures in **t**, moves in a somewhat roving manner through **SMm**, **S/T**, **mD**—all classified as ⑤—and **m**. The abrupt return from the unison A to V of **T** is very dramatic.

Beethoven: Symphony No.2 (D major), Introduction

Beethoven: Symphony No.4 (Bb), Introduction

The introduction to the Seventh Symphony[1] (Ex. 160), though fairly long, does not modulate very far, that is, only to ♭M and ♭SM, classified as ②.

Beethoven: Symphony No.7 (A major), Introduction

160.

[1] This introduction is marked Poco Sostenuto (♩=69). I am convinced that this is a misprint. Evidently the two episodes on ♭M and ♭SM have a marchlike character. If ♩=69 seems too fast I would suggest ♩=52–54. Besides, if one of these masters writes 16th notes he means it; he means not eighth notes, but fast notes, which will always be heard if the given metronome mark is obeyed.

The introduction to the first movement of the String Quartet Op. 59/3 is entirely roving. The same is true of the introduction to the last movement of Op. 18/6 called *La Malinconia* (Ex. 161).

161.

Beethoven: String Quartet Op.18/6.

Mendelssohn's and Schumann's introductions do not move into such remote regions as Beethoven's. Harmonically they differ from established procedures by a more frequent use of substitutes and very short deviations into closely related regions, repetitions of which they do not even avoid.

One of the few introductions in the instrumental works of Brahms, that to the first movement of the First Symphony (Ex. 162), must be classified as employing enriched harmony. At least it does not abandon the tonic region for any length of time. The introduction to the last movement of the Piano Quintet (Ex. 163) is even richer in substitutes and transformations, and the quasi-sequential treatment of some phrases might even suggest the presence of more remote regions. But a correct analysis will consider most of this introduction as being in **sd**; it will deny a functional meaning to some of the harmonies (marked +) whose roving effect derives from the chromatic (melodic) movement of the main motive.

Brahms: C minor Symphony Introduction

Brahms: Piano Quintet, Introduction, 4th movement

The name Rhapsody suggests an improvisatory construction. When Bach wrote his *Musical Offering* he made clear the difference between an improvisation and an elaborated composition. Though he was a great improviser he could not do justice to a theme given by Frederick the Great. The excellence of an improvisation lies in its inspired directness and liveliness rather than in its elaboration. Of course the difference between a written and an improvised composition is the speed of production, a relative matter. Thus, under fortunate conditions, an improvisation may possess the profundity of elaboration of a carefully worked-out composition. Generally an improvisation will adhere to its subject more through the exercise of imagination and emotion than of the strictly intellectual faculties. There will be an abundance of themes and contrasting ideas whose full effect is achieved through rich modulation, often to remote regions.[1] The connection of themes of such disparate characters and the control over the centrifugal tendency of the harmony is often achieved only in an incidental manner by local " bridges " and even by abrupt juxtapositions.

Brahms' three Rhapsodies for Piano—Op. 79/1 and 2 (Ex. 164) and Op. 119—differ from this description only because of a certain similarity with sonata or rondo forms, the recapitulations in which seemed essential to the organizing mind of Brahms; even an improvisation should not lack such formal balance. Ex. 164 shows the modulatory constitution of the G minor Rhapsody. Clearly it is not only the enriched harmony but also the deviation into many regions which is characteristic here.

Brahms: Rhapsody in G minor, Op.79

[1] But why should a musician's brain not work as fast and profoundly as that of a calculating or chess genius?

Liszt's Rhapsodies are looser in construction than those of Brahms. Most of them are also much simpler in modulation and do not move further than Classes 1 and 2. Only Nos. 9 and 14 of the rhapsodies move to regions of Class 5. No. 9 in E♭ (Ex. 165) moves (in the Finale) through **SD** to **SD♭SM** [5], later returning in several steps to **T**. No. 14 in F minor (Ex. 166) moves through **T** to **♯SM** [4], the signature of two sharps indicating D major, but it seems uncertain whether the D major on which it ends is not a dominant. In this case it would also be questionable whether the repetition in four sharps is really in E major, the E being rather a dominant of the following region, **♯m**. These endings on dominants may be due to modal influences in Hungarian folksongs, to which evaluation of regions does not apply.

Liszt: Hungarian Rhapsody No.9 (E♭)

Liszt: Hungarian Rhapsody No.14 (f minor)

166.

(Harmonic Excerpt)

In some inferior examples of rhapsodies, the title merely gives an excuse for abrupt jumps from one subject to another and from one region to another, for superficial relationships and loose connections, and for total absence of elaboration.

However great the difference between rhapsodies and fantasies may be in aesthetic respects, it can be disregarded from the standpoint of structural functions. Generally rhapsodies attempt to please the listener with the beauty and number of their melodies, while fantasies enable the player to show his brilliancy, and so contain much effective passage work rather than an abundance of beautiful themes.

The lowest forms of organization are the pot-pourri-like Fantasies and Paraphrases. Fortunately these are out of fashion today, though, in my youth, they familiarized one even with good music—for instance, melodies from Mozart's *Don Juan* or *Magic Flute*, Weber's *Freischütz*, Verdi's *Trovatore* and even Wagner's *Tannhäuser*, etc. For that reason I keep a certain gratitude for them.

The following three artistically high-ranking examples of fantasies show similarities as well as divergencies: Bach's Chromatic Fantasy and Fugue (Ex. 167), Mozart's Fantasy in C (Ex. 168) and Beethoven's Fantasy Op. 77 (Ex. 169) (curiously called " in G minor ", though not more than the first three measures are in this tonality). Mozart's fantasy resembles Bach's in its chromaticism; it resembles Beethoven's in its use of many contrasting ideas in the regions which are established. Bach's, on the other hand, is to a great extent

roving, and in the few places where he remains in a region—
the Recitative section—he does not formulate a theme. Even
these regions are expressed merely by 7th and diminished
7th chords of a V followed by a I, which qualifies them as
resting points in an otherwise roving harmony. The beginning
and ending are unquestionably established in D minor.

Bach: Chromatic Fantasy and Fugue

Mozart repeats at the end, in such a way as to establish C minor, the motive which roved in the beginning. This is the only reason for considering C minor as the tonal centre. According to this analysis, almost all of the following regions are remote, connected by roving segments. The regions in which he stays for shorter or longer periods are **m** [3], **msm** [5], **msmM=S/T** [5], **♯sm** [4], **v** [1], **SD** [3], **sd** [1], **subT** [4], and **v.** Such modulatory movement contradicts a tonal centre even more than a *Durchführung* does.

Mozart: Fantasia

Beethoven's is an extremely "fantastic" fantasy. The concluding section, 83 of the total of 239 measures, a third of the whole piece, consists of a theme and seven variation and a coda in B major, preceded by a Presto introduction of 68 measures in B minor. Thus more than 150 measures are in B major/minor. One could consider the 156 measures which precede the theme and variations in B major as an introduction and call the piece " Introduction and Theme and Variations ", were it not for the considerable number of themes whose appearance is too independent for an introduction. All this suggests basing the analysis on B major as if it were the tonal centre of the piece. The regions would then be: ♭**sm** ③, followed by a sequence in **S/Tm** ⑤ introducing **S/T** ④, and then ♭**smM** ⑤, ♭**m** ③, **SM** ②, and finally **t** and **T**. This analysis is very artificial and rather serves to demonstrate the absence of a tonal centre.

Beethoven: Phantasie, Op. 77

169.

The Recitative can be described similarly. The so-called accompanied recitative repeats some phrases occasionally. In the secco recitative, in which roving harmony is the driving power, even such repetitions are lacking. The question as to which features here produce the logic and coherence so necessary for comprehension cannot be answered by an harmonic analysis. Here it is probably the amalgamation of tones with words whose meaning and logic are substitutes for the meaning and logic of tonal progressions.

In the following examples, illustrations of recitatives are analysed from Bach's *St. Matthew Passion*, No. 30 (" Und er kam zu seinem Jüngern ") (Ex. 170), Mozart's *Marriage of Figaro* (Act III, preceding the Count's Aria) (Ex. 171), and Beethoven's *Fidelio* (to Leonora's Aria, Act I) (Ex. 172). All three combine secco with accompanied recitative. Again the tonality upon which the evaluation is based is not a real tonal centre but serves only to measure the compass of the regions through which the recitatives move. Bach's recitative follows an Aria in G minor, beginning on the VII of that key. It moves over **dor** [4], to **♯sm** [4]. finally arriving at **♯m** [4].

Mozart's recitative begins in the key of C major, to which the following analysis refers. It moves through **M** ②, **S/Tm** ⑤, **S/T** ④, **D** ①, and again **S/T**. Beethoven's recitative passes, with reference to G minor, through the regions of **D**, ♯**sm** and ♯**SM** ④.

Bach: Matthew Passion: Recitative (No. 30)

Mozart: Marriage of Figaro, Act 3, Recitative

"Hai già vinto la causa"

Beethoven: Fidelio, Act I, Recitative, Leonora ("Abscheulicher! wo eilst du hin?")

An attempt to analyse the relations of tonality within an entire opera or at least a single act would not produce any different result. Besides, it is known that composers of operas very often replaced or omitted pieces or even scenes. Though here, too, one could put the responsibility for the structural logic upon the text and the drama, one must admit that the problem of the extent to which an opera is an homogeneous structure has not yet been resolved.

It is difficult to believe that the sense of form, balance and logic of those masters who produced the great symphonies should have been renounced in controlling their dramatic structures.

CHAPTER XII

APOLLONIAN EVALUATION OF A DIONYSIAN EPOCH

EPOCHS in which the venture of experimentation enriched the vocabulary of musical expression have always alternated with their counterparts, epochs in which the experiences of the predecessors were either ignored or else abstracted into strict rules which were applied by the following generations. Most of these rules restricted modulations and designed formulae regarding the inclusion and treatment of dissonances.

These restrictions purported to facilitate the understanding of music. In earlier epochs, even more than in our times, the inclusion of a dissonant tone—"foreign" to the harmony—interrupted plain, undeviating understanding. "Whence comes this tone? Whither does it go?"—these questions distracted the mind of a listener, and could even make him forget the basic conditions upon which the continuation of the musical thought depended. Similar disturbances could be caused by the addition of an unexpected chord which was not in accordance with existing conventions. This may have been the reason why, for instance, V–VI in a cadence, instead of V-I, is called a "deceptive" progression. Difficulties of comprehension were once attributed to the minor third. It was at best considered an imperfect consonance, if not a dissonance; accordingly it was considered incapable of producing a definite ending to a work.

Classical music was composed in one of the Apollonian[1] periods, when the application of dissonances and their treatment, as well as the manner and extent of modulation, were governed by rules which had become the second nature of every musician. His musicianship was in question if he failed in this respect, if he were incapable of remaining instinctively within the limits of accepted convention. At this time the harmony was inherent in the melody.

But the new chords and dissonances of the next epoch, a

---

[1] Nietzsche establishes a contrast between the Apollonian mind which aims for proportion, moderation, order and harmony and its contrast, the Dionysian which is passionate, intoxicated, dynamic, expansive, creative, and even, destructive.

Dionysian period (provoked by the romantic composers), had barely been digested and catalogued, and the rules for their inclusion had not yet been formulated, when a new progressive movement began even before this last one had settled down. Mahler, Strauss, Debussy and Reger cast new obstacles in the way of the comprehensibility of music. However, their new and more violent dissonances and modulations could still be catalogued and explained with the theoretical tools of the preceding period.

It is different in the contemporary period.

Because of the many attempts to connect the past with the future one might be inclined to call this an Apollonian period. But the fury with which addicts of various schools fight for their theories presents rather a Dionysian aspect.

Many contemporary composers add dissonant tones to simple melodies, expecting thus to produce " modern " sounds. But they overlook the fact that these added dissonant tones may exert unexpected functions. Other composers conceal the tonality of their themes through harmonies which are unrelated to the themes. Semi-contrapuntal imitations—fugatos taking the place of sequences, which were formerly used as " fillers-up " in worthless " Kapellmeistermusik "—deepen the confusion in which the meagreness of ideas is lost to sight. Here the harmony is illogical and functionless.

My school, including such men as Alban Berg, Anton Webern and others, does not aim at the establishment of a tonality, yet does not exclude it entirely. The procedure is based upon my theory of " the emancipation of the dissonance." Dissonances, according to this theory, are merely more remote consonances in the series of overtones[1]. Though the resemblance of the more remote overtones to the fundamental tone gradually diminishes, their *comprehensibility* is equal to the *comprehensibility* of the consonances. Thus to the ear of today their sense-interrupting effect has disappeared. Their emancipation is as justified as the emancipation of the minor third was in former times.

For the sake of a more profound logic, the Method of Composing with Twelve Tones derives all configurations [elements of a work] from a basic set (*Grundgestalt*) [tone-row

[1] See Arnold Schoenberg: *Harmonielehre*, p. 459ff.

or note-series]. The order in this basic set and its three derivatives—contrary motion [inversion], retrograde, and retrograde inversion respectively—is, like the motive [in classical music], obligatory for a whole piece. Deviation from this order of tones should normally not occur, in contrast to the treatment of the motive, where variation is indispensable.[1] Nevertheless, variety is not precluded. The tones in the right order may appear either successively in a melody, theme or independent voice, or as an accompaniment consisting of simultaneous sounds (like harmonies).

Evaluation of (quasi-) harmonic progressions in such music is obviously a necessity, though more for the teacher than for the composer. But as such progressions do not derive from roots, harmony is not under discussion and evaluation of structural functions cannot be considered. They are vertical projections of the basic set, or parts of it, and their combination is justified by its logic. This occurred to me even before the introduction of the basic set, when I was composing *Pierrot Lunaire, Die Glückliche Hand* and other works of this period. Tones of the accompaniment often came to my mind like broken chords, successively rather than simultaneously, in the manner of a melody.

There exists no definition of the concepts of *melody* and *melodic* which is better than mere pseudo-aesthetics. Consequently, the composition of melodies depends solely on inspiration, logic, sense of form and musical culture. A composer in the contrapuntal period was in a similar situation with respect to harmony. Rules give only negative advice, that is, what one must *not* do. He, too, therefore, learned what to do only through inspiration. Is then a composer with twelve tones at a greater disadvantage than his predecessors because the evaluation of the chords which he produces has not yet been carried out?

Theory must never precede creation: " And the Lord saw that all was well done."

One day there will be a theory which abstracts rules from these compositions. Certainly, the structural evaluation of

---

[1] Minor changes in the order are admissible if, because of many repetitions, the mind has become acquainted with the basic set. This corresponds to remote variations of a motive in similar circumstances.

these sounds will again be based upon their functional potentialities. But it is improbable that the quality of sharpness or
mildness of the dissonances—which, in fact, is nothing more
than a gradation according to lesser or greater beauty—is the
appropriate foundation for a theory which explores, explains
and teaches. From such gradations one cannot deduce principles of construction. Which dissonances should come first?
Which later? Should one begin with the sharp ones and end
with the mild ones, or vice-versa? Yet the concept of "first " or
" later " plays a role in musical construction, and " later "
should be the consequence of " first ".

Beauty, an undefined concept, is quite useless as a basis for
aesthetic discrimination, and so is sentiment. Such a " Gefühls-
aesthetik " [aesthetic of sentiment] would lead us back to the
inadequacy of an obsolete aesthetic which compared sounds
to the movement of the stars, and deduced virtues and vices
from tone combinations.

This discussion would fail in its main purpose if the
damage wreaked by the performer's ignorance of the functions
of harmony were to remain undiscussed.

Listening to a concert, I often find myself unexpectedly
in a " foreign country ", not knowing how I got there; a
modulation has occurred which escaped my comprehension.
I am sure that this would not have happened to me in former
times, when a performer's education did not differ from a
composer's.

Great conductors like Nikisch, Mahler and Strauss were
aware of the gradual alteration in the texture which precedes
a modulation and results in a " change of scenery ", the
introduction of a contrast. A musician's culture and sense
of form is acquired by a thorough education and knowledge.
Such a musician will make a modulation lucid by " vitalizing "
the appropriate voices. Then the listener will not awake
suddenly " as in a foreign country ".

Hans Richter, the renowned Wagnerian conductor, was
once passing by a studio in the Vienna Opera House, and
stopped surprised by the unintelligible sounds he heard from
within. A coach who had been engaged for this post, not
because of his musical talents, but because of a powerful
protector, was accompanying a singer. Furiously Richter

opened the door and shouted: " Mr. F---thal, if you plan to continue coaching you must first buy a book on harmony and study it!"

Here was a conductor who believed in harmony and in education.

GLOSSARY

Original	*Equivalent* (*American or English, where either differs from the original.*)
part-leading, voice-leading	part-writing
degree	degree of the scale
artificial dominant	secondary dominant
substitutes, substitutions	borrowed chords, notes
transformations	altered chords
tone (e.g. leading tone)	note
vagrant, roving (harmony)	wandering (i.e. indefinite in key)
deceptive (cadence, progression)	false, interrupted
half cadence	imperfect cadence
cross-relations	false relations
flat mediant, flat submediant	flattened mediant, flattened submediant
v-minor, five-minor, minor's five	minor chord on dominant (V)
registration	indication of region
establishing sections	expositions, sections in which tonality is established (see p. 73).
Durchführung	development, elaboration, working out (see p. 145)
measure, measures (ms, mss.)	bar, bars
half note	minim
quarter note	crotchet
eighth note	quaver
sixteenth note	semiquaver
6-chord	$^6_3$ chord
2-chord	$^4_2$ chord

TABLE OF DEGREES

(Cf. Chart of the Regions, p. 20)

Degree	Name	Symbol in Major	Symbol in Minor
I	Tonic	**T**	**t**
II	Supertonic	**S/T**	**dor**
III	Mediant	**M**	**m**
IV	Subdominant	**SD**	**sd**
V	Dominant	**D**	**v**
VI	Submediant	**SM**	**sm**

N.B. VII, usually called Leading Tone, is not referred to by Schoenberg as a " region-creating " degree in itself; the flat VII in minor he calls Subtonic (SubT)—cf. p. 30.

Flat II is called Neapolitan (Np).

The page references to Schoenberg's *Harmonielehre* apply to the 3rd German Edition (Vienna, 1921); and to the English translation, *Theory of Harmony* (New York, 1948).

APPENDIX

p. 17: Example 31a — additional examples.

p. 17: Example 31b — additional examples.

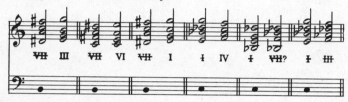

p. 31: In many cases, Transformations and Vagrant Harmonies are used. See Chapters V and VI.

p. 57: Flat Mediant Minor and Flat Submediant Minor are actually classified as "Indirect"; see p. 68.

p. 62: Both "Indirect but Close" and "Indirect" relationships are considered here. See Classification of Regions in Minor, p. 75.

198

INDEX OF NAMES

INDEX OF TERMS

Artificial chords and triads, 8, 16–18, 28, 35, 37, 138; Exs. 30, 31–34, 48

Augmented six-five and four-three chords, 44, 54, 67, 71, 165; Exs. 64, 75

Augmented triads, 16, 44–46; Exs. 30, 64, 66–67

Authentic progression, *see* Progressions

Cadences:
deceptive, *see* Progressions
enriched, 25, 27, 29, 118–19; Ex. 46
full, 29; Ex. 47
half, 14, 25, 29, 115; Exs. 28, 46, 47
Phrygian, 14
plagal, 14

Chord (chords):
artificial (*q.v.*)
constitution, 44–46, 76
multiple meaning of, 44, 111, 164, 165, 168
progression (progressions), xii, 1, 48, 67
succession, 1
see also Diminished; Dominant; Inversions; Neapolitan; Ninth; Seventh

Chromatic:
procedure, 23–25; Exs. 42–46
progression, 22, 54, 55, 67, 101; Ex. 75
substitutes, 18, 36; Ex. 51

Chromaticism, 51, 134, 180; Exs. 73, 167–68

Codetta, 114, 118–19, 138, 143; Ex. 125

Consonances, 4, 5

Contemporary period, 193

Contrasting middle section, 104, 111, 114, 120–24, 127–30, 138; Exs. 126 31, 134, 135

Deceptive progression, *see* Progressions

Degrees, xii, 1, 4

Descriptive music, 1, 76, 80

Development section, *see* Durchführung

Diatonic progressions, *see* Progressions

Diminished:
seventh chords, 16, 17, 35–36, 44; Exs. 30–31, 50, 64
triad, 16; Exs. 30, 33

Dissonances (dissonant):
in contemporary music, 193, 195
emancipation of, 193
harmony, 113
in minor, 10, 11

treatment of, xii, 4, 5, 192; Ex. 6

Dominant:
artificial [secondary], 8, 16, 28, 35, 37, 138; Exs. 30, 31, 34, 48
in cadence, 13, 16, 16n, 28, 30, 31, 35, 37; Exs. 25–28
common, 58, 68
function, 16n, 56
introduced chromatically, 28; Ex. 48
region (D), 20–21, 57, 68, 73–75, 120, 130, 188; Exs. 39, 47, 49, 76

Dorian:
mode, 9, 15–16; Exs. 19, 29
region (dor), 20–21, 68–69, 125, 130, 158, 160, 187; Exs. 37, 41, 47, 75, 76, 77, 80, 133, 135, 151, 152, 170

Durchführung, 69, 71, 73, 75, 78, 114, 138, 143, 145–65, 167, 183; Exs. 145–54

Enharmonic change, 38, 42, 44, 54, 68, 69; Exs. 54, 57, 64, 75

Fantasy, 8, 105, 107, 166–071Ens. 167 69

Five-minor:
degree, 16, 16n, 17; Ex. 32
region (v), 20, 30–31, 51, 56, 57, 68, 75, 120, 122, 160, 183; Exs. 49, 76, 79, 80, 127, 152, 168

Forms:
"free," 114, 165–91; Exs. 155–72
school, 114–18; Exs. 123–24
see also Codetta; Contrasting middle section; *Durchführung;* Fantasy; Introductions; Period; Prelude; Recapitulation; Recitative; Rhapsody; Scherzo; Sentence; Sonata; Symphony; Transition; Variations

Function (functional), *see* Dominant; Harmony

Functionless harmony, *see* Harmony

Harmony (harmonies, harmonic):
enriched, 84, 90
functions, 1–3, 193–95
functionless, 1, 193
meaning, 1
passing, 5
principles, 4–14
progression, *see* Progressions
purpose of, 1
roving (*q.v.*)

Improvisation, 175

Interchange:
of tonic and dominant, 2, 114, 115, 120; Exs. 2, 3, 123, 124, 125

201

Penguin Books

Don't Talk To Me About Love

Craig McGregor was born at Jamberoo,
in New South Wales, grew up at
Gundagai, and went to school and
university in Sydney. He has worked as
a journalist in Sydney and has
travelled and worked in England,
Europe, and more recently in America.
He is the author of the Penguin,
Profile of Australia; *People, Politics and
Pop* and a number of other books on
Australian life. His short stories have
been published in England, Europe and
Australia. This is his first novel.

Craig McGregor

Don't Talk To Me About Love

Penguin Books

Penguin Books Ltd, Harmondsworth,
Middlesex, England
Penguin Books Australia Ltd, Ringwood,
Victoria, Australia

First published by Ure Smith, Sydney 1971
Published in Penguin Books 1972
Copyright © Craig McGregor, 1971

Printed in Australia for
Penguin Books Australia Ltd
at The Dominion Press, Blackburn,
Victoria

FOR JANE

This novel was written with the assistance of the Commonwealth Literary Fund, for whose help I am very grateful.

Orange bowls on the breakfast table, a clean life and well-ordered, two spoons for the children, two forks, the blue-and-white check tablecloth which her mother had given her as a wedding present — or had it been for her glory box? — everything in its place, the last twist of the knife, two more bowls which she reached down from the scrubbed wood dresser, looking past the wall calendar with its encircled dates and the protruding edge of kitchen wall across the open-plan living area with its gold-and-orange Leonard French abstract and the white voile curtains to the window each item focused and transfixed for a moment in her mind until finally she reached the balcony where sunlight was already beginning to trickle and spatter through the trees and a filament of yellow was beginning to dance around the trunks yellow against the orange light which, reflected from the bowls she was holding, coursed across the back of her hand. When they had first moved in the trees had seemed beautiful: precipitous gums with trunks as erect as tomato stakes, reaching up and overbranching the house so that the sun was always filtered through sickle-shaped leaves and strips of bark littered the roof, falling sometimes at night with an indistinct bump which woke Paula where she and her husband lay close under the ceiling of their attic bedroom, and so that the sound of the whistling lorikeets and the crows which she had been so surprised to find in Pymble always seemed to drift down like the sun from hundreds of feet above them, floating down like the leaves which

1

settled gently each night on the outside balcony and that single gorgeously coloured feather, all vermilion, blue and peacock mauve, which she had found there one morning and which now, rather wilted, adorned the calendar with its circles for appointments and all the week crossed off except yesterday, Friday. But now these trees imprisoned her, their trunks black rods which barred the window and shut her from the sunlight like those which had confronted Nolan's Mrs Fraser, who at least had a convict to rescue her, and walled her off, a convict instead of convict-freed, from the world outside; so that even now, as she lay utensils monotonously on the breakfast table and watched the morning yellow begin to trickle down the trunks and across the balcony, they merely emphasized her alienation.

Alienation?

'Alienation, of course, is a Marxist concept,' Johnston had said last night, 'though like so much else Marx got it all arse-up. He believed the capitalist system had alienated the worker from his work; you know, the bloke turning screws on a mass production line can't feel part of what he creates, whereas the medieval craftsmen did. But man has always been divorced from his work; it's not a modern thing. A lot of Lefties think there was a golden age which the industrial revolution destroyed —— you know, merry maidens around the village maypole and master craftsmen beating out bronze scabbards. That's all horseshit. Most people worked on the land, tried to grind corn with machines made from wood and nothing to reduce the friction, and died before thirty. If you'd scratched an agricultural labourer in the Age of Enlightenment you'd have found he was alienated too.'

'But what they're alienated from has changed,' Paula said. 'Surely that makes the character of the alienation different too?'

'Nonsense,' said Johnston. He knocked his pipe out on the heel of his boot, searched in his sports coat for tobacco, failed, pulled out a cigarette and looked around for a light. Johnston had a greater repertoire of

2

mannerisms than anyone but Arch-Alf Cassidy, as Graeme called him. 'Alienation is a relation; it doesn't change according to the objects to which it is related. Angst, alienation, even old Ben Jonson's melancholy, it's all the same. The difference is that in the past only the aristocrats could afford to indulge their melancholy; now anyone can. The better off we are, the higher the suicide rate. Man has always been alienated. Only a fool likes the world he finds himself in.'

'And what about women?'

'Aha,' said Johnston, 'woman has no need to feel alienated. She has man.'

That morning, before her husband or the children had woken, she had stood full-length before the mirror in the bathroom and stared at herself. There was the oval face which she had always thought too symmetrical, too perfectly curved to have any character, the long and somewhat scraggy neck, the breasts with stretch marks on them from feeding the two children and the nipples which when she was younger had been a strawberry pink but which were now a mud brown, her waist still slim but the belly a little too full now her muscles had slackened, perhaps she should have taken more notice of the physiotherapist when the baby was born after all, the black tangle of pubic hair, the thighs still firm but pocked with the buttermilk marks which her husband, whether through loyalty or sheer perversion, said he adored, the legs which always looked better in stockings than out of them and the feet which were simply feet, splayed against the off-white bathroom tiles, and, putting a hand up to draw back her hair which she would have to cut soon and checking the desire to turn a little to one side which, she knew, would have flattered her more, she stared at this her body which she thought she knew but did not know because it changed secretly as each day turned over and which had been loved by how many men and now for some years had been used and no doubt loved too by her husband, and thought flatly and without malice but with

3

burgeoning discontent, 'I am growing old.'

She turned to the shower, placed a floral cap over her hair (which she resolved she would have Pierre cut that week) and allowed the warm water to course down her body, flooding down between her breasts and dividing about the ripe pod of her belly *saw its water break in fear the first murderer* and then join again to create of her body hair a moist plait from which water curved to the floor and tried to wash away in the balm of heat and water the bitterness which she had felt within her when she awoke that morning, her husband's back encased in paisley cotton against her to maintain that contact which, even in sleep, and despite what had happened the night before, he felt he needed from her, the magpies already gurgling with closed throats in the branches overhead and the children, as far as she could hear, still asleep downstairs. She lay there with her eyes half-closed, the dull morning light forcing its way through the attic window onto white walls and dark timber beams, taking care not to wake her husband so she would have some precious minutes to herself, some priceless interval wherein she could simply be herself, before the day's demands and the remorseless routine of her life overtook her, thinking without pleasure of the day ahead, the interminable procession of actions which had to be done and actions which if possible had to be done and finally actions which might have to be done before she could consider any actions which could be enacted for her own sake and, unbidden, there loomed before her mind the island.

Black rocks fracture deny what white Aegean drove against this spit daggered in downtumbling stormblack stone at ocean's bowels which not history time nor surge of tide had won from the island where sheer cliffs of fall smothered seawrack in rubble and flung against the white encirclement of spray a new battlement. From the sea the island looked bare, bereft of human softness, twin granite peaks which jutted gauntly from the immense expanse of water like —— of course, it was *L'Avventura,* and how

4

often had she thought that she too would have liked to clamber over that windblasted timedeserted volcanic rockface uneasily aware of she knew not what: some immanence of Evil? some suspicion that reality lied? that existence was a fragile glass which a stone could shatter, an icerink over which as one skated the upturned beast on four paws like a fly or a magnet followed the intricate manoeuvres of the skater, face to face so that if one peered one could dimly discern beneath the clouded ice the furry face staring upwards?

Which was absurd because on the other side of the island hidden by the spit of land which fingered into the sea were the whitewashed cottages flung against the steep hillside and the harbour where the fishing boats tied up, the curved promenade paved with stones, cafes with chairs pulled back under the shade of awnings, a church confronting the town square, white porticos arching over alleyways, the houses conjoined and tunnelled by stone steps, then bare clay and thistles and behind that again across brutal rock too hot to stand on fracturing in the midday sun as the heat seeped down fissures in the baked stone and reached through invisible seams to hidden weaknesses and prised open the seemingly inviolate granite, behind that again the pine woods where once, on a glittering and sunbursted Sunday, she had finally, with he who was not her husband, achieved surmounted burst open like sun the pressurized rock that act of womanhood which . . . .

Or rather had not, she thought, as she reached across and turned off the shower. She stepped quickly over the tiled footwall and, shaking her hair free, hung her shower cap over the metal hook which Graeme in a fit of handicraftsmanship had managed to fix to the wall and, reaching for a towel, began to dry herself before that mirror which had reflected back such a cruel Picasso portrait of herself but now, dimmed by steam, mistily created an orange Renoir nude.

Had it been the memory of the island which had set off

5

the discontent she felt as she lay there this morning?

She thought not. It was more the aftermath of last night; and more still, perhaps —— and here she stopped, and wiped one towelled hand across the mirror, her face transformed once again into that which, atop her naked body, had so appalled her earlier —— more still the days which passed in an unending stream of predictability, the gracious and perhaps enviable days of Pymble house-wifeliness where, surrounded by those she loved and who loved her, the glad trees and clay-yellow creek and clinker-brick walls and Aegean-white panels, the Vogues and Novas and Graphises piled high on the magazine rack, the blackboard scribbling panels for the children in the downstairs bedroom, the Irish matting in the nursery and the Bernard Leach pots which she had brought back with her from England and the Mike Brown pop collage which Johnston had given them, the sea shells from her schooldays and the photographs of her and Graeme's wedding and the garish gold, orange and vermilion hangings which she had selected as a deliberate and clamorous discord in this antiseptic machine-for-living, in fact surrounded by those things which she had created or chosen or wrought herself, so that they reflected back a multiform and multifaceted image of her own being, she felt, chokingly, as if she were drowning.

There had been a time, at the university, when it had been different; when she had had not only an existence but ambitions of her own; when, walking between lectures across the quadrangle of overpowering, gaunt-grey Gothic buildings which always reminded her, somewhat menacingly, of her schooldays, she felt certain that some vague destiny awaited her beyond the round of lectures, essays, examinations and holidays which delineated the university routine. It was all, she felt, leading somewhere, though she could not have said precisely where, and had felt convinced enough of that to have avoided the Women's College gaggle which divided its time between the Women's Union, the Fisher library and sex on Saint Paul's

6

College Oval (how ironic! she smiled to herself —— and only Buzzy lived up to the saint's jeremiads and became pregnant) and to have taken off the university medal in English in her final year my God! when was that? with her father beaming and oblivious of the stains down the front of his tie and the missing shirt button which revealed a grubby flannel singlet above his portly gut and her mother smiling underneath her new blue rinse, 'I am so proud of you, dear', as she kissed her on the forehead and kept just the teeniest eye out for the photographers, the medal which was now tucked away —— where? in the suitcase in the spare room downstairs, like the rest of her ambitions.

Yet those university days had been important to her. She had felt free there, had felt herself expand, the pores of her skin clogged by tile roofs, clipped hedges, stucco front porches and North Shore Line railway platforms open up and absorb what she found around her. Even those musty, steeply-angled lecture rooms in which the tutor, backed by chalkdusty blackboards and pinioned to his dais by an amphitheatre of eyes, struggled to make the words sing which rang like bellpeals from the pages anyhow —— poor Whitfield, reciting Dylan Thomas and Hope and Frost against a tumultuous undercurrent of conversations and rustling papers until she had reached the point where she wanted to leap onto the desk in front of her and scream at them *STOP IT! STOP IT!* but instead had sat there, furious with indignation, her face reddening, especially on the day when Whitfield plucked up enough courage to read out some of his own poems, until finally she had hurried across the desk tops out of the lecture theatre, her grand gesture of defiance, as always, a defeat —— even there she felt herself grow, was conscious of a selfness confirmed and underpinned, until in her honours year she seemed to become aware, like Mrs Ramsay, of an utterly invulnerable entity who was herself, a wedge-shaped core of darkness that resisted and rebuffed all attempts at violation . . . .

Where was that now?

7

No, it had not been the island. She turned away from the mirror and bent forward slightly to dry the rest of her body, delighting as always in the fullness of her breasts, 'kalò kalò' said the black-dressed Greek woman with a smile in the dark, incense-perfumed waterfront shop where she had bought her swimming costume and had stripped naked behind the curtain of beads and Christ ikons to try it on, it had been, more than anything else, the sudden memory of that child-figure who for two entire weeks had strolled self-absorbedly around the university grounds, holding herself a little tensely as though a sudden commotion might shatter her inviolability, imagining herself as an immaculate and invisible core of darkness, an absurd figure really but one who had at least . . . a future.

But now? And with Graeme?

She straightened herself again, bringing the towel slowly up her body to beneath her breasts so that one hand inadvertently —— or was it inadvertently? —— brushed her nipple, and as the quick erogenous response ran through her the memory which she had chopped short and thrust from her while she was showering suddenly caught her unaware in all its power and she stood with the steam still swirling around the tiny bathroom and rapidly misting over the mirror where the oval face with its parted mouth and orange surround of towel was beginning to disintegrate as beads of water coagulated and ran down the easily shattered glass-reflected skin as indeed they had that day . . . .

She clambered awkwardly over the rocks which tumbled down to the sea, salt water trickling down her body and from her hair which she had cut short with a pair of surgical scissors only the night before, and because that heat-fractured granite hurt her feet she ran across the flat slabs where the Greek women had laid out their washing to dry like so many disembodied arms, legs and torsos to the knoll of pine trees which rose behind the shore and began climbing again. Richard followed, but more leisurely, taking time to put on his rope sandals before stooping

8

under the pine branches which came down so low that, to get through them, they had to drop on all fours to the bed of brown pine needles. Together they forced their way up through the fallen cones and splintered branches till they burst through to the stone battlement which, shaped like the turret of some forgotten Crusader castle, now grown over with clumps of weeds and pine seedlings and the refuse of centuries, dominated the western side of the island.

'That's a climb,' said Richard. A khaki Army towel, souvenired from National Service, was tucked around his waist. She looked away from him. Far below them the Aegean crawled towards the coast; overhead the sky was as washed of colour as the sea where they had been swimming. Richard came up behind her and touched her arm, and together they wandered desultorily across the flat, shadeless battlement. They were looking for a place to lie down, but the thistles and clumps of unfamiliar, spiky grass deterred them. In the end they retreated to the edge of the pine wood and there with the cicadas shrieking mindlessly overhead and the forest full of strange thuds and footfalls and the pine needles harsh against her sunburnt skin, they began to make love. They had begun often enough before. When, in London, she had agreed to make the trip to Greece with Richard she had half-realized what it would entail, and at camping grounds and behind the Herrens and Damens across the continent they had struggled their way towards the fulfilment which all the women's magazines promised and which she awaited with an uneasy mixture of desire and horror, but the Continentals' rigorous division of males from females at the youth hostels had protected her. Now, with this blinding Sunday fulfilling a swollen world and the lines which had straggled across so much distance about to intersect at last, she could see no point in not at last surrendering to whatever time-stream had brought her to this instant and when Richard, with masculine awkwardness, had at last succeeded in rolling her costume

9

which she had bought in that waterfront shop a demure
one-piece in deference to Greek sensibilities down to
below her knees she did not roll aside but conscious of the
incongruity of the pine needles prickling her bare backside
of which she was sure she should not have been aware and
also of the indignity of this final climactic act where
anyone might discover them she lay passively and let him
penetrate into what seemed her guts trying with her eyes
screwed up to blot out that horrific consciousness which
watched every action from some vantage point high above
them so that all her reactions seemed forced and unnatural
and trying by dint of sheer repetition and repetition to
bring herself to some point of pleasure flinging her arms
around his salt-sweaty and still sand-rough back she was
yet unable to wrench any response from her body so that
when after what seemed an infinity of movement and a
growing tightness and tearing inside her during which she
was sure blood was pouring from her and staining her
thighs legs and belly when finally Richard with a noisy
desperation which seemed altogether too melodramatic
reached whatever it was he had wanted to reach and fell
heavily upon her, and actually smiled, suddenly and
without warning tears began sluicing from her clenched
eyes her gargoyle mouth tensed in anguish as she realized
she was no longer a virgin and she had felt nothing nothing
nothing NOTHING

The island. Where was the island? It had meant so much
to her: the white spattering of seabirds, the dark secretive
rocks, the crystal arc of seaspray which cyclones flung
against them ... And Richard. When had she lost the
island? Droplets of water wriggled down the mirror,
dragging shiny trails, snail's slime, across her face; absurdly
disturbed, she turned away and felt the edge of her towel
catch a shampoo bottle. In 19 Arcadia Street, Pymble,
splinters of glass zipped across bathroom floor man stirred
blood began

Johnston had dropped in on Thursday night. 'How are you, my love?' he said, abstaining from a chaste kiss which might have implied too close a relationship but allowing his burly, houndstoothed shoulder to brush hers as she led him through to the living-room.

Graeme was reading by the record player. 'Hullo, you studious bugger. What are y' reading? *The Australian Tradition?* The mind boggles.' Johnston held up his hand in the Boy Scout oath. 'I believe in the Holy Trinity of mateship, egalitarianism and bushmanship, and furthermore that the union buries its dead, and in rattling good yarns, and the Working Class Ethos . . . .'

'Up yours too, baby,' said Graeme, grinning beneath black Celtic hair. He got to his feet, a frail five-eighths to Johnston's scrumpack bulk. 'A drink?'

'Of course. Anything at all —— so long as it's Reschs, Pilsener preferably, in a well-chilled glass, sport, none of your snivelling pewter. Seen the latest *Bulletin?*'

'No,' said Paula.

'Bloody PM, sounding off about what a great little white future we've got Down Under here. Who the hell's his speechwriter? Some superannuated hack from External Affairs, no doubt. Though that's unfair to EA —— they couldn't be *that* bad.' He paced up and down the room, paused in front of the Leonard French painting, pulled a wry face ('a decorator, just a decorator'), resumed his pacing. One of these days, Paula thought sourly, he'll wear a track in that carpet, and it cost us a fortune. 'It's enough

11

to make a man leave the country.'

Her husband came back into the room bearing three glasses and a bottle of beer. 'Are you being serious?'

He handed Johnston a beer. 'Do you want anything, darling?' he asked her. Always an afterthought, she noticed. What if she said 'yes, I'll have a Campari with ice and a slice of lemon please Graeme?'

'Campari and ice, please —— with lemon.'

But at her husband's surprised expression she couldn't help laughing. 'No, it doesn't matter. It's just that sometimes I'd wish you'd ask me *before* you've made up your mind.' She flung herself into an armchair and looked up at him. 'I'll have a beer. A small one.'

'Act One, Scene One: Death of a Marriage,' interposed Johnston. 'Get this into your dirty black gut.' He halted long enough to quaff some beer, wiped the froth from his ginger moustache which, together with his ever-so-slightly greying hair and impressive, not to say portly, bulk managed to give him an air of somewhat raffish maturity. Paula could imagine him in cloth motoring cap, goggles and string-backed gloves behind the wheel of a 1936 Hispano-Suiza. 'Yes, I think I am being serious, strangely enough. Two years in this country is long enough. After that you're fit for burial. A living corpse. Which gives some wenches their first taste of necrophilia, of course.'

'That's a change from when you first came back,' said Graeme. 'You were full of ideas then, baby.'

'I know. I was going to turn this bloody place upside down. But it already *is* upside down, you see; we're all walking around like flies on the bottom of the globe thinking that upside down is downside up and nobody realizes that everything is arse up. How long is it since you two have been back?'

He looked across at Paula. It was one of the things she liked about Johnston; he was one of the few Australians who actually talked to women, who took an interest in them and bothered to listen to what they had to say. 'God, I've forgotten. What is it, Graeme? James is two, and I had him in November . . . oh, it's at least three years. Closer to four really.'

'Jesus Christ, I don't know how you've stood it. Especially you, locked away in domesticity. Why don't you let me take her away for a dirty week-end sometime, Graeme? At least it would provide a break from the shit on the nappies . . . .'

'You'd better ask Paula.'

'Well?'

Paula's laughter was a little forced. 'I'm getting too old for that. I can just imagine it: a sleazy little motel up near the Newcastle tollway somewhere, with fibro walls so thin so you can hear everything through them and signing yourselves Mr and Mrs Smith and the lady behind the desk looking at you as though you're a tramp and one of those ghastly black Bibles on the table next to the bed —— I couldn't face it.'

Johnston pondered. 'What about . . . Paris, then?'

'Oh, you French rabbits are all the same.' She had a sudden vision of Johnston in a tweed coat with huge pink ears poking above his fedora and furry legs plastered with douane labels and laughed again, this time without strain. 'I'd soon be washing shit off nappies again.'

'Remarkably unromantic wife you have, Graeme,' said Johnston. 'Not even Paris.' He sat down, at last, in a chair. 'Bugger it, I'd like to be there now.'

'Why don't you go back, then?' said Graeme.

'I might even do that.' Sprawled in the chair, legs akimbo, his massive frame overflowing the frail Parker armrests, he became unexpectedly sombre. 'There's a limit to what you can do here. You can jump around, make a fuss, kick a few shins, shout down everyone's ear, and nobody takes a damn bit of notice. It washes off their backs. Everyone's too busy having a good time, waddling around in the effluent society. What's up with you, sport? Sumpin' got into ya, has it? Even that ABC's like that. I've tried to push a few things through, but they're scared to death of the politicians. If they're not scared they're

13

asleep. People have been trying to wake this place up for centuries ... what was Penton's book called? "Wake Up, Australia!" A lot of good that did. You could write the same book now. The only thing that will smash this country open is a revolution, and Christ knows that'll never happen. Poor old Coms down in Melbourne, waiting for the Marxist flashpoint to occur. At least here in Sydney they've done a Togliatti. About the only other thing would be a crisis, a really major bloody crisis —— but by that time it'd be too late.'

'An economic crisis?' said Graeme.

'Ah no, the Yanks'd never let that happen. They've got too much at stake here now. They'd prop Australia up, just as they've propped up Britain —— at a price. Napalm for Vietnam, boys. Here's a dollar: go and shoot a Com.'

Johnston stared around the room and Paula felt, guiltily, that every manifestation of her and Graeme's pleasant and comfortable life met with his disapproval: the Parker chairs with their fashionable beige-and-pottery-brown checks ('we don't call it nigger brown any longer,' the camp interior decorator at Interiors had explained, 'too racialist, you know —— though if what's going on in America at present is any guide, we're better off without them here!'), the French painting for which they had paid an extravagantly high price and which they knew, really, they couldn't afford, the custom-built stereogram with its twin speakers built into the bookcase which was topped by the huge, gaudy paper flowers she had fallen in love with at Marion Best, the scattered cushions and low table topped with tiles which she had created and fired herself at the North Shore Workshop Centre and the swollen globe of the Japanese fishbowl lightshade hanging low in the corner by the feature wall, the whole thing 'reeking of good taste', as she had written once to her sister —— what would the revolutionaries make of them? Liberal-lefties, with a small l in both cases. How can you be Left and still indulge in, or worse still display an indulgence in, the best of everything? Donations to Food For Asia, a dollar for

14

every charity that came around, conscience money to the ALP. Had they, in fact, sold out? There were enough wealthy manufacturers and small-scale entrepreneurs, Johnston maintained, who bought themselves freedom from guilt by donating large sums to the Communist Party. Johnston had once mounted a campaign to tap those sources and divert it to support a radical socialist-anarchist magazine he had been thinking of starting. The scheme had come to nothing, because the conscience-salvers had been revealed to be, under pressure, conservatives who were happy to support causes only if they were certain they were lost. Johnston, with his fieriness and his reputation established on TV, had scared them. Were they any better?

'I don't know, what the hell can you do?' Johnston was saying. 'The Labor Party's a joke, the CP I wouldn't trust as far as you throw a grand piano. You're up against the great bloc of committed neutrals in any of the parties these days: the blokes who want to keep the status quo, don't rock the boat, bhoys, we're right as we are. Show me the union organizer who wants to pull on a strike which might jeopardize his position? Do you think any of those soft-palmers down at the AWU want to work with their hands again? Not bloody likely. Political action's out as far as I'm concerned.'

'And what's in?'

'Silence, exile and cunning,' said Johnston. 'Another beer please, sport.' He lapsed into moroseness, ignoring Paula completely. Johnston, apparently, felt much as she did — but for a different reason. He felt helpless before the massive immobility of the political machines; she felt helpless swathed in the cocoon of family life. They had both been reduced to impotence.

Graeme, oblivious in blue-jeaned self-sufficiency to what had been going through her mind, came back into the room bearing a frothing Pilsener. Johnston accepted it, swallowed, and stared out the picture window to where the last of the light still caught the edges of the tree trunks.

15

'I've begun to wonder whether Australia has a future at all,' he said at last. 'I know that sounds like heresy. Especially after what we came back from London to do. But I don't know —— are we going to be left alone? What chance have we got of keeping our precious isolation from the world? We're a few hundred miles from Jakarta, a couple of thousand from China. We can't go on forever living as a Tight Little, Bright Little White outpost. Do you think?'

'Sounds a bit like the old domino theory, man,' said Graeme. 'Do you really think we're going to be over-run by a Yellow Horde sailing up Sydney Harbour in sampans?'

'No,' said Johnston. 'But history has some sort of inevitability to it. Look, it isn't our fault. We were the last of the imperialist colonies, set up as far away from the bloody homeland as the Establishment could make it. We've grown up in the twentieth century, when all the others grew up in the nineteenth. It's not our fault we're a couple of decades —— a half century —— too late to establish ourselves as an independent Asian nation, but we are. The die's been cast, sport. We might dismantle the White Australia policy eventually, but it'll be too late. We might finally pull out of Vietnam and get onto the right side in Asia, but it'll be too late for that too. We're twenty years, thirty years, a half century behind the destiny we should have had. It's a pity, but history's full of ironies like that. Born late, die young and have an affluent corpse.'

'Do you really believe that?' Paula asked.

'Too right I do,' said Johnston. 'I'm leaving for London next month.'

There had been a time, she thought, when the world was safe. Black swans on Deep Creek lagoon, and pelicans too. Tent towns strung out along the beaches and headlands of the North Coast, water from rusty camping ground taps, sand bars where the river looped like an uncertain question mark into the sea, paddle boats and canoes for hire,

16

FRESH BAIT on the kiosk wall. Her father, an old rope tied around his khaki shorts, worn sandshoes which displayed the bunions on his feet, had taken them there on Easter holidays and on long week-ends in the car. Sometimes Mother had come too, but days spent over a primus stove in a row of car tents had not been her idea of a holiday, and more often than not her father packed the children in the back of the Ford and took them off by himself. She remembered wet knickers and bare feet feeling for oysters in the sand, pink bows in her hair, huge black crabs which scuttled over the rocks as her father sought remote possies for rock fishing, nights spent on camp stretchers with a mosquito coil burning in the far end of the tent and her father arguing with the fisherman from three tents down.

That had been in another world; another century almost. She had been younger, the world had been younger. The coast had been a sand-and-bottle-brush infinity stretching up to heaven knows where, the tropics, the northern tip of Queensland, and imagination could not circumscribe the limits of that immense continuation. It had been like that for aeons and for aeons, from the time of dreaming till the time of comprehension, the jagged white edge of the dust-red continent, the infracture of land and sea, which was and always would be, world without end, forever and ever, amen. Australia was the land where time had achieved its final expiation, the movement of the sphere dwindled imperceptibly to a standstill.

But now ... now, when she took the children for holidays on the coast, the old immutability had disappeared. Even in the far North, where strands of sand shaped like gumleaves dwindled to perspectives of nothing and carbuncular bluffs thrust bluntly across saucer-smooth horizons, even there where all distance seemed stretched and mountains were smudges lost in the sea's curvature, even there, now, she felt vulnerable. Time had broken free of its stasis, she felt. Sand grains and sea shells were no longer safe. This scalloped coast was no longer the edge of

17

the world, a heat-frozen contour line confronting infinity, but the simple frontier of a simpler nation, agape and eyeing an alien Asia. Would her children be able to live and play there, grow old and untroubled as she had, composing sandcastles against the encroaching tide under a sky which had forgotten time?

No, they would not. The world had overtaken even that. She could give them life, yes. But she could not give them, as her father had bequeathed her, long, long ago, when she was a child, safety.

'London? That sounds like a retreat,' said Graeme.

'That's where it's happening,' said Johnston.

'But that's where it began,' Graeme persisted. 'In fact that's where it began for all of us, didn't it? You, me, Paula, Don, George and Sonia . . . .'

'We live where we must. I thought I had good reasons for coming back here; now I can't get out of the place quick enough. Don't tell me you've turned into one of those expatriate-baiters?'

'Of course not.'

'You know why Australians don't like expatriates?' Johnston said. 'Because they feel they should never have left in the first place. It's not envy. They don't envy the exiles their success —— those who do turn out to be successful, that is. What sticks in their gullet is that they should actually have preferred somewhere else. Australia? She's the You Beaut Country. It's so You Beaut even Olsen has to get out of it every year or so. And Nolan. He only comes back for the film previews.'

'And you,' said Paula. 'You feel you have to get out too.'

'No, not necessarily.'

'Why go then?' said Graeme.

'Because I'm not a bloody Australian, sport. I'm *me*. Being an Australian no longer defines me, the sort of person I am. I left that behind when I first sailed out of the Heads with a P & O sticker on my suitcase. I'm me whether I'm in Earls Court or Brooklyn or . . .' his mind reached for somewhere suitably bizarre ' . . . even Pymble.'

Graeme smiled at him. 'Okay, baby, so you're you. And you've decided to go back. Well, I'm sorry. Not just because we won't have your ugly face around here, but because — — well, we were going to change things, weren't we? We were going to make a difference. That's why we came back.'

'You're talking more about yourself than me,' said Johnston. 'I came back on a sentimental pilgrimage, doncha know . . . .'

'Of course.'

'Anyhow, I haven't noticed you doing so much since getting back — — except make money.'

'My failure doesn't excuse you,' replied Graeme, rather too quickly. 'This place can't afford to lose people like you. What do you expect — — instant acclaim like instant coffee? You've already made a breakthrough.'

'A five minute spot on Four Corners,' said Johnston. 'That's a hell of a breakthrough. Christ, one of these days I might get fifteen minutes. Or a programme of my own. Carefully quizzed by Canberra, of course. Any more victories like that and I might die of ecstacy.' He took a long swallow of beer. 'Humphrey Stearns Johnston, the national network's Eric Baume.'

Graeme crossed himself piously. 'God rest him.'

'God damn him!' said Johnston, with sudden ferocity. 'If the man believed what he said he was a fool, if he didn't he was a hypocrite. Politics isn't a game — — it shapes people's lives. He's better off dead.'

Johnston relapsed into silence. It was easy enough to say, of course. But how many people didn't have to act out a public role to recognize themselves? Each social situation was a mirror, and each time it reflected back a different self. And what did those selves have in common anyhow? Was there a unifying quality, an essential selfness? One man's many parts, or each a different unity?

The ego exists only for an instant, he premised. A split second later, a different individual. How then guilt for the

19

past, or responsibility for what has been? They were someone else's acts. The instants trace pinpricks in carbon paper which leave upon the white sheet of history the illusion of a line, but under the magnifying glass the dots were separate, distributed almost at random. There was no forward movement, nor backward neither.

Nor was there any self, for that matter, but only selves. It was the effort of keeping them in some sort of reasonable relationship with each other, of forcing upon them at least the illusion of unity, that denoted maturity. If they ricocheted too far apart, broke up, disintegrated, you got — — schizophrenia? Breakdown?

London. Graeme was right. That's where it began: to walk out of the station on that wintry November afternoon, the black taxicabs scurrying past like hearses and people dressed like mourners beneath the great iron crematorium-arch of the terminal, lugging a suitcase heavy with winter underwear and ambition past the unfamiliar bookstalls and magazine stands and the newspaper posters with their outlandish handscrawled headlines onto the footpath and the cobblestones yes! cobblestones, and then his first shock: that utterly grey, impenetrable, foggy sky hanging like a great dirty dish-cloth over the city so that even at that time, at two-thirty in the afternoon, the sun was a dim grey orb vainly attempting to pierce the gloom — — it was then and only then the full realization struck him that at last he had reached it, the starting point, the hub, the dark grey Empire City of museum facades and anachronistic street sets left over from some nineteenth century stage play and department stores like overgrown cottages which actually had roofs on them, pitched roofs of slate and tile so the snow would slide off, he supposed; he had almost expected to see a hansom trot around the corner driven by a cabbie in a top hat.

But instead it had been Donald Woodfall himself, bloody old Don in a duffle jacket, Plymouth Hoe symbol of the new Elizabethan Age, smiling his Cheshire smile and making his Persian gestures, looking incredibly elongated and thin, thinner even than Johnston had remembered him, in that damned jacket which ended well above his knees and saying, without any trace of accent, thank God, 'How are you, Humphrey? It's very good to see you again,' and who, grabbing Johnston's valise, hurried him along the pavement, talking the while, to where Rosinante, veteran of some half-dozen European trips and exuding an unmistakeable Quixotic aura, stood staidly parked beneath a giant **SKOL LAGER** hoarding; thence to Don's bedsitter or rather to the rabbit warren of rooms, bedsitters, communal kitchens and bathrooms in that Oakley Street residential which, glorying in the name of Gunn's Gully, had been taken over by expatriates fleeing from Kangaroo Valley who had created, amidst the swingers, art students, beats, intellectuals, folkies, ravers, actors, guitarists, junkies and other Arnotts Assorted outsiders of Chelsea ('all of them waiting for success to happen', as Paula put it) a new, equally provincial and equally incestuous Earls Court. Who had been in the top flat at that stage? Don, of course, who had pride of place as the oldest identity; Richard, shy, withdrawn, a damned fine guitarist, whom Don had met on the Fairsky a year earlier and, sharing Don's passion for chess, had ended by sharing his room as well; George, of course; and that was about all until he had turned up, the others arriving even later . . . .

Though he, Johnston, had certainly not been one of those who simply waited around for success to happen but had pursued it grimly from the start, or if not grimly (which was rather too harsh a description to apply to himself, surely) then at least relentlessly, realizing immediately that in that bloated, cancerous, all-devouring, smog-grimed city of nine million units any single unit distinguished itself from the other eight million nine hundred thousand nine hundred and ninety nine only by application of the meritocratic equation, $IQ + effort = merit$, and even merit was no real guarantor of success but merely the first throw on the Monopoly Board —— Christ yes! the street names, straight out of Walther &

Stevenson's toy emporium, so familiar he half expected to see them labelled with their appropriate purple (Park Lane), blue (Islington) and green (Regent Street) backgrounds; and so had, eventually, achieved what he wanted, trounced the Poms on their own ground, become a byline man with trips to Cannes for the film festival and to Geneva for GATT, the BBC for talks and the Evening Standard for the occasional Londoner's Diary item, the Cheshire Cheese or the Cogers for lunch and occasional cocktails with Fleet Street deputy editors, with the breakthrough into telly always a possibility; if it hadn't been for the trouble with Jackie he might have stayed . . . .

London. That's where it had begun; but that's where it had ended, too, in a gas-filled room in the swinging city, Graeme's utter disbelief, the window smashed with a frying pan, a dish towel under the door, London, City of My Desire, each with the same thought: who will tell Paula?

'The hell with it,' said Johnston.

'What?' asked Graeme.

'A thought-train with no junction,' Johnston replied, and turned to Paula, who had been sitting with both knees tucked under her in the cerise-covered armchair which, discovered at St Vincent de Paul's, she had covered with mod Marimekko. 'Another drink?' he asked solicitously, knowing it pleased her to be treated with even a semblance, nay even a parody, of gallantry after her husband's obtuse and determined disregard of the feminine psyche.

'Thank you, Humphrey, I will,' she said, and, smiling, proferred her empty glass to Graeme. 'Another beer, darling.'

Johnston studied her. She had grown older, no doubt about that. The thin, expanding lines around the base of her neck gave her away. But with her fawn, still richly tinted skin, the perfectly oval face with the hair cut fashionably short to reveal boyish ears, the suggestion of fulness beneath the loose drape of her garish dress-top and the mature heaviness about the hips and belly, she was still beddable. No doubt she still magnetized her quota of young men; or even, he thought, with a quick shift of consciousness to himself, of ageing —— the word eluded him for a moment —— adulterers?

Though Graeme, retreating to the kitchen to replenish the beer, had caught from eyes' edge his speculative look.

After Johnston had gone silence settled on the room. Graeme, his book forgotten, poured another Pilsener into one of the tall grey Orrefors glasses for which he had exchanged, against Paula's wishes, the cut-glass Crown Crystal set her mother had given them for their anniversary, Paula protesting that they should not exchange gifts from friends and relatives who had chosen them personally and would be hurt to find them swapped for something else; but then his wife had a thing about gifts and possessions and loyalty which was no doubt one of the moral extravagances the North Shore could afford but which he, brought up from good lower-middle-class stock, certainly could not. He had a hard day ahead of him tomorrow —— an appointment with Cassidy, the managing director of Consolidated Enterprises Inc., in the morning and a brain-storming session with Solly Sternberg, the photographer, about the layout for Solly's new book in the afternoon, neither of which prospects gave him any joy —— but he was reluctant to retreat to bed, slouched on the settee with half-formed images and snatches of remembered conversation and a jumbled, idiotic sequence of memories passing in disarray through his brain, too tired to order them into coherence and yet not tired enough to chop them off completely and move for the stairs. He looked across to where his wife, who had taken out some needlework, was bent over it in her utterly absorbed, concentrated way. What was it Johnston had said, about them all changing since London? Of course they had

24

changed! What did he expect: complete stasis, non-growth? And thank Christ they had changed, remembering the uncertainty and lack of any sense of identity which had afflicted them then, the constant worrying and introspection about who and what they were, what they were doing there anyway —— Richard had been the worst, of course, though not having met him until he went overseas he had not known him as well as the others. And what were they all doing overseas anyway? In search of themselves in another country? He rejected the answer. Certainly he had not gone for any such reason, and he doubted if any of the others had either; it was more the sort of thing which was expected of one, or which one had intended to do for some time, to seek not one's own origins but rather the origins of one's culture, the beginning, omphalos, father, which art not in heaven, British be thy name, give us this day thy Union Jack tar, who will defend us from all evil, especially the Chinks, for thine was the power, though hardly the glory, for never the sun set never, not on this red blotch slapped like homestead roof-paint across the world's map, Amen. But once there, it was true, confronted for the first time with an alien culture and an alien way of life, the question of who you were and where you belonged burnt into your mind. In the beginning (omphalos, father) it had seemed exotic and little more; a country to see, a Continent to tour, the four-minute Louvre and the eight-day Europe, the Tube was cute and the Metro messy, this, these are not my countries. And so they had gathered together in burrows in Chelsea and South Ken and Notting Hill and in a vast warren at Earls Court and shouted from the tops of their voices at the Down Under, the Overseas Visitors, the Surrey, the Stag and Antler and other gathering grounds 'WE ARE AUSTRALIANS', and slapped each other on the back and drank cold Foster's Lager when they could afford it and complained when they couldn't, and greeted each new boatload of mates and mates-to-be with embrasive good humour, the expatriates huddled together for comfort and selfassurance creating thus in that wintry isle of discontent and black-bowlered strangers, an outpost, a colony, an Other Australia.

But then slowly, after a year or two, you were modified by the land in which you found yourself, entered into an ambivalent relationship with it because even the condition of being an outsider implied a relationship with what one was outside, so that one became not so much an expatriate, an ex-Australian, but merely an un-Englishman, like so many other un-Englishmen, from those with black Jamaican faces who punched your ticket in the tube to those who wrote Das Kapital in the British Museum, and being at that stage neither Australian nor English it was virtually inescapable that you should be forced to consider, finally, who the hell you were anyhow, for until then nationality had (despite Johnston) defined your being, or so much of it at least that the loss of nationality created a corresponding loss of being as well. Of course some, like Carrington, escaped the pincer by transferring completely to the other side, becoming not merely permanent expatriates but rather full-blown Englishmen who had happened to have had the misfortune of being born in the wrong place and who, upon finding the right place, had embraced it as readily and unreservedly as Carrington his goloshes, weskit, umbrella and High Church proclivities. But there were only a few who were able to do that, though for a while he thought that Johnston, despite his masquerading as a professional Australian in Fleet Street, might go the same way, with only an empty shell of sports, diggers, roll-yer-own cigs and Primary School Aussie history to disguise the Englishman underneath; which might still happen, after all, because though Johnston had eventually found his way home he was now, apparently, about to scurry back overseas again, which was perhaps indicative . . . of what? Of the fact that he had finally turned over, like a card with the Knave on one side, to reveal the King on the other? Or that he, more damagingly than most of the others, including himself, had

26

been caught between two identities?

Of course, you always found good reasons for postponing the decision as to which identity to choose. There were countries you hadn't visited; it was the wrong time of the year, or you needed more money for the return fare (unless you were one of those prudent Australians who had kept the return fare in a padlocked bank account at home); you had at last found a job you liked, made the breakthrough; or, if you were honest enough, you admitted that you had actually begun to like England, its freedom and sophistication, a pint at the Blues and Barrelhouse, guitars and black coffee at the Gyre & Gimble, dollybirds in Kings Road and Toorak girls opening their legs in newfound freedom in Earls Court, the Thames near London Bridge with its grey barges and sootgrimed railway stanchions, even those bitterly cold nights when, huddled in duffle jacket, gloves, scarf and disposals boots, you walked back along the river from Charing Cross to Chelsea because you didn't have the fare. And all the time the country was entering your soul, the actual feel and look of it, the grey overbearing streets and peak hour tube crowds and late-night guitar pickers, the elevator ads (at London Bridge, TOP PEOPLE TAKE THE TIMES, with scrawled across it in graffito magnifico, I LIKE FUCKING MARRIED WOMEN) and Sunday qualities and the Statesman on Fridays and the Crystal Palace on Saturdays and the Troubador on Sundays, working men in clodhoppers and caps begriming the seats where houndstooth dormitory commuters, Southwark housewives, Notting Hill spades and Richmond pooves would later sit, London in the snow, bus lights in fog at half-past four, that railway line which wound north through acres and acres of netherworld terraces, residentials and chimney pots, clattering across overhead bridges beneath which black-skinned children played in desolate streets or sat in doorways or glanced momentarily upwards until it emerged dramatically into flat and blasted fields, wind-and-winter-stricken skeletons of trees posed melo-

27

dramatically against a grey and featureless skyworld, hedges and fences and rooks and the occasional unexpected two-storey stone house at some junction of barren lanes . . . this other country, where the wench was dead, slowly entered like iron into one's soul, until in the end there was no choice between identities, no crisis of allegiance —— one had simply become someone else.

He had fought against that transformation, as conscious of his Australianness as Carrington had been of his unAustralianness, or rather had been caught up and stretched like elastic by the conflict between the person he had been and the person he was becoming. It had put them all under a strain, which explained the peculiar intensity and bitterness of the feuds which rent the entire expatriate community —— including the motley crew which, under the aegis of Johnston the Oracle, had established its own selfcontained world in Oakley Street. Each of them had reacted in different ways. Carrington had succumbed completely. George had wrung what he could out of the place (and out of Sonia —— not realizing she would follow him home) and then bounced back to Australia. Richard . . . Richard had broken apart. Johnston, at that stage, had seemed completely impervious, choosing where to live as calmly as he might choose a sports coat. And Don, characteristically, had tried to have it both ways, by marrying an Englishwoman and then bringing her back to Australia, which was probably the worst compromise of all. They none of them liked Don's wife and the fact that she was English somehow made her doubly insufferable because, though they had all been involved with English women and felt that anyone English deserved some sort of loyalty, Don's Wife (or That Bitch, as Sonia affectionately called her) with her Oxford manners and county accent and that poisonous, insidious curiosity about everyone else's affairs, seemed a betrayal of their loyalty. At first meeting she seemed charming and easygoing enough and Graeme could understand how Don, who had always had so little to do with women and had met her quite by chance at Oxford, should have become entangled; but whenever any of the group had come to close quarters with her in Australia, or had made any sort of imposition upon her, as Sonia and George had once by sleeping in Don and Don's Wife's lounge room after they had been thrown out of their Paddo digs following a particularly wild and fornicatory party, the fornications unfortunately taking place on the tiny square of grass (it hardly deserved to be called a lawn) which fronted the crumbling Goodhope Street terrace and was, therefore, visible to the street, passers-by and, eventually, the inevitable Black Maria, then Don's Wife revealed herself as a born troublemaker, attempting to secure agreement from some members of the group that others in it, who might in fact be close friends, were rather this, that or the other, which put those who were dependent upon her hospitality in a rather difficult position; though Sonia, as forthright as ever, had refused to play the game and told Don's Wife what she thought of such sewing-circle shit-slinging and had thus found herself and George asked, in none too subtle terms, to find themselves another flat as soon as possible, because they certainly weren't welcome there cluttering up the polished and white-handwoven-Indian-rugged floor of Don's Wife's immaculate (and charladied) lounge room.

Don had compromised, survived; whereas he, Graeme, caught in the struggle to preserve a link between his past and present selves, had slowly come to doubt his identity altogether. *Who am I?* was the eternal solipsistic question which confronted everyone, but in London it had confronted them all more brutally and unforgivingly than ever; which was why, in that airless coffin of a room at Oakley Street, he had woken one night clawing at the wall and trying to run as in a dream and asking: who was he? Was he still the blind and mucus-ugly rabbit which had butted its way out of the uterus to be born? Or a bare-foot boy of twelve wriggling his toes in the dust of an Australian summer? Or a tense student in borrowed gown waiting for his name to be called at graduation? Or was this only and truly him, alone and vulnerable in London, temporarily finite yet this his present being soon to be abandoned like the others? Was he his father's son, or his brother's brother, or merely the accidental excreta of one night's conjunction of sperm and ovum . . . ?

Which was why, also, he had shouted at Paula that night when she had refused to sleep with him, Paula displaying the reaction to that first sleepy coupling which he had feared all day and which, because he had expected it, seemed all the more unbearable; had shouted at her 'I am my father's son and my brother's brother and I want to sleep with you because I am both those and I am also Graeme . . . .' Christ! It made him, even years afterwards, squirm with embarrassment. What had he meant? Somehow he had been trying to reach back and link himself with what he had been, explain to Paula who only knew that present self that he was also other and worthier people, worthier because younger and more innocent, trying to explain: I am really all these, I am son brother child adolescent and now Graeme who is the sum of all these and yet more please accept what I offer you please accept me child and man please. She had not understood; or, understanding, had rejected him nevertheless; had turned away from him to whom she had surrendered her body only a few hours before and had finally slept alone in her defiant and unimpeachable bed, muffled beneath the blankets and the dark rugs with her hair darker still against the white pillowslip, so that impotent and furious he had slammed outside to let the wind blow coolly through his mind and had walked home along the Embankment sweet Thames run softly watching his shadow jump forward and then slide back beneath the riverbank lights swearing never to leave himself so exposed, so defenceless again, especially to Paula . . . .

But had, of course.

'Why are you looking so morose?' Paula said from across the room, bent over her sewing still, not looking up.

30

'Am I?'

'You haven't said a word since Johnston left.'

'I'm sorry.' He reached down for his drink. The room was absolutely silent except, from the kitchen, the faint ticking of the clock. 'I was thinking of the first time you refused to sleep with me.'

This time she did look up. 'Did I ever do that?'

'Don't tell me you don't remember.'

'I can only remember sleeping with you, rather against my will, not long after Richard . . . .'

'A few months.'

'Was it as long as that?'

'Yes.' Then: 'Don't you remember the night after?'

'Refusing to go to bed with you? Not very well.'

'Jesus Christ,' Graeme said, taking a long swallow, the scene beginning to reform itself, but at several removes, like the sixth (file) carbon copy of a badly typed business letter. 'All that agony for nothing.'

Paula smiled at him. 'Don't worry, darling, we're together now.'

The irony in her voice did not escape him. 'What's the matter with you?' he asked.

'The matter? Nothing at all.'

'You sound a bit fed up.'

'I am — but it's nothing you can solve. Tell me, what do you think of Johnston going back to London?'

He was about to pursue his original query, changed his mind, and instead switched over to the more amenable problem of Johnston.

'Do you think he means it?'

'It sounds like it, don't you think? Not that I blame him at all. I think he's being perfectly sensible getting out while there is still time. But it's something of a surprise, nevertheless.'

'He's been talking like this for —— oh, for months now.'

'Yes, but he's never said he was actually going to go back. I think he will.'

'Are you sorry?'

31

She held up her sewing to the light, squinted at the ribboned edge of what seemed to be a bib for the baby, and worked at it on her lap again. 'I haven't thought about it. Yes, I am, I suppose. We've seen a lot of him lately. But whether I'm sorry *for* him —— that's another matter. I can understand his reasons. But perhaps it is a retreat, as you said. It means it hasn't worked out here for him. I'm not sure if it's Australia or his own lack of success which is most to blame . . . .'

'He's been successful by most standards: he's a bloody smart journalist.'

'Yes, but not by Johnston's standards. He wanted to turn the place upside down when he came back —— he said as much tonight. Johnston's very ambitious.'

'And so?'

'Nothing, really. Perhaps Fleet Street will be kinder to him.'

Their conversation flickered, died out. Graeme thought of the morrow, flinched, took another mouthful of beer and decided to throw the rest down the sink. It tasted stale and unenlivening. His watch showed quarter of an hour after midnight.

'I'm tired —— and I've got a hell of a day tomorrow. I think I'll go to bed.'

'Very well, darling. I'll be up in a little while.'

He walked over, kissed her briefly on the forehead, yawned, turned for the stairs.

'Goodnight, darling.'

'Goodnight.'

Their marriage, she decided, apparently intent upon her needlework but only half-conscious of it, their marriage had not been an easy one. Was she to blame? Because in a way she had forced them to get married, or rather had forced Graeme to make up his mind one way or the other about the whole thing, by refusing to live with him any longer in that horrid flat at Elizabeth Bay; though it was

he who, after that, insisted they get married despite the
fact that, living alone for a change, she had begun to doubt
whether she really wanted to marry him after all. Perhaps
she had been right to hesitate, too, considering what had
happened to them since. Graeme, in his usual jack-in-
the-box and headlong fashion, had overborne her doubts,
but they had persisted nonetheless and had turned their
honeymoon on the North Coast into a prolonged torment
such as they had never suffered when they had been living
together. For she had never been certain just what her
motives had been in marrying Graeme: love?
possessiveness? or her crippling and neurotic desire for
safety? She had always sought absolute security in
everything in her life, from examination passes to her daily
emotions; and she feared that, especially after what had
happened with Richard, she had allowed herself to be
bullied into marriage, or rather (for that was over-
dramatizing it surely) had allowed herself to slide
unprotestingly into it because it had offered her a refuge
from uncertainty — — a retreat as much as Johnston's
return to London was. And she had been too honest, or
too naive, to keep her fears from Graeme, who, thinking in
the manner of all men that he had made a great gesture of
commitment and self-abnegation in marrying her instead
of insisting that they merely keep on living together,
suddenly found that what he had committed himself to
was as shifting and uncertain as the sands on that
seashaped crescent of beach with its long line of purple
mountains disintegrating into the distance on the other
side of the bay and a curdled sky blowing in from the east
and a wavecreased bowl of sea which turned to molten
pewter in the brazening afternoon sun where, day after
day, they played out their rituals of seeking and courtship
(for they had never had much courtship before) and denial
which should all have come before and which, whatever
honeymoons were ordained for, were certainly not for
that. Each day, seeking certainty where she could offer
none — — or should she have lied? — — the scales suddenly

and, to him, inexplicably reversed, he had asked 'do you love me?' And each day she had replied that she knew what she felt for him, and that it was more intense than anything she had ever felt for anyone else before (except Richard, which she did not say), and that it had made her marry him, but that beyond that she could not in all honesty, which is surely what he wanted, go. Love? How did she know what love was? How define it, how be certain that what one felt was in fact what the books and novelists and churchmen and sex manuals called love? She could not bring herself to give him the lying reassurance he demanded, partly because she knew it would be dishonest to herself, but mainly because she felt, intuitively (though she believed in no such nonsense as women's intuition, but simply felt certain within herself without actually testing it intellectually) that it would also be dishonest to their relationship, might even damage it by trying to impart to it a gloss, a nomenclature which it did not deserve. And so to all his bitter questioning, which grew more bitter as the days and the weeks passed and the sun hung like a reproach in that curdled sky and the pewter seas washed and rewashed the sand from one end of the crescent of beach to the other, uncovering rocks here and piling up great overburdens of gritty shell-rough drifts beyond the point where the fishermen came at dusk on the falling tide and cursed the shallows which had been built up by the waves' motion, she had been able to offer nothing but a willingness to sleep with him in that low-wheeled motel bed which slid around like a dodgem car at Luna Park and an unspoken reassurance that, even if she did not love him, she was with him at least; which was, after all, a beginning.

But hardly a satisfactory one. That first uncertainty lay between them like a knife in the months that followed, in fact throughout the first year of their marriage; and the situation was aggravated because Graeme at that stage was trying to break out as a freelance, with drawing boards, anglepoise lamps, shelves, library books on design, overseas magazines and brown manila files strewn all over their tiny

Paddington flat, and after each exhausting day with news editors, publishers, business executives and other clients had few reserves left to grapple with a recalcitrant and unselfcertain wife. Even so she could not bring herself to tell him the words which, she supposed, he wanted to hear; which would have been the easy way out. How could she? For she was still not sure that they should have married at all, that it might not have been one gigantic mistake brought on by her own fearfulness and selfish need for a world of fixed and immutable dimensions (which she had not gained by marrying Graeme anyhow). And all the Marriage Guidance advice in the women's magazines, which she had begun to read then because she had no one else to turn to, except her mother, which was out of the question because she, having destroyed her own marriage years before, was hardly in a position to offer advice, all their talk about 'understanding' and 'initial problems' and 'marriages need tact and sympathy to survive' helped not at all; because what was the use of trying to make things work out, trying to compromise and give in here and stand firm there and allow for the failings and weaknesses and cruelties of your partner if in fact it was all a mistake, if you really were unsuited to each other and should never have been married in the first place, and the sooner you found out the better? For heaven knows how many marriages ended up in the Divorce Court, was it one in seven or one in five? Anyhow whatever it was some of them were destined to fail from the very beginning, were *meant* to fail because people were genuinely unsuited to each other and how did one know one's own marriage was not among those? There was no one around to say to her 'stick it out, you'll be all right' (she would have doubted them anyhow) and, what was perhaps worse, no one to say 'you should never have married, separate and see what happens'. Though her mother had, just once, hinted that she should do just that . . . .

And end up like her?

Her mind flicked back to her mother, the heavy,

matronly figure in the formal navy blue one-piece dress clasped in front of her rather stout bosom (which Paula feared she inherited) by a formal brooch, the slight blue rinse to her hairdo by Alexander which seemed to become bluer as the years wore on, the plucked eyebrows arched a little above the natural line, Saturday evening socials at the Royal Yacht Squadron, Kirribilli, and card nights at the Liberal Party and the little circle of Killara divorcees, widows and wives who entertained in each other's homes and flew down to Melbourne for the Cup and lived on their husbands' alimony and trust fund dividends and superannuation investments and, if they could afford it, took short P & O trips overseas to Noumea and Hong Kong and even England, and attempted bravely to pretend that their lives were sufficient without males to despoil them; she was fond of her mother, though she did not get on well with her and had not ever, if she were really honest about it, forgiven her for divorcing Percy over a petty infidelity; for she, Paula, had spent the major part of her life, especially when she was a teenager and needed him most, without a father to turn to or advise her or even simply to admire, and had been left with this terrible and stupid and, even though, now, she could admit and analyse it, inescapable craving for the sort of emotional security which she had been denied as a child and which, more than anything else, she was determined to have as a grown woman; and had found herself married, by an ironic quirk of fate, to someone who demanded precisely the same of her, who demanded a certainty which she, so far from being able to give, remorselessly pursued herself . . . .

Sometimes, after one of their interminable scenes, she felt like giving up altogether, retreating, abandoning marriage completely. Heaven knows she had offered Graeme his freedom often enough, told him there was no need for them to stay together if he felt marriage was not giving him what he wanted; nor had done this selfishly, nor bitchily, but because she felt genuinely guilty about not being able to provide what he so clearly wanted, an absolute and unconditional love. Was she, perhaps, protecting herself against his ego in doing so, holding on to some frail independence because she knew that, if she gave that up, he would overwhelm her, demand everything and more, reduce her to subservience — and then turn elsewhere for other women to subjugate? No, it wasn't as machiavellian as that. And, paradoxically, because they both needed certainty so much and had failed to find it in each other they were more reluctant, perhaps, than others in the same situation might have been to break asunder and thus lose what little they did have: each other. And so had persisted.

Which, no doubt, was why she was here now, sewing an apron for the baby, with the children asleep in the room above and her husband, in all probability, asleep also by now. The usual, predictable, tiresomely familiar and yet —— well, fond almost —— domestic round.

When had things improved between them? With the birth of James? It would be nice to think so, that the arrival of their first infant and Graeme's one and only son had been the catalyst which transformed their relationship. But that, she thought, only seemed to happen in the women's serials. Graeme had been singularly untouched by James, which was a gauge of his selfishness; indeed had resented him more than anything, which was not lost on James as the child grew older and would be the cause of no end of tension between them if Graeme was not more careful, and of course it had all exploded that first time when, in the middle of their lovemaking, she had been forced to break off and go and attend to James who was yelling his poor little lungs out in the next room. It was a situation which she had tried desperately to avoid, knowing how afraid he was that, never having really won the certainty of her love from her, the baby would do so by default and would be yet another barrier between them . . . .

Sitting there, bent over her sewing which she held up occasionally to the fishbowl light, she might have seemed to someone passing by utterly absorbed in what she was doing, the needle flashing deftly, catching the light every now and then on its curved silver sabrepoint; but in fact the sewing was almost automatic, like driving a car on a long journey, carried out by one tiny and surface section of her mind only, while the rest of her was concentrated on that scene: James whimpering and grizzling, demanding his feed earlier than usual, while she and Graeme pretended they couldn't hear him and tried to make love with her leaking all over the place from her over-abundant breasts (which almost drowned James when he suckled her, poor little blighter); but Graeme was never one to hurry and James's whimpers had turned into such full-blooded yells that, unable to bear it any longer, she had slid away from beneath her husband and reached for her nightdress hanging behind the bedroom door, while Graeme, with an oath, had flung himself back on the pillow and, crossing his arms beneath his head, had half-shouted: 'Go on! Go on to your bloody infant! It's more important to you than your husband —— I've known that all along.' Which was most unfair, because she had been trying to avoid just that situation and it was sheer bad luck that James should have chosen to cry at the particular moment, and besides she had never been able to indulge in sex when anything else distracted her, even a light in the room, which was another source of conflict between herself and Graeme who, eroticist that he was, liked to fuck her with the bedroom light blazing so he could watch her move and might, for all she knew, come home one day with a magnifying mirror to put on the ceiling!

No, it had not been James's arrival which changed things.

It had been —— well, nothing, really, now she came to think of it. Time. Sheer persistence. Perhaps they had just, very slowly, come to know each other, to find out just what had occurred in the past to make each the person he or she was; and, understanding, had come to accept; and, accepting, had come to —— love.

Love?

The word still hung like a question mark in her mind.
There were times when everything seemed well between
them, when she would not have wished it any different:
neither the achingly dull domestic routine, which became
bearable only when she could feel it sustained their
relationship, nor the children, despite the way they bound
her life so tightly to their petty demands and desires, nor
Graeme himself, who was still capable of surprising her
with the intensity of his involvement in her; sometimes,
with Graeme home early from work, having bypassed the
pub for a change, the children in bed, a jazz fugue playing
quietly on the stereo as the two of them sat out on the
balcony watching the light fade from the treetops and her
husband talked quietly to her about the day's work,
involving her vicariously in the world of ambition and
conflict and disappointment which was denied to her, life
seemed almost as sweet as it had in those girlish days
which seemed so utterly distant now and which had
acquired a distinct patina of nostalgia for her, so she could
hardly bear to look at those early colour slides and
black-and-white Old Girls' Ball flashlight shots which she
kept, amidst a confusion of letters, notebooks, scribbled
reminders, mementos, unwanted gifts, unused perfumes
and lipsticks, autographs, signed menus and heaven knows
what other junk in the suitcase in the spare room. But
between those high points there were long stretches of
boredom and sourness when her existence seemed to have
lost all its savour, when she and Graeme seemed to be
operating on different wavelengths and he spent more and
more time at work or at the Windsor Castle or with those
of the push he still kept in contact with, while she found
herself wondering just what the hell she was doing here
anyhow and just what the future held for her, or for them
—— or if they had any future together at all.

So, with a sigh, holding up the apron, which only
needed the red lace trimming on the pocket now, she

thrust her sewing away in the chest of drawers which she had bought at Bric-a-Brac, walked upstairs to the bathroom, cleaned her teeth, glancing at herself in the mirror and noticing the dark, oval face staring back which seemed a little dry but she felt too lazy to put cleansing cream on tonight, looked in on the children, drawing the blanket up over the baby who had crawled down to the wrong end of the cot and was lying there, thumb in mouth, floral nightie caught up around her waist and one foot poking through the slats, which she didn't move for fear of waking her up, and James curled up with both his arms under the sheet for a change, and then upstairs to the attic room; where to her surprise, she found her husband still awake, in bed, reading.

'What are you doing awake?'

'Couldn't get to sleep. Kept thinking about the interview with Cassidy tomorrow —— what a bastard! So I thought I'd wait for you.'

Turning to the walk-in wardrobe she caught his sly, half-grinning expression as she began to undress. 'Oh no, not tonight. I just don't feel up to it.' Feeling, suddenly, unbearably bone-weary.

'That's a pity. I was.'

She kicked off her shoes, walked jadedly across to the bed and turned her back to him. 'Here, unzip me.'

Graeme did as he was asked, slipping the dress down over her shoulder, and kissed her lightly on the arm. 'Sure?'

She sat there on the edge of the bed, shoulders slumped forward, the dress down around her waist, rubbing her face with her hands, the day's chores and the couple of glasses of beer and Johnston's demanding, importuning conversation mixing to create a feeling that she could not go on, simply could not go on like this.

'Positive.'

She sat there a while, expecting him to grow angry, but her husband went back to reading. 'Thought I'd bone up on the organization men for tomorrow. Beat 'em at their own game, I say.'

After a while she turned and looked at him. He was lying back with his paisley pajama top unbuttoned, black mat of hair curling out of control against the pillow, the beginnings of a day-old beard showing through his swarthy skin, eyes intent on the page and his eyebrows frowning a little so that they seemed to join in a black scar across his forehead, biting absentmindedly at the nail of one forefinger while the other hand held the book open. He looked like —— heavens, what did he look like, something out of a bad French film, not handsome enough to be a Belmondo or Jacques Courier but rather the nasty guy, the seducer, third angle in the triangle —— maybe it was English, Alan Bates, that kitchen sink stuff, North Countree. Bates? Yes, he did look a bit —— 'Do you know you look a bit like Alan Bates?'

'What?' said Graeme, not looking up from the page.

'You look a bit like Alan Bates.'

'Bates?'

'Bates. Yes, BATES. The film star.'

This time he did stop reading, momentarily.

'Cor! I've always wanted to look like a film star!' And went back to reading.

'Oh, what's the use of talking to you, you get your nose buried in a book and there's no hope of squeezing a sensible conversation out of you! I've had it, I really have, I've absolutely had it! It's bad enough being cooped up here in this mausoleum of a house day in and day out with nothing to do except wash shitty nappies and listen to the commercials on the radio and watch telly with the children without having a husband who doesn't talk to you!'

'A husband who what . . .?'

'You're absolutely hopeless. I'm sick and tired of it, I really am.'

She stood up swiftly, pausing only momentarily to gather her dress around her, but it was long enough for Graeme to thrust the book aside, jerk himself upright and grab her by the arm.

41

'I heard every word —— and I completely agree! You've married a real shit. What'll we talk about?'

'Too late,' she said, and wrestled her arm free. 'You're always too late.' She undressed to her bra and pants, reached down a floral dressing gown from the wardrobe and slung it over her arm. 'I'm going to have a shower.'

'It might wake you up,' said Graeme. He chanced a smile.

'If it does I'll take a barbiturate. I'm too tired,' she said, and flounced out the door towards the bathroom.

Alan Bates indeed! She should have her head read. Perhaps she just had a weakness for men with dark hair; which was pretty corny, now she came to think of it. And beards —— she liked beards. Perhaps Graeme should grow one? No, she decided immediately, he was too swarthy, too madly Ancient Briton for that. Naked, he would be all hair and no body. The thought of Graeme, spindly-shanked and hirsute under the shower, cave man's hairy face soused in water, made her giggle. Alan Bates indeed!

Still, she had to admit she didn't feel quite so sleepy.

Morning sunshine skating in through the window, waning and brightening as clouds drifted over the chimneypots. Bars of shadows striped the ceiling, yellow panels bending around the porcelain sink in the alcove and straightening themselves against the red and turquoise Ortega poster, beneath which a mantelpiece supported two striped bowls from Italy, a Michelangelo nude, a charcoal drawing by Gromolski the artist downstairs, yesterday's bottle of milk (unopened), a pile of letters and a Pernod ashtray souvenired from a dockside cafe in Marseilles. On the wall next to the door a single large Renoir nude for which he had reluctantly paid twenty francs at the Musee d'Art Moderne in Paris; on the door itself the torn woolly dressing gown his mother had given him 'to keep you warm over there'.

To wake in sunshine. It was one of the things he missed most about Australia: to wake slowly and know without needing to look but simply to know by the wafer-thin slice of light escaping around the edge of a drawn blind that outside blue arced overhead and everywhere a sense of space. Here the sun was cool, though lying in bed watching it panelling across the ceiling one could almost imagine it had warmth to it. At least it was the right colour. Yellow of sunshine, yellow of Queensland sand and pineapples sliced across the grain, yellow of .creek clay after the rains had set in, of tractors at the Royal Easter Show, of bleached summer grass, of hair, my true love's hair. A children's song started up in his mind:

Oh, my yallow oh my yallow oh my yallow gal,
Yallow oh my yallow oh my yallow gal

She got pretty hair, the yallow gal,
She got pretty eyes, the yallow gal.

Oh, my yallow on my yallow on my yallow gal
My yallow oh my yallow oh my yallow gal . . . .

Except his true love's hair was brown. He lay thinking
about her, the calm symmetrical face, irises so dark they
seemed to swell and annex the pupils, the slim body
which, apart from the extravagant breasts, reminded him
of a Rodin bronze. Her unfamiliar odour, a subtle yet
unmistakeable muskscent, clung to the white cotton
where, only an hour before, she had lain in drowsy
half-sleep. I'll ring her later, he thought. I'll ring her and
see how she is.

Fling back the bedclothes, jacknife over to the fire, light
heater, turn it up, arms in gown, feet in slippers, slam out
the door and down the half-flight of stairs to the kitchen.
He went through it half a dozen times in his mind before,
reluctantly, transforming it to a reality, wary still of what
the English, God bless 'em, still thought of as the best
climate in the world. He pounded against the kitchen door,
which was latched —— against the cold? 'Hey, what's going
on?'

Don's unshaven and glassless face. 'Not today, thank
you,' and shut the door.

The hell not! Kicked, the door opened, Graeme
stumbled, almost fell inside. Don, clad in unbelievable
white dressing gown which revealed, obscenely, both
jutting kneecaps, was flattened ogre-like against the
cupboards. 'Gentlemen, THE KING!' His high falsetto
warbled a Royal fanfare.

Johnston was hunched like a hairy bear over the frying
pan. 'Bon jour, mon petit Graeme,' he said, arching a
Boyer eye. 'Desirez-vous une saucisse?'

44

'You are too kind,' Graeme said. He reached high onto the shelf for the cornflakes, poured them into a bowl. They fell with a loud clatter. Yes, he decided, he did have something of a hangover.

Don burst into a singing commercial for Weaties, the Sunshine Breakfast. 'For Christ's sake, Donald, shut that bloody awful racket up,' shouted Johnston, relapsing into the tongue vulgaris. A racquet: two strings and a mister. 'Why've we got him here? Who can tell me? Didn't his father read the Durex ads?'

'Johnno, you working today?'

'Yes, frig it. The Big Fart is opening a new church vestry or pissing in a new urinal or something, so Johnno boy here has to go along and make sure he doesn't release a foreign policy statement at the same time.' The Big Fart was Johnston's private epithet for the Australian High Commissioner in London, whose doings provided some of the copy that Fleet Street's colony of Australian journalists dutifully relayed home. Policy through piles. 'What a life. Some day I'm going to get out of this rat-race.'

'You're Robinson Crusoe.'

Johnston switched his attention back to the stove. He had sausages spluttering in one frying pan, eggs in another and tomatoes under the griller. 'Talk about a culmination of orgasms,' he said, not without pride —— 'everything's reaching a climax at the same time.'

'Indeed a plenitude of pussy-puckering,' Graeme defined from the table.

Johnston served the food onto three fluted Woolworths plates and carried them across to the table.

'What did you think of the grog-up last night?' Don asked nobody.

'Passable,' said Johnston.

'You seemed to be enjoying yourself with Sonia in poor old George's absence' Don said slyly.

Johnston looked up. 'You keep your lecherous bespectacled frustrate eyes off her, Donald. I'm warning you —— you can find a sleeping bag of your own. Anyhow, she wouldn't be much use to you right now.'

'Why not?'

'She's got her rags on.'

'Good Lord above!' Don exploded, choking on his toast and golden syrup. 'Do you have to give us the gory anatomical details at breakfast, my man?'

Johnston ate on unconcernedly. 'I saw our dear landlady yesterday.'

'Old Harpic? What was she on about?' asked Graeme.

'Something about the gas meters. Reckons she's not getting enough from them. Don must have lost one of his string-and-sticky tape bobs down the slot. Caught me in the bathroom, she did, and wouldn't go away from the door!'

'She's a neurotic.'

'Like all spinsters —— waiting for the big defrost,' said Johnston.

'She's a widow, not a spinster.'

'Same difference. Been serviced once and can't wait for it to happen again.' Johnston mopped up his plate with a toast crust. 'What are you doing today?'

'Nothing much. I've got to go into the ad agency this morning.'

'Do you want to have some lunch with me? I'll be free about twelve-thirty.'

'Okay.'

They finished breakfast and Graeme went back to his room, shaved, dressed quickly in a grey Marks & Spencer suit and topped it off with a sincere-looking tie. Knotting it, he glanced at himself in the mirror. Ho hum, manners makyth man. Almost.

He walked over to the mantelpiece, jammed a couple of felt pens and a wad of drawing paper into his inside coat pocket and glanced quickly through the pile of letters. Most of them were from home, including one from his father. He picked it out and put it in his pocket. At the bottom of the pile was a black-and-white photograph of

Don, Richard and Johnston which had been taken in France the previous summer. They were leaning against Rosinante, the battered 1933 Austin which Don and Richard had bought in a Battersea secondhand car yard to take them on a trip to Provence, and which Richard, heroically, had later taken Paula to Greece in. Johnston, as usual, was acting the fool and was staring into the far distance with one hand to his brow like a shipwrecked mariner; Richard was his usual cool, photogenic self; but Don was gazing straight at the camera with the embarrassed, goonish grin he seemed to reserve for snapshots only. In the background was the low stone bridge which crossed the Rhône at Vienne.

Graeme picked up the photograph and the remaining letters and thrust them into the top of his sole chest of drawers, awash already with bills, letters, receipts, scribbled ideas, drawings, layout sheets, biros and used Pentels which he could never bring himself to throw out believing, against all logic and reason, that perhaps they could be resuscitated by standing them in a jug of water for a few hours. Then, as an afterthought, he took the photograph out again and propped it up against the wall behind the yellow Pernod ashtray.

He looked hard at Richard's face, which, turned in semi-profile in that withdrawn, self denigrating way of his, revealed nothing; then at the other two. Disparate, idiosyncratic, his closest friends; and yet apart from him. Hand to the photograph to study it, he noticed the short, purple scar from his time at the nursery garden which ran across the back. It was the hand of a worker or a farmer, stubby, wide; thick-fingered, though paled now by two long English winters. He had always envied, though he was loth to admit it, the easy affluence of the others. At university, scrabbling his way through on a Common-wealth Scholarship, he had begrudged Don his unquestioning acceptance of the cloistered, warm-stone privileges of life at St Paul's College while he himself worked weekends in the nursery to get some spending

47

money; and later he had sweated his way across to England as a deckhand on a cargo ship while Johnston, who had sold a year of his life to the Melbourne Herald for the price of the berth, went first class P & O. But would he have had it otherwise? He had concentrated on what he thought worthwhile, was a free man still, owed no one, despite the advertising agency, his integrity . . . or did he?

Downstairs Johnston, resplendent in heavy tweed overcoat and pigskin gloves, was calling him.

Lunch time. He caught the tube from Piccadilly to Blackfriars, walked unhurriedly up Fleet Street past the streaming commuter faces, the tourists with their inevitable cameras and exposure meters slung in leather satchels around their necks, the City clerks in waistcoats and bowler hats, the faces of men with moustaches and greying hair which might have belonged to Guardian and Reuters journalists and might not, and found Johnston jammed behind a desk in the nearly-deserted Melbourne Herald bureau, tie undone, shirt unbuttoned, cigarette in mouth and trying hard to look like Walter Wagner's version of a newspaperman. He was battering away at a decrepit portable Remington which made more noise than a jackhammer and which he had used ever since Graeme had first met him, many years before, in Melbourne. Graeme wondered why he still kept it; the keys struck down instead of up, the capitals printed half a space above the line, and when you hit the keys your fingers practically dropped a foot. Johnston typed heavily, with two fingers only; perhaps the machine was the only one which could stand up to such a pounding.

'You can quit posing —— nobody's looking,' Graeme said over his shoulder.

Johnston looked up. 'G'day, sport. Sorry, I'm running late. I'll be another half-hour yet.'

'Okay.' He glanced across at the yellow, closetyped cable sheets lying besides Johnston's typewriter; for some

48

reason his mind flicked back to the morning. 'What did you make of Don asking you about Sonia this morning? Very strange, I thought.'

Johnston leant back in his chair and grinned. 'I don't know. Poor old Don —— maybe he's just frustrated. I don't think he's ever had a woman in his life; probably a covert camp. Either that or the sight of Sonia's too much for him . . . . By Christ, she's a whore if ever there was one; fucks like a rattlesnake, she does. You've got no idea what she gets up to.'

Graeme laughed, a little forcedly. Johnston always talked about his sexual conquests in crude and extravagant detail; Graeme had never quite worked out whether it was because women meant nothing whatsoever to him except as vagina vehicles or whether it was all a pose and that he was quite mushy and vulnerable, like an oyster with the shell ripped off, when alone with women. The second theory was the more creditable to Johnston, but the first was the more likely.

Johnston, his cable forgotten, had by now launched into a vivid description of Sonia's bedspring antics which made her sound like a combination of Messalina and Fanny Hill. Graeme interrupted him:

'I thought you said she had the curse?'

'Ah, that was just for Don's benefit,' said Johnston. 'I know it gives him a thrill.'

'You shouldn't talk about her like that, anyhow.'

'Why not?'

'Because I don't want to hear it.'

'You? The blushful and virginal Graeme Turner? Christ, you'll have to do better than that, sport.'

'Well, for a start, she's George's woman and George is supposed to be a mate of ours. And even if she hasn't any other virtues she's at least let you sleep with her. So she's got that claim on your loyalty.'

'Come off it! That's the bloody trouble with you, Graeme, you're too much of a Puritan. Or a Romantic, which is worse. You and Shelley would have made a great pair —— Graeme Bysshe Turner, the great twentieth Century Romantic. God Christ Almighty!'

'Have it your own way, baby.'

'She's been handled so many times she's grubby. She's got dirty fingermarks all over her.'

'Maybe. Still, you owe her something.' Graeme could feel himself getting angry, but Johnston persisted.

'Listen, you anachronistic Childe Harold, just listen to this! You know the night George left for Scotland, and Sonia came back to the flat after seeing him off, and was sitting on my knee there? In the main room? Well, do you know I had nearly all my hand up her! I hadn't even kissed her and I had four fingers scratching her womb! What sort of a woman is that?'

'Johnno,' Graeme said, 'sometimes you appal me. Don't you understand?' He grabbed Johnston's hand and held it beneath Johnston's eyes. 'Whose fingers were they?'

He dropped Johnston's hand and swung away. 'Anyhow, I've got to ring up. See you when you've finished.'

He moved towards a telephone, then changed his mind and walked out of the reporters' room down the long corridor to the men's washroom. That bloody Johnston. He didn't feel like ringing Paula now. Instead he walked into the tiled shower-room which the Australian newspaper bureaux, after much negotiation with the owners of the building, had installed for their staffs, flung his clothes off, tied a towel around the overhanging showerpipe and turned the water on. It cascaded down his body, drenching and warming him, a welcome change to the grubby and rust-stained enamel bath which was what he and the others shared in Oakley Street, where showers were unheard of and demanded only by health faddists like Australians and other crazy colonials. He made no attempt to wash himself but stood there idly with legs crossed, one arm resting against the tiled wall of the cubicle, watching the water stream off the point of his elbow. The luxurious heat of the water gradually washed his anger away; he threw his head back and let the water pour into his face, then stepped out of the cubicle, gasping. That Johnston.

Drying himself, he caught sight of his figure in the long shower-room mirror. It was like his father's, really, thick and powerful-looking in the body but with legs and arms which were too long and thin for the trunk. I look, he thought, like an unflattering combination of Don's gawky limbs and Johnston's scrumpack barrelchest. Side-on, however, he looked wiry and proportionate, the clean descending line broken only by the inevitable ugliness of his cock. It ruins the harmony of a man's physique, he thought; it's quite ugly, and it's the only reason why a woman's body is more beautiful than a man's. We should be like women, smooth and unobtrusive; no wonder the Hellenic and Renaissance sculptors had shrunk the size of their gods' genitals till they were fit for nothing but a figleaf —— form came before realism. It was as though God had fashioned the body of man and then as an afterthought had thrown a blob of hair and gristle at it as you might throw mud at a wall, not caring much where it landed.

Back in the reporters' room, splotches of water marking the front of his shirt, he found Johnston still jackhammering away. Upon a sudden impulse he walked over, touched him briefly on the shoulder:

'What're you writing, daddy-oh?'

Johnston, hunched over the typewriter as though to devour it, accepted the peace offer. 'John Osborne. A profile for Melbourne of the Original Angry and whatever-happened-to-the-cult-of-petulance. They don't like nothin', mate, not even themselves.' He poised two pugilist fists above the keyboard. 'But like me, come to think of it. Sometimes I give me a pain in the neck. Though you're wrong, of course.'

'I'm going to ring up,' Graeme said.

'Very well, cock. I'll be through in five minutes. Then you can buy me a beer and lecture me about' —— he looked up, grinned briefly —— 'morality.'

51

Graeme walked across to one of the reporters' telephones and dialled Paula's office number, FLAxman 2488. He had to wait a long time to be put through to her, the line clicking, a subdued conversation murmuring on in the far distance. When Paula's voice did come on it sounded startlingly close and sweet.

'I'm terribly busy, I can't talk for long,' she said.

'What's the matter?'

'I'm doing dictation for my boss, and he doesn't like to be kept waiting.'

'Okay, I won't keep you long. I just wanted to make sure you were all right.' He paused. 'Is everything all right?'

'Of course it is —— but it was nice of you to ring.'

'No aftermath?'

'No aftermath.' She paused, then laughed. 'Not much anyhow.'

'What are you laughing at?'

'I don't know whether I should tell you, Graeme. It sounds too crude for words.'

'What is?'

'I hope the switchgirl isn't listening,' she replied, lowering her voice a tone, as though that made any difference, 'but every time I stand up it simply pours out of me. It's terrible.'

'What does?'

'You do. It's disgusting —— I can't seem to stop it. It's left a wet mark on my frock, and I have to keep sitting down all the time so no one can see it.'

He sat there with the phone in his hand and he felt himself become very tense and hot, his stomach contracting into a cavity which hollowed out his body behind the ribs and behind the navel, and he suddenly desired Paula fiercely and lustfully and quite crudely.

'You're incredible,' he said. 'To think I was worried about you.'

'I'm glad you rang, Graeme. Please ring me again. Will you?'

'Of course.' He wanted to call her darling, but couldn't; the words stuck in his throat. 'See you later.'

'All right. Bye.'

'Bye.'

When he put the phone down he noticed his hand had left a black, sweaty imprint upon it. Paula, he thought; Paula Paula Paula. He was filled, transfigured, by a sudden, fierce exaltation. Paula Paula Paula PAULA. Christ, he thought, and stood up. A high, wild strand of jazz melody started up in the back of his brain, unformulated but shocking his nerve-ends into a naked, precocious sensitivity. Paula.

Johnston, looking across, knowing what time Paula had left that morning, perceiving more than he had ever allowed his friends, or anyone for that matter, to suspect, absorbing the expression on Graeme's face, paused momentarily in his typing. Ave atque vale, Richard.

But this was another morning now, four and a half years later.

Graeme finished his coffee, glanced at his watch, and looked across to where Paula, in dressing gown, ruffled hair and bare feet, was rinsing the children's plates in the sink. Paula? Yes, it was the same Paula. A little older, somewhat heavier around the breasts and buttocks, considerably more discontented, with two children to drag her down and a familiar husband instead of an unfamiliar lover to stain her dresses, but still the same Paula. On a sudden impulse he got up, walked across to where she was standing disconsolately poking at a Walt Disney mug with a dishmop and kissed the faint lines which creased her skin between the neck and shoulders.

'Will you be late tonight?' she said, without looking up.

'Shouldn't be. Why?'

'Nothing.'

'I'm glad you weren't so tired last night after all,' he said.

Paula didn't reply so, turning, he hurriedly kissed the baby, who was sitting slimy with Farex in a high chair at the end of the table, and James, who was munching toast with both legs curled up beneath him like a yoga devotee, walked into the hallway, picked up his briefcase, shouted goodbye and, outside, the sun glittering through the gumtrees, the turned earth in the garden still wet with dew, climbed the series of stairs which led to where his car was parked on the top roadway. He glanced at his watch again. Five to nine. Half an hour into the city, another ten minutes finding a parking spot, another ten walking down from near the Quay, which was the best place to find a meter at this hour of the morning, under the railway and up Pitt Street to Bridge Street, where Consolidated Enterprises Inc. had its suite in the glossy new Mercantile Assurance Building —— he should just make it.

At eleven minutes past ten precisely, puffing a little, he walked into the glossy outer office of Consolidated, decorated in International Functional style with rubberplants, low modular furniture, embossed but oh-so-plain Japanese ricepaper serving as a backdrop to the framed early-period Picasso copy ('The Harlequin') and the Jeffrey Smart original, and an equally tasteful secretary in severe bun, frosted nailpolish and clingtop stockings barely but enticingly visible amid a hint of white flesh beneath a skirt not so much mini as Cooper S. She paused fractionally before her massive electric typewriter as Graeme, with such insouciance as he could muster, tossed his battered and, as he now realized, ex-university leather briefcase (when everyone else in the building no doubt had those snappy American-style clip-lock models) upon the immaculately conceived teak settee, which he half expected to yelp in protest, and smiled cheerfully:

'Is the Old Man in?'

The unexpected familiarity unfroze the secretary just the teeniest little bit because, somewhat unsure who this bugger was (a salesman, one of the breed she had been instructed to keep out? or a penniless relative, whom she had also better keep out? or a client, which was hardly likely?) she asked in her best telephone voice: 'Whom shall I say is calling?'

'Graeme Turner.'

'Oh yes. Mr Cassidy was expecting you at ten o'clock. I'll tell him you've arrived.' The rebuke could not have been clearer. It was as though Mr C. had had his room entirely cleared of bugs, tape recorders, secretaries, files, graphics and even furniture at ten o'clock precisely Eastern Standard Time purely for the sake of this upstart window-dresser, layabout or whoever he was and had since been prowling up, down, across the ceiling and around the walls of his office chomping on cigar ends which she, personally, would have to clear up later and working himself into a lather of temper which she, personally, would have to assuage later through the expenditure of God knows what sexual expertise and degradation which, after all, she had been saving for her boyfriend at the Drive In that night .... 'Mr Cassidy will be free in a few minutes. Would you take a seat?'

It was the waiting that got you, thought Graeme, just as it got Schulberg's Scott Fitzgerald; it was the interminable sitting around waiting for Great Men to take notice of you, waiting for them to be Free, waiting for interviews like patients outside a dentist's surgery with one grubby copy of last year's Punch little compensation for a jawful of bloody and soon-to-be toothless gums, so that your bowels knotted inside you and when, at long last, you were wheeled up before the Commanding Officer, GHQ, to answer a charge of cowardice in the face of battle or whatever it was the hearing was already over, the case lost, the verdict pronounced and the firing squad oiling their barrels. So he preferred to stand, prowling around the outer office like a caged Cassidy, watching the secretary's frosted fingers flicker caressingly over the hairtrigger typewriter keys (would that be the ideal gift for Johnston? just a cool thou or so, and for two or three Pernods you might get the secretary thrown in), and when at last Mr C.

55

was Free he walked in bearing an upturned, jolly, well-here-I-am-boss-who's-for-de-high-jump-today James Cagney face which would have melted the heart of lesser men than John Sean Cassidy, no initials.

It was wasted, however, on Mr C.'s wooden desk leg, because Mr C. himself did not look up but was busily shuffling papers on his desk and gazing fixedly at a file of papers which his Personal Secretary, who was at the moment tip-toeing out of the other door, had left for him. There was a chair on the firing-squad side of the desk which was fully a foot and a half lower than Mr C.'s own personal blackleather-backed swivelchair from Artes, and which put whoever sat in it in the position of staring supplicatingly up towards Mr C. over the desktop as though towards a Bureaucrat God; Graeme sank into it and stared with coolly Berenson eyes at the ceiling, thinking, Ho-Hum Ploy One, the Old Man's sore, up-your-bum.

After fully five minutes Cassidy looked up, leapt to his feet, smiled, took off his hornrims, strode quickly around the desk, held out his hand, pumped Graeme's, 'Hullo, Graeme! I didn't hear you come in!' (the old egalitarian trad is not dead, dad, even in Consol Ent.) replaced his hornrims, smiled again, walked back, gestured Graeme to the chair, sat down and picked up his papers once more. Back to Square One, baby; though he noticed now that the papers were in fact his own working roughs of the graphics for Consolidated's new downtown multi-storey office project, which at the moment was little more than an enormous cavity surrounded by a white fence and gawping clerks on the nether side of Pitt Street but which, as the line drawings with garish colour-wash hanging on the walls of Mr C.'s sanctum attested, would surely outrank in splendour even Consolidated's Friendship House (so named because, as a PR stunt, Consolidated had given over half an entire floor at the very back of the building to a local charity).

At last, and not without some deliberation, Cassidy spoke. 'Graeme, I'll be very frank with you' —— still gazing at the papers held in both manicured hands in front of him and shuffling them intermittently —— 'you've put me in a very difficult position. You know we've liked your work before; we think you did a splendid job on Friendship House, absolutely first-class. And at our board meetings on The Project I pushed very hard to have you in on this one too, though the price you were asking was, I must admit, a trifle on the high side. Still, that's in the past now. The Board agreed, and I personally was very happy about it. But . . .' and here Mr C. leaned back in his swivel chair, took off his hornrims (if he starts polishing the lenses, thought Graeme, I shall scream positively scream) took out a folded white handkerchief, luckily only wiped his nose, and continued at a rather more measured gait

'. . . I've just been looking through your initial sketches here and I can't say I'm very happy with them; no, not very happy at all.'

'Well, they're only roughs,' replied Graeme with a casual wave of his hand, hopefully implying that Cassidy simply didn't like the powerfully abrasive, auto-erotic yet poised calligraphy of line with which he had rendered such immortal statements as CONSOLIDATED ENTERPRISES PROJECT and SYDNEY COVE CITY —— ANOTHER CONSOL. ENT. PROJECT. But Mr C. was not to be deflected.

'I know, I know, and I can see what you're getting at —— oh yes, I can see that. But I feel they're not quite, how shall I say it, not quite *dramatic* enough for what is, after all, going to be the biggest Project in that part of the city —— and certainly the biggest thing we've ever tackled. They haven't got enough *punch,* if you see what I mean. Not enough eye appeal. We wanted something very special for this, Graeme, and I don't think these have got it.'

Cassidy leant back, convinced that now he had formulated his opinion so explicitly no one could possibly disagree with it, and tossed the graphics across the desk in a gesture which was both dismissive and an instruction for Graeme to pick them up.

'You mean you wanted a big CALTEX sign on the roof and an illuminated spectacular saying CONSOLIDATED BUILT THIS up the side of building,' said Graeme, smiling sweetly and ostentatiously refusing to touch the leprosy-and-Cassidy infected drawings. He felt in a good mood this morning, and he was not going to be jostled out of it by an ulcerated executive heading fast for a Wood Coffill apotheosis.

Cassidy looked at Graeme, refused his invitation to smile and said, just a trifle more slowly and rather more than a trifle more menacingly:

'No, you know I didn't mean that at all. But we do want something good for our money. Something outstanding. This hasn't got it.'

For an instant, just an instant, Graeme's confidence faltered. Perhaps Cassidy was right? Perhaps they weren't any good after all? He looked across at the grizzled grey face opposite in its grizzle-grey suit, the leathery jowls and stubby gravedigger's fingers and the subtle odour of lather and iron filings which he had always associated with his grandfather and thus with death, and dismissed the thought as absurd. Cassidy? Cassidy wouldn't know the difference between a shrdlu and a Billy Tea ad. Question: how to make the point without losing the commission? Answer: be friendly, baby.

'That surprises me, J.C.,' Graeme said.

'It surprises me too,' replied Cassidy. 'We don't want something vulgar: you know that as well as I do, Graeme. But they must have *impact.*'

Impact? Good Christ, Cassidy could actually comprehend TV! Favourite program: Rin Tin Tin. Favourite film star: Mussolini. Graeme leapt to his feet, relieved to be no longer staring up Cassidy's blackhaired nostrils, and launched out on an instant Melodious Thunk improvisation in Persuasive Variations which surprised even himself:

'Look, JC, you business tycoons are all the same' he began, (familiarity and flattery) 'you say you don't want

58

something ostentatious but in fact you do' (Packard sociology) 'the only thing is you don't want to *appear* to be ostentatious in being ostentatious' (glib intellectualism) 'right? Now the way to achieve this is by understatement; and those graphics of mine' (pride) 'fairly scream with understatement'. (paradox) 'Now take a look at that signature graphic:' (sheer professionalism) 'it's small, it's quiet, but it bears repeating.' (analogy) 'It can be repeated a million times and it won't look cheapskate,' (subliminal fear technique) 'it won't look *tired;* you can blow it up, blow it down, expand it, write it across a million letterheads' (vision of Splendid Future) 'and *it will still look good.* Because it's got something to it. It's a big U, right? It's in fact the shape of The Project, right?' (flattering takeover of terms) 'And each part of the U is made up of a C —— C for Consolidated.' (fanfare, flourish of trumpets, exit, pursued by a bear) 'Now, it doesn't knock you right out' (artistic licence) 'as soon as you see it, because it isn't meant to. It needs to be looked into. But that's where the Design' (my own private monopoly) 'comes into it. As soon as the symbols click, you never forget it!' (Triumphant coda) *'And that's what you want.'* (Clincher)

He picked up the papers at last, leafed through them till he came to the big U letraset from ultra condensed compacta Cs, and slapped it confidently on Cassidy's desk. He felt a little winded, and besides he didn't know what to say next, so he added a little lamely:

'Don't you agree?'

Cassidy replaced his hornrims, glanced at the Big U symbol, let the paper fall and replied:

'I must say I don't mind the —— er, the key design so much. But what about these others? All small letters, too much white space; if you've got advertising space on a building, your *own* advertising space, why not use it?' That's an elementary business principle, Mr Turner.'

Graeme, who had not failed to notice the change to Mr Turner, momentarily cabled UPSTICK JOB ARSEWARDS to Consolent from Alice Springs, changed his mind for the sake of a mere two thousand dollars, and replied:

'But if you want to understate, Mr Cassidy, you have to have something to understate with. You take up all the space on your excavation surround, or on your letterhead for that matter, and you've got nothing left to play with. You need that white space to focus down on the lettering. You see? It gives you contrast.'

Mr C. seemed doubtful. His face, beneath the grey, short-napped hair, was an Irish-Catholic exercise in asymmetry, a nose stuck on here, an ear there, one side noticeably more lined than the other. A selfmade man from Ashfield who had only had the benefit of three years at Sydney Grammar to give him the business contacts he needed to start with, he had a reputation for brutality in his dealings with people; but Graeme had decided from the start not to take him too seriously, and lightheartedly played the Bohemian-Artist-with-a-Flair role whenever they had to discuss anything —— though he had not yet got around to calling Cassidy baby.

On the other side of the table Cassidy, the passionate sceptic, still looked sceptical. The time had come, perhaps, for a concession. After all, he had the payments on his car to keep up . . . .

'I'll tell you what, J.C.,' said Graeme, 'you're probably right about some of those letter-lines. Maybe they're *too* understated. What about' —— he indulged in a mock-pause as if he were considering some profoundly perceptive suggestion Cassidy had made —— 'what about using caps instead of lower-case there? It'll certainly change the character of the lines. But it will still be understated, which I think's important.'

Cassidy looked up, the shrewd Irish face seemingly ill at ease with the hornrims despite the virtuoso play he made with them, and Graeme wondered whether he had been taken in by the bluff or not.

'Perhaps that would be an improvement,' he said noncommittally. 'I feel they need *something*, Graeme.'

'I think you're right,' replied Turner né Graeme né Bert the Bumsucker. 'I think capitals would be better. Make it more —— more dramatic.' (Good Christ!) 'But I hope you agree with me about the general principle of understating these graphics, JC. When you've got a building as impressive as The Project you don't need to shout.'

'All right, take these with you, make those changes I suggested, and let me have them back next week.' *He* suggested? Don't say anything, baby. Graeme stuffed the graphics in his briefcase and headed for the door. He had almost reached it when Cassidy, one finger already pressed on the buzzer for his secretary, called out:

'By the way, don't change that big U design. It's kind of cute.'

Bread-and-Circuses Turner, who could scarce forbear to shout hosanna or throw up a stinking sock or two at Caesar's generosity, gave a sickly smile, nodded, and escaped to Miss Frosted Fingers. He waved cheerily at her, whispered 'don't look now, but your pants are missing', grimaced at the Jeffrey Smart, and strode down the corridor towards the lifts. A bell tinkled and doors opened, revealing a Brueghel composition of figures, male and female, tall and short, in snappy grey hats, floral buttonholes, sad overcoats, sincere ties, string baskets, grubby white collars, Executive Suite pallors, mottled jowls, trim-set secretarial breasts and nicotined fingers standing in line, silently, face outwards, bereft of all expression, hope or reaction, waiting for the doors to shut. What a shot, he thought. It's moments like these you need Nikon. He got in, turned around, and waited in the deathly silence which afflicted the glossier lifts in the glossier business edifices to descend, in immolation, to the ground.

Exploiting the exploiters, Graeme called it. But sometimes he wondered.

Outside in Bridge Street the sticky, soupy heat swamped him. People swirled past, buffeting and bruising each other in their rush to extinction. MORE TROOPS FOR VIETNAM shouted the *Mirror* poster on the corner and

61

then, more reassuringly, Southerly Soon. Someone had been sick on plonk and prawns into a urinal-shaped copper sculpture decorating the office block wall. Next to it was a Red Phone. Graeme walked across and dialled Johnston's number. What he would need before this day was out was a drink.

The night air caught him by the throat like fire like smoke like the white light of headlights which flaring down Ocean Street picked out the bizarre silhouettes of terrace house roofslopes twilight on grey slate cast-iron balconies with glassed-in embryonic bedsitters and box trees like toy farmyard pieces and the fragmented multiform reflections of headlights in windows which refracted each jagged image until it slid down to cool grey perspectives of housefronts footpaths gutters yesterday's papers and this curved black but occasionally light-strewn road. Night swirled up out of the bowels of Paddington's valleys and hilltop terraces and deposited itself like a fine grey mist on this street snare of his certainties and uncertainties which once he had felt so secure of that he had wanted to film it, explaining that this street here, this single street in a single provincial city, had been pieced together, brick by brick, crumb by crumb, instant by instant, by the labour of men who had with their hands created something permanent and they had hoped lasting, that terrace with its Georgian purity of blank-fronted form and sloping farmhouse roofs which perhaps a century and a half ago men had built from warm stone and cool slate and clipper-ballast iron, and which had contained within itself a century and a half of living since, a century and a half of lives which even now behind slatted shutters and rectangles of curtained light contained an infinitely textured warp of life which he, passing, could only grasp at but which, with persistence, could be recreated in images even more enduring than these stone slabs —— but the film had been unmade; and the street had been reduced, now, to this single Coutard hand-held shot of changing focus which was him, now, striding along Ocean Street towards the Windsor Castle in this encroaching twilight as a million other twilights had fallen on this harbour-gutted city.

He turned off down Jersey Road and into the deeper gloom of Paddington proper, past the Royal Arms with its quota of Alfas and milkwhite E-types and occasional red custom Camaro parked longitudinally outside, the meeting place of City wealth and Paddo artiness, with a sprinkling of camps and interior decorators thrown in for colour, remembering

'And what did you do then?' said the Police Prosecutor. In the witness box, twitching and jerking, an eczema-faced youth. 'We went up to the Royal Arms.'

'With the girl?'

'Yes.'

'What happened there?'

'Well . . . she tried a few blokes in the bar but it was no good 'cos they were all peds . . .' his voice trailing off.

The magistrate intervened. 'What?'

'They were all peds.'

The Police Prosecutor with his three stripes glistening knowingly shuffled his papers. 'Pederasts, Your Honour.'

The magistrate looked down again and the Police Prosecutor continued with his examination of this youth who had come from Condobolin or Nyngan or some other caste-ridden poor-white town and had picked up with a girl whom he had taken soliciting around the Cross, living in some cheap rat-stricken room at the back of the Glamour Capital of Australia and had himself been picked up by those incorruptible eagle-eyed and pinioned defenders of the Majesty of the Law, the Darlo plainclothes squad, and had been hauled quivering into this last final sink of human bankruptcy, the Central Police Court, which had been renamed the Court of Petty Sessions to preserve the fiction that it was not a police court though everyone

inside except the magistrate (and why not he too?) wore
uniforms and the great dank sandstone pile with its vast
ascension of steps outside to emphasize the infinitesimal
stature of all those whom Justice brought there still had
POLICE COURT chiselled in sandstone capitals across the
pediment, had been hauled up here on a charge of living
off immoral earnings and now, poor bastard, after a bit of
a slaparound by the sadists at Darlo and a weekend in the
cells and maybe the irredeemable promise of a bond if he
pleaded guilty, was thrust naked before the whole panoply
of an Establishment which did not know what a ped was
and later, with his courage finally drained away, was led
off to four years at Long Bay so that the reporters put
their wirebound notebooks in their hip pockets and
shrugged, half in cynicism and half in what was left of pity
and conscience after years of watching the Police Courts
dispense what laughably passed for justice to those who
could not afford Justice (spelt with a capital QC) and said
'that's Kelly law for you', and filed out, while here at the
Royal Arms the peds mutually and illegally consenting in
private and mutually and illegally soliciting in public but
protected embalmed emblazoned by wealth from the
strictures of the Darlo squad carried on their whisky-and-
soda affairs and sought expanding arseholes to wipe their
mothers' faces clean.

'It's so clean,' explained Harold, who was nice but
bitchy, preferred boys to girls and men to boys, sought
West End parts in a hundred poofter lavatory cellars and
wondered why he had never made Stratford

Took her home I nearly made it

Sitting on a sofa with a sister or two so what if Baby
Jane Holzer does think Paul McCartney's got a fat bottom?
*he de best white rhythm-and-blues singer in de whole
world, Uncle Tom,* two sisters? of course Henry Miller
went one better, with Maude and Mona in the same bed, or
was it draped over the same table? what does it matter,
one cunt's the same as another in the dark and you can
never tell the hair colour till you clean your teeth the next

65

morning . . . .

Past, of course, the Royal Arms, climbing slowly past
the row of houses with their friendly stepped-back,
side-by-side, cement rendered and sandstock fronts, a huge
Union Jack (shroud for my Jolly Jack Tar) draped across
one balcony like a gigantic pop-art symbol, turn right at
the Congregational Church with its reassuring gold-lettered
minister's Notice Board and past Rudy Komon's gallery
where by day a fashionable plumber's mate was wilfully
and obscenely exposing plastic aortas and tubes by
Fallopius to Sydney's sherry society but which now peered
shortsightedly with white-and-stained-timber good taste
and immaculate proportions at the gloom-masked
housefronts opposite, past the lane and down through
those familiar hollows with blue streetlights strung on lines
and leafy overshadowing branches and iron pike-topped
pickets guarding the basements of three-storey residentials,
past the silent cars wrapped for burial in tarpaulins and the
greengrocer's, closed, his pace imperceptibly quickened
now as the slope steepened until striding around the
corner, the Hungry Horse rising whitely on his left and the
lit boudoir of the Dandy Dog opposite, there before him,
in all its glory, glamour and ghastliness, was the Windsor
Castle.

The Windsor Castle?

You've got to make it, baby.

Three sporty types came blo-ooo-o-oming up the hill in
an open Sprite with the centre character waving to no one
in particular and calling out to the bearded drinkers sitting
on the footpath. He escaped inside and looked cautiously
around the bar, which was not crowded but in which
everyone turned around to see who had arrived in case it
was Somebody but seeing it was Nobody turned back to
their grogs; whereupon Nobody eked his way forward and
discovered in the corner not Johnston but George with
back to wall and beer to face calculatingly eyeing off the
birds in the bar ('I had a mate,' said Johnston once,
grinning behind his moustache with the lines creasing

upwards, downwards, sideways across his face, 'I had a mate who used to poke his head into any bar he walked past in the street and shout out "G'DAY THERE, MATE" and every bloody Alf in the bar would turn around and reply "G'day there" in case it was someone he knew . . .' Johnston's grin split open in a laugh, ripped his face in half and turned his bushy eyebrows like a satyr's into his hair. 'That's bloody Australian egalitarianism for you, sport! That's about as far as it's got, too.')

'G'day there, baby,' said Graeme.

George smiled. 'Baby yourself. What'll you have?'

'Middy. Been here long?'

'Not really. Since about six o'clock.' He tried to catch the barmaid's eye. Graeme glanced briefly around the bar. He couldn't see anyone he knew, though over in the bigger Public Bar on the other side of the pub he noticed a Famous Writer standing with a group of others who could not have been quite so famous, most of them in dark suits with the occasional check shirt or Harris tweed to denote nonconformity, the Famous Writer rocking back on his heels with his moustache quivering a little as he told some anecdote which was no doubt insupportably funny as the acolytes listened with shorts in fists.

Watch yourself, baby, Turner told himself, you're getting envious. Fame's a must to avoid. Fame? Phone. But how do you avoid being a phone, once you're in the gogglebox eye? You have to choose which of the multitudinous me's to present, and that means acting out a role. And if you think it's all shit, and say it's all shit, and walk onto the screen scratching your arse and saying you don't give a bugger, why that's acting out an anti-role. You can't walk into a fisheye lens and not get distorted.

George came back into focus with a brimming middy.

'For the worker,' he said, and smiled his thin smile. He had a dark complexion which perhaps betrayed a Spanish ancestry, a narrow and almost aristocratic nose, balding hair, a lithe, wiry frame and a quick, twitchy nervosity —— all of which combined, for some extraordinary reason, to make him absolutely irresistible to women. It was a trait which Graeme both admired and envied.

'Strangely enough I have been working,' Graeme said, accepting the beer. 'Pictorial book —— complete layout. I've had a bit of trouble with the type faces, wanted to get away from Compacta but I needed something equally bold. You know? Of course, Solly Sternberg won't mention the designer. Nor will the critics. DESIGN? That's sumpin' y' see in overseas glossies, ain't it?' He pulled a sour face, swallowed some beer, wiped the froth from his top lip. 'Of course I'm not cynical. You understand that, don't you?'

George smiled. His eyes flickered around the bar again while his right hand ceaselessly twirled, fingered and caressed the short-stemmed whisky glass.

'Have you seen Johnston? I'm supposed to meet him here tonight' Graeme asked.

'No, I haven't —— but I only just got here. I've been working back at the uni till quite late these last few weeks. Heavy load this term. Lots of new students.'

'That should suit you.'

'All those fresherettes? Haven't the time, old man; only wish I did.'

Graeme followed George's eyes around the bar: beery faces, whisky faces, young hip kids in denim jackets and Zapata moustaches, girls with discotheque eyes made up to reflect the artificial glamour of whatever was IN, a couple of artists whom he knew vaguely arguing against the mirror which read RESCH'S BEER IS BEST, the usual clutch of dollies, art students, high camps and layabouts and, near the doorway into the Public Bar, Pedro the Pusher in his knee-length John Hunt coat with the astrakhan collar, who must have sidled in after him . . . .

'What a collection of phones,' said George, dismissing them all.

'The whole push?'

'The whole push.'

'Johnston too?'

George sipped his whisky with utmost delicacy. 'Johnston too. He's a phone.'

'And we too ——'

'Speak for yourself.'

'Then why do we come here?'

'To eye the women off; what else?'

Graeme glanced around again, nodded at Pedro, ('gas, man'), gulped his beer. He liked the Castle. He liked the human smell and warmth of it, the clamorous sense of cameraderie, of bodies jammed too close together for freedom and people shouting too hard to be heard, of spilt beer and barmaid smiles and the fluorescent-lit glory of Red Mill, Pernod, Johnny Walker, Vickers, Chateau Tanunda and Corio bottles beatified above the cash-register, the hard and axed-out Paddo faces in the Public Bar, the men with their open-necked shirts and pushed-back Albert Tucker hats and the dartboard swinging against the chalk hieroglyphics on the door, the voices which bounced off the ceiling and ricocheted from wall to wall, the sense of something *going on,* something happening, life being lived, here, actuality, reality, reactuality, unabstractuality, that which exists, which *is*, not that secondhand glimpse at secondhand affairs which the telly cinema art drama the novel all represented, tied up in a square Pye box with a ribbon around it and an inbuilt life-intensity control.

Which is why, he reflected, he had never got around to making that film on Ocean Street.

And why further, he reflected, not without regret, he would probably never get around to doing anything.

Earlier that day, after his appointment at Consolidated Enterprises, he had drifted down to the Quay where the massive concrete-grey bulk of the overhead railway effectively excommunicated the city from its harbour entrance so that the jetties, the old-fashioned double-ended ferries, the ropes and buffers and capstans and kiosks which he knew so well from childhood trips to Taronga Park and Manly (did the old man still play the

69

violin and pass the hat around the Mums, Dads, beachgoers and holidaymakers crowded into the weekend ferry?) were invisible until you reached managerial level in one of the new waterfront skyscrapers which peered over the expressway and blotted out even more of the harbour from the city's walled-in and street-constricted heart, the glint of sunlight upon the oily waves which lapped around the jetty piers and against the moss-buffered rock invisible, so that there, barely a few feet away, one might as well have been in Blacktown or Green Valley as within wavespray distance of Port Jackson, with its yachts and Japanese tramps and island traders and big twin-funnel liners which disgorged every few days a flood of hope-sick, whitefaced migrants into the You Beaut Country; what price philistinism? He walked across the blazing acres of tarmac, concrete, bluemetal roadway and yellow pedestrian stripes, under the shadow of the railway with its massive, rotund pylons of unfaced Labor Government brick, out into the sunshine again and across to the ironbark wharf which, a hangover of an earlier, less glossy and less rumbustious era, was the cool refuge of Maritime Services Board clerks eating sandwiches from brown paper bags, electricians in blue overalls and fishermen in khaki shorts and sandals.

The interview with Cassidy had disturbed him, soured the good humour with which he had woken that morning; he felt much as he used to, years ago, after one of those interminable arguments with his father about the need to 'get on in the world'. He had drifted through his Arts course at Sydney University much as he had later drifted overseas, with no particular sense of purpose and no particular destiny in mind, a little worried really that he should be so directionless when everybody else seemed already to have fixed their goals in life and to be pursuing them with considerable remorselessness; and at least once a week his father had demanded of him, 'When are you going to settle down, Graeme?', unable to imagine that there could be anything in life as important, as

70

fundamental, as the need to get on and make a name for oneself, carve out some sort of niche in the uncaring and unyielding world. Of course that was the neurosis which the lower middle class, to which he and his father irretrievably belonged, carried around with them like a nervous disease, the itch to get on, drag oneself out of the rut, be a success. It had driven his father off the land into a clerk's chair with the AMP, and from there into twenty or thirty salesman's jobs, from irrigation machinery to Zambuk to vacuum cleaners, with a five-year interregnum in the Middle East and at Moresby during the war with Army Transport, and then back into civvies again with a bad gut and a non-com's pencil moustache and a taste for status which had led him into a variety of bizarre money-making ventures, from flogging machinery for clearing brigalow scrub in Queensland (but had been ahead of his time there) to a dozen other engineering designs and patents which were always going to make his fortune but, somehow, had never quite worked out; the only thing that had succeeded had been the property bought cheap from Henderson's down at Kiama and then subdivided for week-enders, which had kept the family afloat for some years and financed his father to other land speculations which had proved not nearly so successful; and so had never broken through, really, ending up on the pension and a fibro house (which at least he owned) in Yagoona — and his mother, worn out by a lifetime of hard work raising five children and taking part-time jobs whenever his father was unemployed, which was pretty often, getting a visit from the Pensioner Medical Service each week, and depending on the money Graeme sent her every month to be able to live any sort of life at all, even to be able to afford a dress at Bankstown or to buy the food for the family get-together at Christmas.

But lack of success had only made the Old Man all the more eager that he should taste it, vicariously, through his children; nothing had pleased him more than Lucy's getting married to Colin Beresford, who was not only an

71

old Fort Street prefect but a civil engineer who had done well with the Department of Main Roads and was now living in a smart two-storey Lend Lease project home at Carlingford and traded in his maroon (it was always maroon) V8 Falcon for a new one every two years. The whole of his father's class was riddled with guilt at not having got on when so many other people so patently *were* getting on; it had taken him a long time to break free of his father's attitudes, and even now he wondered whether he had really managed to excise the suppurating boil of materialism with which his father had afflicted him —— or why did he care so much about his and Paula's home in Pymble, and accept commissions from crass philistines like Cassidy, and divide his time between graphic design and the Windsor Castle, when what he should really be doing was living as a pauper and trying to make films, experimental films which would really clutch at the subtle, indefinite, spider-spun intricacies which characterized human existence and which he would like to crystallize in images that were as far removed from the blunt statements of everyday cinema as . . . well, as graphic design was from what he really wanted to do. It should be possible, he thought, to create a cinema as abstract and yet as emotional, as forthright, as a Jackson Pollock or an Olsen. All you needed was time, imagination . . . and persistence.

Graeme Turner looked out across Sydney Cove, conscious of the sunglint of oilslick wavetops, the white parabolas of the Opera House, the low black horizontals of wharves and jetties and landpoint, loops and whorls of cloudshape, and slashing across them all the single black line of thought: that was what he had always lacked. Persistence. He was no Johnston. He had none of his immensely self-confident, assertive pushiness, a quality which he knew Paula, at least, admired. It was as if in freeing himself from his father's successmanship, sleeping on the floors of push Balmain terraces after the traumatic shouting matches at home, drifting purposelessly from job to job, he had also discarded any capacity for enterprise;

72

his cure from ambition had been almost too complete. It was only after a year in London that he had achieved any sense of direction at all, when he had suddenly found himself caught up in an excitement in all things visual, from painting to films, which was heightened by his discovery during a haphazard year at St Martin's art school that he actually had a flair for shapes and pattern-making and could even draw tolerably well, which a dozen or so years of primary and secondary schooling in Australia had failed to reveal. In the end it was the cinema which had claimed him and he had followed the well-trodden path which led from the British Film Institute to Sight and Sound to Cahiers du Cinéma to his own secondhand 16mm camera and projector, making a living the while doing Press layouts and then more advanced design work for the advertising agency in Piccadilly which was half-owned by an Australian, Tony Rushkin, who still had a soft spot for Australian stenographers (whom Rushkin regularly knocked off after a dinner at some cheap but flashy joint like Talk of the Town or, if he was feeling expansive, the Savoy) and, rather less so, for expatriate copywriters and layout men. Thus, almost by accident, graphic design had become the stock-in-trade in which he became progressively more skilled though it was the cinema in which he became more and more involved, from studying up on the technical side to helping organize special National Film Theatre programmes to weeks spent in Paris simply to catch up on what was happening in the cinemas off the Champs-Elysées . . . .

But all that had ended as soon as he came back to Australia. Once again the remorseless necessity to make a living, especially after marrying Paula, had forced him into graphic work. The link, of course, was visual; and he enjoyed much of it even though it became, inevitably, the application of tried formulas to familiar problems. But the sum total was that, four years later, he was still immersed in graphic design, making more money than ever and able to pick and choose between commissions, while the film

which he had come back to Australia to make, which he
had been so certain on that rainy, saltlashed day he and
Paula set off from Tilbury with the music blaring over the
ship's loudspeakers and Johnston and Carrington and Eljay
and the others waving from the wharf, his arm around
Paula and three weeks of separate cabins and clandestine
fucks in the shower-room because the ole P & O certainly
didn't believe in unmarried couples sharing the same bed,
no matter what went on in Oakley Street and Buckingham
Palace and the Guards Barracks at Whitehall, he had to get
back to Australia, omphalos, the beginning, father, to
make, was an aborted foetus wrapped in twenty-two sheets
of paper scribbled with scenario notes, frame lists and
script ideas in the third (inside) pocket of the leather
briefcase which lay, even now, bulging at his feet. What
had happened? In London everything had seemed possible:
he had grown confident, even ambitious. He seemed to
know where he was going and what he was going to do
with his life. He was going to make films. But here, back in
Australia, he had got lost somewhere, stumbled off the
path, slackened momentum —— reverted to type?

There was a sour taste of defeat in his mouth, and it was
not all of Cassidy's making. Perhaps, he thought, he should
stop kidding himself. He would never make a film; he
didn't have it in him. The time had come to act as an adult
at last, to put aside childish things. That, surely, was what
maturity meant: the ability to face up to your own ——
mediocrity.

He reached down for his briefcase, unclipped the two
straps, fumbled inside, took out a sheaf of papers. As he
walked off the wharf the slurp-slurp of waves stirred up by
a passing ferry slowly receded, washing against the stone
wall with the sticky sound of brushes pulled from a
gluepot. Behind him a lizard's tail of torn sheets, looping
like confetti across the wavetops, drifted out towards
mid-harbour, absorbed water, submerged, sank without
trace . . . .

Three beers later his regret had been drowned somewhat; so that when Gina, in dark glasses, extravagantly long hair, bad teeth and Vaucluse mannerisms burst, or rather erupted, into the bar and George, whom she was looking for, played it cool as usual and chose precisely that moment to immerse his eyes, mouth, consciousness and all varieties of memory in his beer, Graeme smiled across the tops of the heads and waved her over and expansively bought her a Scotch which, with her background to live down, she rarely if ever drank, opting always for masculine middies, but which Graeme knew she still rather liked on account of having seen her get quite rotten one night at Buckley's pub on Scotches because, as she put it, 'I can't stand having to go for a piss in the Ladies', it's *hideous'*.

George noticed her at last. 'Hello.'

'You big prick, is that all you've got to say after not having rung me for two days?' with a slight pout of her half-bitchy, half-lascivious mouth. 'I might have died for all you'd know —— or care, for that matter. What've you been doing?'

George had the grace to look faintly embarrassed. Ho hum, thought Graeme, so it's reached that stage, has it? No wonder Sonia was driven almost neurotic at having to compete with the multitude of women, both beautiful and unbeautiful, who found her husband attractive; and though George carried out some of his infidelities with a certain discretion, it was impossible to be discreet if you got mixed up with an old-time libertarian like Gina.

'I've been very busy,' he said. 'I've just been complaining to Graeme about the heavy teaching load I've got this term . . . .'

'Heavy teaching load! That's French for a cool-down period.' Gina tossed her hair and glared at her reflection above the Pernod-Corio-Vickers-Red Mill bottles, seemed not unpleased with what she saw, adjusted her sunglasses, which were very large and square and tinted a pale Zbigniew Cybulski beige so you could see what her eyes

75

were doing behind them, and returned to the attack.

'What's the matter, Georgie? Did I hurt you last time?' She smiled. 'Oh, these modern men! They like to think they're great hulking brutes in T-shirts with their singlets torn off like Marlon Brando or somebody and underneath it all they're just babies who want to be loved. And not too hard, either!'

'Marlon Brando?' said George defensively. 'That dates you. You might at least have chosen Steve McQueen.'

'It's not my fault I belong to the alcoholic generation,' Gina said, taking a long swallow of Scotch. I'll buy her beer next time, thought Graeme. Suddenly she smiled, and despite the bad upper teeth she became almost attractive. 'Oh come on, let's stop this smart nonsense. How have you been, darling?'

'Fine. Just fine. I really have been busy,' said George, undeceived. 'Actually I tried to ring you. Once.'

'Once.'

'As I said.'

They argued on amiably, joined later by one or two others from the university, and as the circle widened Graeme found himself pushed further away from George. They were talking faculty politics, anyhow, and how the new senior lecturer in philosophy, a surprise import from Adelaide of all places would fare surrounded by Andersonians, and he felt somewhat out of it. He had always regretted not going to university full-time which might have led, perhaps, to some sort of university tutorship, always assuming he got the necessary honours degree. The academic world protected people like George; it gave them a solid field within which to operate. All they had to do was keep up with the journals, keep abreast of a certain amount of research information, and the automatic ingest machine which their university training had bequeathed them took care of the rest. Their source material was limitless. But he had to rely on ideas, an ability to perform; all he had to fall back on was his own talent. Which was fine while the ideas lasted, but what happened when they ran out? What happened when you found yourself still stuck with the techniques which were really hot when you grew up and which you used to push older men out of the way, and then you still had them ten or fifteen years later, maybe they gave you fifteen years before they started primping you for the scrapheap, when the new men started pushing up with *their* ideas and you didn't have the creativity to match them, and then people started saying Graeme Turner? Well yes, he's OK still, but if you want someone really hot, someone really on the ball why don't you get in touch with . . . .? Because you used yourself up all the time, poured everything out of yourself till you ran dry and the new men pushed up like weeds through the concrete, through the cracks in the pavement, the new men are cool as spreading fern baby and then —— why, suddenly you couldn't see the concrete any longer, it was all overgrown, that path? why, nobody's walked along that way for a long time, Sir, no Sir, it doesn't lead anywhere, it was just one of those offshoots of the —— was it the 1960s? —— you know, Sir, one of those dead ends . . . .

Which was why he was envious of George. A little.

And why he was glad when, in the midst of his morose reverie, the smiling and universe-confident face of Johnston, leering and expanding purposively beneath a snappy fedora, came swimming into view and Johnston's heavy hand clasped itself on his shoulder and Johnston's heavy voice rasped: 'Got a drink for an old digger, sport?'

Graeme turned towards the bar but Johnston stopped him. 'It's too bloody crowded in here, let's go into the beer garden,' he said. They pushed their way through the throng and walked outside, along the sudden cool of the street, to the corridor which led down to the rows of hard-railed garden chairs, spilt beer, wilting oleanders and bitumen floor which constituted the Beer Garden. At the other end was a battered bandstand sporting an even more battered piano and a slightly askew sign saying THURSDAY NIGHT MERV ACHESON. There was no one on the bandstand but as, armed with beers, they made for one of the red-and-green painted tables beneath the hanging basket ferns and tree cabbages a quartet of young musicians straggled onto the bandstand and launched into an uptempo version of what Graeme thought at first was 'Sweet Georgia Brown' with the melody turned upside down but then recognized as Monk's 'Bright Mississippi'.

Johnston put his hands over his ears. 'The neurotic music of a neurotic civilization,' he half-shouted above the din. There was no point in talking, so Graeme turned his attention to the music. The alto sax was a competent musician whom Graeme thought he had seen at one of the university jazz festivals and who kept jamming 'new thing' inflections and runs into his basically straight phrasing, more Jimmy Woods than Ayler, and who annoyed Johnston considerably more than Merv's mainstreamers would have. Johnston had a limited tolerance for jazz, being a blues man from way back who had been raised on Bessie Smith, weaned to Billie Holiday, corrupted by Ella Fitzgerald and had then taken a purist leap backwards into Lightnin' Hopkins and Muddy Waters.

'The blues,' Johnston was saying in the gaps between numbers, which were quite long because the quartet, obviously students or beginners, took a long time sorting out what the next number would be and then what chord changes they would use, 'the blues are life-affirmative as well as melancholy. They aren't even melancholy, because that is too European, too angst a word for them; melancholy is for the romantics and Gray's Elegy and all that sort of shit —— they are sorrowful and they can be despairing but they are never merely those things because they are also *for life*. You know, you sing the blues because you sing the blues away. It's cathartic —— the sun's gonna shine on my back door someday, I'm gonna make it, baby, all those lyrics, you know? But these blokes . . . .'

Johnston shrugged, dismissing with one huge shoulder the band, the bandstand, everyone who was listening, the entire corpus of jazz from, say, Bix Beiderbeck onwards, in fact just about the whole universe which could take any such anarchic noise seriously, while Graeme thought, irrelevantly, that at least IT'S CATHARTIC, BABY would make the title of a damn fine film . . . .

'they're just expressing the anxiety neuroses of an age which has really got something to be anxious and neurotic about. They're right about that at least. But it isn't creative, they're not reconstructing anything, are they? They're just psychotic, mixed-up form-destroyers, musical Nazis: they want to tear the world down and themselves with it. They've all got Samson complexes and all you bloody Delilahs can do is sit back and applaud —— here it is, folks, step right up, pay your trahison des clercs money and watch the destruction of music as an art, Parker the Wrecker is Here . . . .'

'You're out of date, man,' said Graeme. 'Parker started the process. It's gone a long way since then.'

'It's got worse.'

'Depends on your point of view. The new men' —— the new men are cool as spreading fern, baby; but of course they weren't —— 'the new men pay less attention to form than Jelly Roll, but so what? What you don't understand is that they have just taken the trad thing a step further. The blues is the music of an oppressed, alienated race —— so it became the pop music of an oppressed, alienated civilization. But the old singers had something to look forward to; the new men don't. Blokes like Ayler and Coltrane and Coleman, they've been freed, man, but they're still alienated. So they've dropped the hope bit. Their music is total alienation: and as such they're the most perfect expression of our age.'

'Precisely,' said Johnston.

'But you can create art out of alienation,' began Graeme. 'Even great art . . . .' But then the alto chopped in with a phrase which might have made Jelly Roll's hair stand on end and might even have made Bird blanch, and Johnston and he settled back to their beers.

An hour and a half and some middies later, with Johnston gone to the Men's before leaving to meet a contact at Vadim's up at the Cross, Graeme wandered back into the small bar and discovered most of the circle had disintegrated, George had disappeared, and thus found himself, a little unsteady and somewhat drunk, standing next to Gina who was saying '. . . you don't get any of the signs' in a contemptuous but also peevish way, to which he replied, gallantly, 'You're dead right. Where's George?' to which Gina, with rather a heavier injection of contempt and rather less peevishness in her voice, replied 'Gone home to his wife.' Graeme ordered two more beers and handed one to Gina.

Johnston's crinkled face reappeared around the corner.

'You staying for long?'

'Don't know —— I've got to get home for dinner some time.'

'See you later if you're still here.'

Johnston backed out the door. Graeme waved, burped, and stared across the bar at the drinkers lining the opposite counter and then at those close by his elbow, perceiving them with a clarity which sharpened and defined every line and angle of their faces, investing each wrinkle and mark of suffering and experience with an extraordinary charge of emotion so that he felt he almost partook of their lives, understood them, knew what they had endured and tolerated and seized eagerly in their pursuit of mortality, and felt so compassionate towards them, towards what they were and what they had been and what, in all ugliness, they were destined to become, that he suddenly understood how Christ must have felt, how one man could suddenly decide by his death to take on all the past sins, guilt and murderous wrongs of mankind, wipe the slate clean, give the race of men a new start simply because he loved them; and thought, staring at the faces over the top of his beer glass, watching these people who were for this instant sharing this crystalline unity with him, watching them laugh, frown, jerk unsmiling heads, hands reaching for glasses, fingers sprawled across the bartop, thumbs and forefingers clutching darts, watching them turn to speak to friends, turn to speak to no one, move, act out, reflect; thought, I love you all, whoever you are, no matter what, I love you all.

Which, he supposed, must include Gina, who was haranguing him about some obscure and personal subject in which all the correlatives were known only to herself, and who required only a listener to set her off on one of her sessions of tortuous self-revelation, and wondered idly what George found in her. But then, leaning against the counter in the comparatively deserted bar, the sound of the alto slicing in through the door from the beer garden, standing next to Gina and listening to her talk in her dramatic, self-obsessed way, a rampant and unshamed ego which was only rendered tolerable by her humour and a certain saving self-awareness, he began to be more conscious, at first coldly and rather analytically, of that rather untarnished sensuality which softened the edges of whatever neurosis drove her to seek out men so avidly and unashamedly, and then, having become aware of this, he found, to his surprise, that he had also become faintly susceptible to it; so that when the time came, finally, for him to finish his drink quickly, slap the empty glass down on the bar and say firmly, 'See you later, Gina', he instead bought her and himself another round, and then another, noticing that the Famous Writer was still in the other bar rocking back on his heels to a rather smaller circle of acolytes around one of whose shoulders he had an arm draped in what was perhaps the teeniest bit too familiar a fashion, and in the end felt in his pocket for five cents and walked over to the phone to tell Paula he wouldn't be home for dinner and might in fact be rather late . . . .

81

Sometimes after they made love she felt too exhilarated, too alive and resensitised to think of going to sleep; at other times she felt languid yet comforted, drained of energy and emotion, as if she had seen a film like *Ashes and Diamonds* or one of those Shakespearian tragedies which she and her fellow form-mates of the Upper Sixth had marched off to in a long crocodile of white uniforms and fawn gloves and straw panamas with the red and white stripe around the inside brim —— what was the word which described it again? It escaped her, as so many other words with which she had been familiar escaped her, words which one retained only by reading the books which she had had no time to read or seeing the films which she had had no time to see or even by talking to the sorts of people she had had no time to talk to since . . . well, for two or three years at least —— really, if the truth were known, since getting married. But last night, after Johnston had left and she had found Graeme waiting for her upstairs, she had felt reactivated, her skin almost translucent with the intensity of the emotion she had experienced so that she could feel the blood tingling just beneath the surface of her skin like some artesian reservoir which had been tapped and drawn upwards, upwards until it overflowed and spread out through her body. She had leant forward in bed and drawn her knees up towards her, allowing the blankets and the sheets to drift down from her naked arms and shoulders, feeling her cares and preoccupations and uncertainties drift down with them, sloughing them off like an old skin which

she, the snake —— the Serpent? —— had no further use for;
and stared at the faint glimmer of moonlight, she supposed
it must be, which shone against the white plasterboard wall
of their bedroom and against the teak-stained shutters of
the walk-in wardrobe; and thought, why can't it be like
this always? knowing full well that it couldn't be, that
neither she nor serpent nor she-serpent could ever regain
Eden; and yet wishing that the certainty which filled her
now, the sense of balance, the jigsaw fragments of the
chaos at last sorted out and ordered and constructed into a
comprehensible and completed pattern, a unity, a oneness
which she always thought of as a sphere, could last longer
than merely the warmth which their sleeping together had
generated; and thought of what her life might have been
. . . .

> You go your way and I'll go mine,
> That's what ya tellin' me all the time,
> You know it ain't right, you know it won't do
> Baby, baby, 'cos I need you . . .

She switched the radio off almost automatically, glanced
at the clock on the kitchen buffet and walked over to
where the casserole was bubbling gently on the simmer
plate —— Graeme was late tonight —— listened for a
moment for any sound from the children upstairs, then
walked into the living-room and picked up a copy of
Vogue

gifts galore YOU WON'T FEEL A
THING BUT BEAUTIFUL what makes a
marriage fail? *kinky geometrics* you
can't fake the real thing FALLING IN
LOVE *dress to kill* WET LIPSTICK a
week in the life FASHION seduction
Italian style women should be OP
SCENE your stars DID YOU KNOW
zingy zip-ons help your tortoise
hibernate safely *Oxfam needs* which In

Love will you choose

then laid it down and, leaning back on the settee, tried to recapture her mood of the night before and stifle the doubt which, however unreasonably, always assailed her when Graeme was late

. . . with Richard perhaps?

Richard was tall, thin, almost English in a mod sort of way with his hair hanging blondly forward like early photographs of Prince Charles and his liking for fawn jeans and old khaki shirts, a London University student whom she had met on one of the Aldermaston marches which she, despite the ridicule of some of her friends at the Overseas Visitors Club and the total noncommitment of others, had decided to go on —— had it been that Lindsay Anderson film at the Academy which had prompted her go to, those shots of the long line of young people with duffle jackets, guitars and CND symbols on their backs marching past Marble Arch where three black-frocked clergymen, as black as sin, stood reading from their black-sin Bibles and declaiming against those who would march against the Bomb? or had it been the conversation with Jackie, one of the few Englishwomen she had known at that stage, who had announced, drawing on her calf-length leather boots and leather jerkin with the gold-and-silver Greek ikons on them, that she and her young brother, who was only eight years old, would certainly go on the march that year

'But why? Who's going to take any notice?' Paula asked.

Jackie stood up, ran a hand through her long dark-brown hair and then, dissatisfied, began brushing it in front of the broken shaving stand which served as a mirror in their Earls Court bedsitter:

'Why? Well, you have to start somewhere, deary.'

'But it's *useless*. Nobody's going to give up the Bomb just because you walk from up there to London.'

'But at least it's something. You're doing something, aren't you? You're not lying at home with your legs in the air waiting for the Bomb to drop.'

'So it's just a matter of personal satisfaction,' Paula said.

Jackie stopped brushing her hair. 'All you bloody Aussie women are the same. You're scared to death of making fools of yourself. If you don't want to come, you don't *have* to.'

'No, it's not that. I believe in what you're trying to do. I'm just not sure it's effective.'

Jackie swung round and Paula, who thought she had got to know Jackie reasonably well in the short time they had been sharing the bedsitter, was taken back by the violence in her eyes. 'You prissy little coward! Don't you understand it's not what *they* do that counts, it's what *you* do. It's a personal matter, a question of whether you're going to stand up for what you believe in. If you don't, you don't really believe it.' And, a little later, had left the room . . . .

Which had been, really, a revelation for her, who had always measured acts by their consequences and not their intrinsic being, and had thought everything useless which was not successful, and therefore — like most Australians, she reflected — had been frozen in a rigid state of do-nothingness; and who, also, with her PLC background and distaste for politics or making a show or anything like that, had always been afraid — yes, she supposed, Jackie was right — had always been rather fearful, really, of making a public display of herself.

So she had gone. And had met Richard. At a morning tea break, by the side of the road, not far from Hexham. And though the trip to Greece with him, months afterwards, had been disastrous, and, after the island, there had been nothing to do but pack up and go back to London with the strain between them becoming worse instead of better, until finally when Rosinante had chugged to a stop in Earls Court and Paula had got out with her dusty and much-travelled haversack slung over her shoulder and duffle jacket under her arm they had been glad, really, to escape from each other's company, still, despite that, and despite everything later, he had been the one person whom she had really, whom she had *known*, with absolute certainty, that she had, utterly, loved.

The thought seemed unfaithful to him who lay breathing irregularly beside her with one bare arm flung out beneath his head in a pose which she found only too familiar, who . . .

was, she thought with something of vexation, getting terribly late; FALLING IN LOVE; walked into the kitchen, 7.30 p.m., picked up the Vogue again

Would her life have been different? Of course. Though how much it was difficult to say. Richard was studying architecture at the time; no doubt he would have returned to Australia, taken up practice, might even have designed the sort of house which, now, she lived in at Pymble, with moonlight, if that was what it was, drifting down through the cunningly sited ceiling light-well and creating oblong Mondrian patterns against the wall; it would have been, — well, saner, more reassuring, and therefore, para-doxically, she might not have felt so imprisoned, so incarcerated as she did now because she would have felt surer of the world in which she found herself; for, though Richard had been a romantic, he had had that understanding of women, or at least that concern for them, which was so rare in Australia, though Johnston had some of it as well. Richard had been committed, too, genuinely committed, whereas Graeme was at best anarchic, with his affiliation with the push and all that, and at worst simply weak-willed; so that perhaps upon their return to Australia Richard would have moved into politics or something like that and she would have been part of his life in some way, caught up in it, *involved*, behind every great man a great woman and all that sort of nonsense, though she didn't really believe that; the point was that she would have had some sort of life outside her husband, the house, the children.

Husband, house, children. What the hell made people think that was all women wanted out of life? How terribly unfair, she thought, how terribly unfair that it was women

who were expected to play the secondary role, be the
helper-bedmate-housemaid-nurserymaid all rolled into one,
condemned to lead a vicarious life through their husbands
and therefore, if their husbands failed in life, condemned
to a vicarious failure in life as well. No wonder so many of
her friends had turned, deliberately and in a sense of
desperation, to trying to create a life of their own outside
their charmed home circle of kids, washing machines and
once-a-week sex: Buzzy, who had worked her way through
most of the palliatives, from yoga to cookery classes to
pottery lessons at the North Shore Workshop Centre;
Judith, who tried to paint canvases in the upstairs
bedroom of their terrace while her kids tore the place to
pieces downstairs and who had finally given up exhibiting
altogether, the texture of her paintings, like her life,
becoming more and more jagged and fragmented; Maria,
who had taken to other women's husbands and who was
now, she suspected, under treatment from a psychoanalyst
though she had never said as much in so many words; and
one or two other mothers she had met at the kindergarten
who, once that first synthetic mother-of-three affability
had been penetrated, were only too ready to reveal too
much, really, of their lives . . . .

   She looked at the Vogue, threw it down in disgust,
FALLING IN LOVE indeed; like most of the women's
magazines they were sops for deprived housewives, arty
acute-angled photographs by people like Lord Snowdon of
haute couture fashions they would never wear, beautiful
homes they would never own, hair styles they could never
afford, film stars they would never meet, and love-is-a-
swinging-affair stories and serials about romantic situations
in which they would never find themselves — masspulp,
not religion, was the opium of the people. The housewives'
LSD; *take a trip with FLAIR*. No wonder all those skinny
models like Twiggy and the Shrimp were photographed in
places like Saudi Arabia and The Falkland Islands . . . .

   Where on earth could Graeme have got to anyway?

   With that stupid clock in the kitchen ticking the

minutes away, ticking her life away, tick-tock tick-tock
tick-tock over the white-marbled wipe-down serving unit,
the floor-to-ceiling wall cupboards with the built-in oven,
the four concealed cooking rings next to the two-unit sink
on one of which her casserole, which she had begun
preparing at about three o'clock that afternoon, while the
baby was asleep in its cot in the nursery, was now bubbling
away to nothingness.

It was not, she thought, that she minded in itself the
wife-and-mother role in which she found herself; what she
objected to was being cast into it willy-nilly, without
choice, without even being presented with an alternative.
You grew up thinking that happiness in life consisted of
being with another person, sharing your life with them,
love was *the* thing. You never really questioned it, and not
just because of all the Women's Weekly serials and films
with happy endings but because you grew up in a family
which was at least based upon the theory of love even if
the love had died long ago and your parents slept in twin
beds with hot water bottles hanging behind the bedroom
door and a dead wedding dress in the attic, or in a family
like Maria's whose parents still slept in a double bed and
lived some sort of life together, entertaining at home and
First Nights and candids in the Sunday Telegraph, but
who, when they finally got to bed at 3.a.m. on Sunday
morning Father (seen together, Mr Douglas) jammed
earplugs in his ears and Mother (and Mrs Geraldine
Lloyd-Bonnyton) slapped face cream on her face and a
black mask over her eyes to keep the daylight out in the
morning, *BLACKOUT* —— in fact all the families you saw
around you and grew up with, even those which had
splintered and disintegrated and suffered the Divorce
Court-Weekly Truth treatment, they were all founded
(foundered?) upon love; so that you never really
questioned whether love was what you wanted out of life,
whether love really was as the mags and all your friends
said a swinging affair FALLING IN LOVE, what with your
girlfriends coming home with diamond rings from Prouds

on the fourth fingers and a foetus in its fourth week in their stomachs

no, that was unfair, she thought, pulling herself up, that is being bitchy, am I turning into a bitch?

and when did that all start, for heaven's sake, why, almost as soon as they left school, Buzzy was the first, of course that was predictable, but then it was Maria, which was quite a surprise to the whole class of '59 because she was the quiet and sober one of their group, the Holy-causts as they called themselves, and she certainly was not pregnant, in fact was still childless, I wonder what went wrong there?

so that it took quite a bit of, well not courage really, but confidence to withdraw from the matrimonial stakes and whizz off overseas, still thinking that love was the thing, love makes the world go round, not the phony synthetic love of the magazines and TRUE ROMANCE comics but *real* love, that was what counted; and love, of course, meant loving *someone,* and if you loved someone, why, you got married, or you lived with them, which was sort of marriage without the benefit of certainty, and you had children —— well, eventually, you supposed, and you never really questioned that that was what you wanted to do with your life

so you ended up in Pymble in a three-storey architect-designed machine-for-living-without-love with two childrem whom it took most of your time simply to look after, washing their nappies and making sure they didn't pull the plug out of the electric iron and things like that, and a life which narrowed down to a tight, unbreakable, inescapable circle of constriction, like a camera narrowed down to its smallest aperture, all those metal discs overlapping and closing in tighter and tighter till only the tiniest pinpoint of light was left

I am a camera, she thought, at f22 and a husband who comes home late for dinner.

And yet

And yet, she thought

89

And yet, she thought, there were times like last night when, sitting there with her knees drawn up under her chin, the past seemed to make sense at last and images of contentment ran through her mind

It must have been a Sunday, they had been in Battersea Park, looking at the sculpture exhibition put on by the Arts Council, one of those blowy, gusty days which sometimes you got around Battersea and Chelsea with the river surface churned to a muddy grey and charcoal cloud masses moving past the four rigid uprights of Battersea Power Station but with those occasional lulls which suddenly gave an illusion of spring calm as they stood before one of the sheet-bronze masses on spindles by Armitage or those granite-solid junk metal welded assemblages by Paolozzi, the crocuses broken through from freshly tilled earth around the Men's Lavatories and those beautifully grassed lawns which petered out into dirt and tree roots as you got towards Battersea Fun Fair. They had walked back that way, past the amusement stalls and dodgem cars and ferris wheels with their overtones of Saturday Night and Sunday Morning, did people really have such unadulterated and unselfconscious fun at fun fairs or was it just another of those cinematic cliches? then over Chelsea Bridge with its stone lion sentinels at either end, past the Royal Hospital and along the embankment to Oakley Street with its lamp-posts and grim canyons of residentials and then up to his room, which by then was so familiar: the Renoir and Ortega posters pinned to the wall, the dirty cream mantelpiece with its burden of ashtrays, Italian bowls, photographs, letters and litter, the bed pushed against the wall to help prop up the crumbling wallpaper, the alcove with its cracked porcelain sink, grimy work surface and inevitable gas ring, though Graeme had the use of the kitchen a flight of stairs further down as well, those yellow, dirt-stiff mesh curtains made specially for London landladies, framing a window which looked

out over rooftops, chimney-pots, clotheslines strung
between brick false-fronts, and the tops of telegraph poles
which at night cast a tram-stop orange light upon the street
below.

After the bluster and windnoise of the park it seemed,
despite its masculine tawdriness, a haven. She walked in,
tossing off her coat and headscarf while Graeme opened
the window a fraction at the top and bent over to light the
gas fire on the far wall. He came back, kissed her gently
and led her over to the bed, which she had expected; and
then began gently undressing her, which she hadn't,
drawing off her black Marks and Spencer sweater and
unzipping her plain grey skirt at the back until, although
she complained 'It's too cold' and sat on the edge of the
bed with her arms crossed in front of her like the
bandoliers of a Mexican to protect her nakedness she had
finally relented and climbed into bed with him, drawing
herself down against his bare flesh for warmth with the
frill of the rug tickling her cheekbone and the gas fire
burbling quietly away in the background somewhere. But
she had not felt like making love, though they had done so
— — oh, several times before, and finally Graeme, disgusted,
had given up his attempts at persuading and/or exciting her
and had taken down from the wall the dulcimer which he
had bought secondhand at Camden Town some months
ago and had been desultorily trying to play ever since,
regarding it as an appropriately way-out instrument to
conquer when everyone else was picking twelve-strings,
and, lying on his back with his head propped up
awkwardly against the bed headpiece which also served as
a bookshelf, began singing in that rather off-key voice of
his some song which he had been learning from the
Penguin Book of English Folk Songs, the name of which
escaped her now — — no, of course, it was *Queen Jane,* or
was it *The Death of Queen Jane?* anyhow of course that
was it:

Queen Jane was in labour
Full nine days or more

91

Till her good women hmmmmmn
And wished it were o'er

King Henry, King Henry,
King Henry if you be,
Will you hmnm hmmmn hmmmnnn
And mind my baby

There was flamboys, there was dancing,
On the day the babe was born
But Queen Jane beloved
Lay cold as the stone . . .

She could not remember all the words, she could not
even remember the tune quite, but she remembered that,
lying there, with the wind blowing outside and sometimes
billowing the curtains drawn across the window and the
room darkening ever so slowly, and Graeme singing in that
reedy uncertain voice of his and the dulcimer strings
making that rather plucking modal sound, she had felt
indescribably sad, utterly and uncontrollably sad, and
there had loomed up in her mind quite unbidden, because
she had not thought about him for —— well, for a long
time and had not wanted to, there grew in her mind,
unbidden, and unexpected really, Richard

and suddenly she had been crying, not desperately or
anything, but crying, just crying, with the tears rolling
slowly down into the corners of her mouth, as she thought
of Richard, and what had been, and what might have been

crying so quietly Graeme had not noticed at first and
had been appalled when he had, putting the dulcimer
down with an oath and saying:

'I'm sorry. I'm a bloody fool.'

'It's all right. I'm being silly,' she said, and groped under
the pillow for a handkerchief, which she could not find;
and dried her tears on the sheet instead.

'Is it Richard?'

When she nodded he had the sense not to say anything
but, instead, lay back with his hands crossed behind his

head and stared up at the ceiling.

After a while, when she was sure she was in control of herself again, with the skin across her cheeks seemingly drawn tight with the strain of crying and her eyes, she was sure, horribly screwed up and red, she felt guilty about what she had inflicted upon Graeme who, after all, could not be expected to bear her burdens and carry about, vicariously, her grief, and who must have suffered, felt something, about Richard himself anyhow; and, quite a long time later, when the room had darkened to a London twilight and the gas fire threw its own unsteady light against the wall, she turned slowly round towards him and ran a hand as unsteady as the gaslight itself down his bare chest with its black growth of hairs down between his ribs to his navel and then lower still until it came to rest against his groin.

He did not move and she let it lie there, thinking both somehow of Richard and the body of the man who lay beside her now, herself caught between memory and the present, incapable of action, time-stricken, an odalisque; until at last the moment passed and, leaning over him so that the weight of one breast fell against his side, her hair drifting forward, one arm reaching to the other side of him to bear her weight, she lowered her lips and ran them along his skin till her mouth closed upon his bare nipple.

For a while he let her make love to him, hands behind his head still; but then, distracted at last, he reached over and with masculine crudity hoisted her on top of him, fastening her in arms white from the long London winter and forcing her down towards him. And at last, at long last, the caul which had always seemed to coat her emotions in a thin membrane of reserve since —— since when, since the island? —— broke away, fell away from her like a dried and shattered skin, so that she found herself clinging to him with her face buried against his neck because she dared not look, questioning nothing at last and jerking her body as he made her with nothing held back and she not really conscious any more, conscious of nothing really except words which welled up from her and seemed to explode in her mind Graeme Graeme Graeme or was it Richard? no it was Graeme with the words swelling and ballooning and gyrating madly Graeme Graeme Richard GRAEME GRAEME Richard GRAEME Graeme Graeme she was saying GRAEME GRAEME GRAEME until suddenly the words stopped exploding and like a lightning flash, like a rooster tail of foam whipping across the surf as wave and backwash met, like the flick of leaves across treetops struck by wind, at last, at once, she reached there, came, yes came, fell timelessly down, Graeme, Graeme Graeme, Richard finally exorcised now, surely, Graeme Graeme, only Graeme, Graeme, Graeme

She looked across at her husband, his arm flung out, quite inexpressibly fond of him. But he was already asleep.

In 19 Arcadia Street, Pymble, the telephone rang.

Johnston was much possessed of death. In the mornings, when he found hair follicles wedged between the teeth of his comb, he ran a ginger-freckled hand over what remained, and which he had had cut in a somewhat youthful fashion to disguise his advancing years, and thought regretfully of decay, boyhood, and the disintegration of the physical being of man. He was not afraid of death, he reasoned. He had had too rich a life, had stuffed too many pleasures into each passing moment, to complain about that. If most men died before thirty a mere three centuries ago and Paris was but a downyfaced boy who was taught how to cleave a man to the testicles before he learnt to shave, what right had he, at thirty-six, to testify to whatever god sat on whatever marble de Mille throne that he had deserved to live longer? And yet it was but human to wish to prolong the time one spent on this earthly sphere; once when, absorbed too deeply in an imagined confrontation between himself and Hal Patten, the head of the Melbourne Herald bureau in London, he had almost been run down by a London cab and had been buffeted against a parked Humber Snipe with intimations of mortality branded upon the forefront of his mind, he had been forcibly reminded that the barrier between living and non-living was but an elastic band which, stretched too far, whether with fine and feckless deliberation by mystics like Malory or accidentally by Alf who, deciding against the disc brakes option in his new Holden wagon, found it transformed on a rather idiosyncratic bend of the Hume

Highway into his and his wife's and his children's sheet
metal funeral pyre, snapped and catapaulted the luckless
life-stretcher into

What?

Why, mere non-being. Nothingness.

No, it was not so much death which worried him as the
remorseless degeneration of the years, the knowledge that
he was growing older and the more profoundly depressing
knowledge that he felt older, he who had once, as a boy,
found a day an eternity to endure and, as an adolescent,
had thought thirty the final point of no return, with
nothing to anticipate after that but a slow slide into
senility. He had long since given up the struggle to preserve
his young man's body so that, as thick about the trunk as
Michelangelo's later Christs but whiter and flabbier, he had
resigned himself to knee-length shorts and single-breasted
tweed sports coats and undressing himself in the dark
whenever he had some wench to seduce; and he had even,
after much research and detailed interviews with chemists,
pharmacologists, trichologists, phrenologists and astro-
logers, relinquished his hair to that goat-thighed Pan or
whatever deity it was who had such need of hair to bristle
his bollocks that he magnetized it from the earth-mortals
who served his philosophy; but he had not yet resigned
himself, though no doubt he would also bring himself to
that in time, to the gradual dwindling and diminution of
sexual energy which Kinsey, with such statistic-sodden
certitude, had ordained for all men and which he, though
he had not yet uncovered one skerrick of evidence of it,
indeed not one single shred of tangential or circumstantial
evidence, was forever worriedly watching for and which
quite jaundiced some of his more ambitious exploits
because of the continual fear that, suddenly, the ground
would open under his feet, or to be more explicit, that he
would find he could not have an erection, and would
tumble, silently and without a tear shed by anyone, but
perhaps with a stifled laugh from some woman whom he
had at some stage of his life wronged, into that

stake-bedded pit of sexual derision which awaited, despite the cold comfort of de Sade and the impossibly unattainable example of Casanova, all libertines . . . .

The baroque rhetoric of the term made him grimace. Why, it was positively Johnsonian. But who would be his Boswell? No one: he would have to be his own discographer, his record a succession of newspaper articles, radio talks, TV programmes and the occasional inclusion in an anthology, his ultimate monument a file of yellowing cards under his byline in the Melbourne Herald library. Johnston, Humphrey Stearns, journalist.

Once he had wanted to be a writer, and had even, in a fit of bravado, dashed off 'author' against his occupation in his passport, but some time later, at Dover customs on the way back from Italy, he had guiltily changed it back to 'journalist.' Veritas super omnia, sport. Nevertheless, he had tried. Which was more than one could say for the majority of bleary-eyed, beer-sodden, elbow-bending roundsmen who leant conversationally against the tops of slops-wet bar counters and declared that they could have written a bloody beaut of a book if they'd ever got around to it, a bloody beauty, they had the theme worked out and everything, fantastic story to tell, just never got around to it, just never had the time, you know how it is, wife and kids, broken shifts, night work, a man gets old, you get out of the habit, you lower your sights, you know what I mean? but it would've been a bloody beauty, not the Great Australian Novel maybe, but still something which would've made people sit up and take notice . . . and more than one could say for the wild men in beards and shoulder-long hair who decorated the Windsor Castle or crept defiantly around Buckleys clutching copies of Ionesco and Pinter and announcing darkly 'it's all up here, man, it's all up here', pointing significantly to their heads, implying that there, fully formed in all its glory, waiting but for the opportune moment of birth, was the opus which would set the world aflame, which would out-Nietzsche Nietzsche, which would out-Saul Bellow, which would even perhaps if he didn't pull his socks up and look to his style and polish up on his grammar make Dostoevsky look pretty bloody sick too, man. From which it was but a short jump to Meher Baba, Zen and the whole non-art thing, art is strictly for the Alfs, man, it's not what you *do* but what you *are* that counts, life is art, man, that's what it's all about, that's where it's happening, my *life* is a work of art, man . . . .

It was, admitted Johnston, a doctrine of some force which he had never entirely, to his satisfaction, refuted; so that he called for another beer, and paid for it and sank his mouth into the foaming middy, and wiped the froth from his moustache, and thought: still, life wasn't just an abstraction, it consisted of doing as well as being, doing things like eating, sleeping, making love, working, writing — the act of creation was itself an aspect of living, so it was not so much that life was art but rather that art was life. And it was arguable that those whose lives encompassed some artistic activity, who created as well as consumed, were richer than those who had attempted to retreat to a state of merely being (which was impossible anyhow).

But then, thinking that, why had he not succeeded as an artist?

Ah well, you see, the wife, the kids, a man got older . . . he smiled inwardly at his self-parody. He had no wife or kids, though he was certainly getting older. Well, he had tried. He had put together that collection of short stories in London which nobody had wanted to publish; not, mind you, that they were not good enough, oh dear no, he remembered, the dark mahogany walls, the huge and richly polished desk, the luxurious armchair, the tiers and tiers of books behind glass doors, the fatherly voice issuing from behind the publishing editor's spectacles, oh dear no old boy, it was simply that nobody read short stories any longer, there simply wasn't a market for them, and so far from publishing the short stories of an unknown author, why — and at this stage the soothing, fatherly voice allowed itself a tremor of lightheartedness — — why, the situation was such that if one of their bestselling authors came in and announced he wanted to put out a collection of short stories the publisher simply blanched, and swallowed, and tried in all good faith to talk him out of it, and if the author insisted, well then, dear boy, you may rest assured that they would lose money on it, oh yes, indubitably, not just break even, but actually lose money.

LOSE MONEY! Good heavens! Well that, of course, was the very last thing that Johnston would have wished such an honourable and multi-million-pound-sterling publishing firm to do, and so he had not put them up to anyone else, but had instead kept them in the drawer of his desk at the Melbourne Herald bureau in London and had finally made a bonfire of them a couple of days before he came back to Australia, consigning them to the grate in Oakley Street along with letters, articles, rejection slips, scrapbooks, memos, notes, scribbled ideas, story drafts, chapters of novels and all the other impedimenta of six years of expatriate life in London, City of My Dreams; besides they were no bloody good, he realized that, otherwise he wouldn't have burnt them.

And, to be fair, the publisher might have printed them. But if he had failed as a writer he had at least succeeded as a newspaperman; at the thought of which Johnston turned, and rolled some phlegm in his mouth, and was about to spit on the floor of the Windsor Castle but catching momentarily the eyes of two white-shirted turds in grey suits and Australia Square hornrims next to and slightly behind him — — advertising execs slumming it, no doubt — — decided against it and swallowed the phlegm with a mouthful of Resch's. What with all those articles for the *Express*, AN AUSSIE LOOKS AT US, THE VIEW FROM DOWN UNDER, even WHY YOU POMS WON'T WIN THE ASHES — — he winced at that — — and the series in the women's magazines about HOW AUSSIE MEN TREAT THEIR WOMEN and A MAN'S COUNTRY WHERE WOMEN RULE THE HOME. After which it had been fairly easy, trading as a professional Australian whipping off to Cannes (THE BIKINI FILM FESTIVAL) and Scotland (WHERE THE QUEEN MUM LIVES) for the pulps and rewriting fictional adventure series (THE GIRL WHO RODE DOLPHINS —— NAKED!) but turning out some reasonable background features for the qualities at the same time, so that slowly his byline became better known and the *Observer* paid him a retainer to research for *DAYLIGHT ON THE WEEK* and the BBC began ringing him up to join panel discussions on AUSTRALIAN ART TODAY and CAPITAL PUNISHMENT: THE PROS AND CONS, and actually reprinted one of his talks in the Listener, so that to most of his colonial mates and certainly to his Fleet Street confrères he had it made, but had come back . . . .

Why?

Partly because he had the cash at last; in fact quite a stash of it, because the Fleet Street pulps and especially the women's glossies paid their freelances well, so that he hadn't had to work very hard since returning to Australia. And partly because of the trouble with Jackie, who had buggered everything up by getting pregnant and refusing to go to an abortionist and might have, had he stayed, slapped a paternity suit on him, being a typical English bint in her readiness to resort to the armoury of the Welfare State. But really it was Richard's death which had decided him, scared him as it had scared the others. With that everything had broken up. Don had moved to Oxford to meet his destiny and Millicent; George had gone back to Australia, pursued a little later by Sonia; then Graeme and Paula had left too. Soon there hadn't been any of the old push left in Gunn's Gully except Carrington, who had decided never to leave England anyhow, and Thompson, and Eljay —— but then they had been on the fringe. He, Johnston, had really been the last to hold out. For a time he had gone back to working for the Melbourne Herald bureau, it being summer and the freelance world practically dead for the duration, but even after the season had picked up again, and he had set out once again on the Fleet Street circuit and life had resumed its usually frantic, frenetic, exaggerated, constipated round, nothing had been the same again. Richard's death had proved them all vulnerable, they who until then had thought, or rather had simply assumed, that even if life was not eternal death was something that happened to somebody else

Smoke and a thick darkness in the air, people hunched on the floor or leaning against the walls, barely discernible in the half-light filtering down from the ceiling grate over which, every now and then, high heels or a man's brogues clopped. Gromolski was sitting on the floor, a pannikin of cider in one hand, watching Richard's fingers walking jerkily up and down the frets of the big twelve-string guitar and whining dark ripples of plaintive, questioning melancholy into the people-warm room. Gromolski looked like the artist he was: luxurious, full-face black beard, high yellow forehead, a flattened slavonic nose. Somewhere in his multifarious travels about which, drunk on ouzo, he could sometimes be persuaded to tell and act out hilarious tales, improvising grotesque charades and convoluted mimes which limned out every detail of the crisis he was describing, playing six simultaneous roles with virtuoso agility, as once he had stormed his way down the centre of a crowded near peak hour Central Line tube juggling, in imaginary succession, a Scottish caber, six oranges, a pane of sheet glass, a chest expander and a tandem surfboard-rider, much to the bemusement of the honest burghers who stood strap-hanging with copies of the Evening News tucked under their chicken-flap elbows, somewhere he had picked up a fake San Francisco accent but behind that and the aggressive black beard lurked a shy painter's soul. Murals of jazz club abstracts which he had painted in deep blacks and burnt reds gave a jaunty dissonance to his room, which was in the basement of the Oakley Street residential; another wall he had papered with clippings from the *Observer,* the *Sunday Times* and the other qualities in varying stages of disrepair, upon which collage of blacks, whites and yellows he had hung, unframed, one or two of his latest canvasses.

Johnston eased his way in through the door and peered through the fug of cheap cigarette smoke. He couldn't see anyone he recognized except Gromolski, Richard —— and Don, white and etiolated, eyes unblinking behind their rimless glasses, leaning forward over near the sideboard in the habitual long-necked stoop which made him look like an ageing vulture. Sonia and George were nowhere to be seen, nor Paula. Most of those crammed into the basement were friends of Gromolski's: a gaggle of Sorbonne-eyed girls from the Chelsea Art School down the road, plus some folkies from the Troubador and the Blues and Barrelhouse in jeans and Zapata moustaches, and a few older men, artists no doubt, who were strangers to Johnston. Oil paint and guitars, yoked in natural juxtaposition ever since Picasso . . . .

'Nobody knows me, nobody seems to care

Ummmnn, nobody seems to care,

Blues, hard luck and trouble, man I've had my share . . . .'

Johnston caught Richard's eye and beckoned him. Richard finished the blues he was singing, propped his big guitar up against a chair and came over.

'Where is everyone?' Johnston asked.

'Don't know —— maybe Grom didn't ask them,' said Richard; 'There's Don over there.'

'It was an open invitation to everyone,' said Johnston. 'What about Paula?'

Richard didn't reply, but instead took a packet of Gauloises out of his faded khaki shirt and lit one with the air of a man performing a ritual which could not, under any circumstances, be interrupted. By the time he had finished he seemed to have forgotten Johnston's question.

'Would you like a drink?' he said. 'There's some whisky over there on the sideboard —— or there was a little while

102

ago.'

At that moment Gromolski caught sight of them and wandered over brandishing a quart bottle of beer. 'Cor, if it ain't the Oracle wiv an empty pintpot in 'is hand. Want a drop o' this?' he asked in demotic Cockney.

Johnston shook his head. 'I'm looking for some whisky,' he said, squinting through the gloom at the sideboard.

'What's happened to the music?' Gromolski asked.

Richard smiled, 'Duty calls. Any requests?'

'Something religious,' said Johnston, and went off in search of the whisky. After all, he calculated, there were only one hundred and twenty-eight shopping days left to Christmas. Behind him Richard began playing a slow Negro spiritual.

Five minutes later, his hunt for Johnnie Walker a miserable failure, he was reduced to contaminating with mere brown ale the imitation cut-glass Watneys Red Barrel pintpot he had stolen from the Stag and Antler several weeks before, vouchsafing at the same time a Long John Silver oath to the perverted taste of Poms who preferred warm ale to cold beer. The sound of the guitar stopped suddenly. Glancing across the basement, he was surprised to see Richard's back disappearing through the door.

Gromolski squeezed his way through the crowd.

'What's up with him?' he asked. He turned to where Don, tall and cadaverous, was leaning against a decrepit chest of drawers and arguing about Spinoza with a dapper CND official.

'Hey, Don,' he shouted. 'Hey, what's the matter with your buddy? Is he sick or something?'

'Where is he?' Don said, turning around.

'He just whammed out of here like a woman with a miscarriage. You think he's had too much to drink?'

Don shrugged. Gromolski swung around to Johnston. 'You think he's all right?'

'He seemed to be,' Johnston said, gulping down the first few inches of his pint of ale in case he should spill and thus unforgivably waste it. He glanced around the room, trying to sort out which of the Chelsea art school women were by themselves; but most of them seemed to have men at least several years younger than himself attached to them, so for the moment compassion won out. 'Maybe I should make sure.'

He started out across the room, teetering uncertainly over the couples carpeting the floor between him and the door, then suddenly reversed and souvenired a bottle of beer. 'Might need it for the patient,' he explained to Gromolski, grinning. Or, of course, for himself.

On the roof it was cold and quiet. Johnston shut the stairwell cover behind him, watching the distorted rectangle of light thrown onto the tarmac squeeze shut. London lay around him: row upon row of rooftops, downpipes and blank brick walls, chimney-pots silhouetted starkly against the faint lightness of the sky. Upright edges of buildings and squares of lighted windows, diagonal slashes of street canyons and disintegrating curves of car headlights strove to achieve a cubist lithograph.

He could just make out Richard leaning against the far parapet wall, the guitar propped next to him. He walked over and stood beside him, gazing down at the treelined roadway, the streetlamps turning the leaves a vertiginous green like the chestnut trees in Paris.

'Something the matter?'

Richard didn't reply at first, then slowly turned towards him. 'I don't want to burden you with my troubles.'

'That's all right.' Johnston took a long swig from the bottle, wiped his mouth with the back of his hand, and waited.

'I got a cable from my sister this morning,' Richard said. Johnston waved the bottle at him, but he shook his head. 'About my mother. She's been sick for a long time, in and out of a convalescent home every few months. We've been expecting something to happen. Two days ago she had a stroke and was admitted to the Mater Misericordiae. She died this morning. Friday morning in Australia, I suppose that is. She never regained consciousness.'

'Christ, Richard, I'm sorry about that,' said Johnston. He immediately regretted his crass offer of the beer bottle and composed his face into something resembling sorrow. 'I really am. What a terrible thing to happen.'

'It's not so awful, really,' Richard said. 'One of the reasons I came over here was to get away from Mother. She was a —— demanding person, I suppose you'd call her. My sister takes after her. They even look the same: it's incredible. Between the two of them they were suffocating me.'

Johnston had a sudden picture of a dark heavily curtained sitting-room somewhere in Cammeray with a polished rosewood table, lace doilies under the vases, family photographs and tasseled cushions which were straightened if ever a guest disturbed them, the whole scene varnished in sepia . . . was that Richard?

'What are you going to do?' he asked.

'Go home, I suppose. It'd be expected of me. My sister's a spinster; I'll have to look after her.'

'What about Paula?'

Richard shrugged 'She knows already. It's over.'

'And Don?'

Johnston had the distinct impression he had overstepped the mark. 'What about Don?'

'He'll be sorry to see you go. We all will be.'

Richard didn't answer. Instead he swivelled around and leant over the parapet.

'It's not fair. It's just not fair, is it?' he said. 'Somebody's always getting hurt. Your life's not your own. I can't get away from it even here . . . .' Johnston wondered momentarily whether he was talking about himself or his mother. Richard stopped; when he resumed his voice was something more like normal. 'I'd have liked to have seen her before she died. Just once. Said all the things I should've said to her while she was alive. I suppose that's always the way. Christ, what hypocrites we are! It's not right that she should die while I'm over here. I can still hardly believe it.'

Nothing moved. The city seemed to have gone to sleep. From below came the faint buzz of the streetlights. Johnston, who had begun to feel unaccustomedly embarrassed, took his pipe out, looked at it, and returned it to his pocket.

' "It is the blight man was born for,
It is Margaret you mourn for" '
he said at last.

'Yes?' said Richard scornfully. 'Cold comfort from a Jesuit priest whose struggle for faith killed him.'

'You can't change things like death, mate,' Johnston said. 'I don't like the way things are ordered any more than you; but you can't do much about it. I suppose if you were some fat-bummed prelate you could at least blame God for it all —— or the devil. When you're an infidel like me, you haven't even got the comfort of someone to blame. You just have to accept the universe as it is.'

'Well, I don't,' Richard replied slowly. 'I refuse to accept it. Look what it's done.'

Johnston shrugged his shoulders. 'You've got no choice. You have to buckle under —— or get wiped out.'

'Maybe. That's a risk I'll have to take. I refuse to serve.'

Johnston reached down between his feet and came up with the bottle of beer. He took a couple of swigs and then passed it across to Richard.

'Sounds like a third-rate play at the Royal Court,' he muttered.

'I know,' Richard said, laughing almost gratefully. He drained the beer bottle with an abrupt gesture and put an arm around Johnston's shoulders. Together they walked across the dark tarmac-covered roof towards the stairwell. 'I can just see the reviews —— "this brave but melodramatic dot dot dot anger dot dot petulance dot dot look forward dot dot . . . . " Johnston chuckled, and side by side they descended the rickety wooden stairs which led down from the roof. 'But I mean it.'

And had, Johnston remembered.

Which was the terrible thing about it. That he had meant it and nobody had realized it, nobody had understood just how precariously Richard was balanced between normality and abnormality, stability and neurosis, life and death; least of all he, Johnston, who might at least have been expected to perceive something from Richard's confession that night, might have been put on his guard or warned the others or suspected what was to come. What if Don, instead of he, had sought Richard out on the roof? Would he have understood? Would he have been able to alter anything?

Or was it Richard's relationship with Don which was the crux of it all? He had always taken it for granted that Richard was at least bisexual —— assuming he had knocked Paula off at all —— and that he and Don had more in common than the only shared room in Gunn's Gully; had Richard, with his mother dead, found that Don too had failed him in some crucial and specific way? Unless it had all been repressed, and Richard had been making covert demands which his friend had not even recognized, let alone met. Which would explain much; an unsatisfied homosexual relationship could be more destructive than an overt one. But whatever it was might not he, Johnston, have been able to succour him, strenghten him, change with one act . . . .

Johnston brushed the thought aside. It was a fruitless speculation. He had not done anything; nor had anyone else. And Richard had died, and the circle of living had been shattered, and they had all suddenly and brutally been confronted with their own mortality, had been forced to stare into a mirror which reflected back not their own but Richard's immobile face, and had fled home for safety.

And at last he too, had come back (he wouldn't call it home) to find, as he had expected, the disintegration of the group carried a stage further: Don a successful barrister, gone his own way now, meeting the rest of the push but infrequently; Graeme and Paula married and incarcerated in a suburban hell —— poor Paula, first Richard and now Graeme, were things really as bad between them, he wondered, as they seemed to be, with Graeme chatting up birds like Gina and Paula stuck at home there, plugged into domesticity like an automatic washing machine? George —— well, George hadn't changed much, and though he had finally relented and married Sonia, the two of them might as well have been still independent of each other for all the difference it made. And that was that, but for the on-the-fringers back in London still and he, Johnston, the only link between them any longer, shuttling between the two like a bloody ping pong ball and with about as much sense of destiny or purpose.

But that, he reminded himself, was how he wanted it. Once someone from the Young Socialists, trying to force him to commit himself ('commitment! Christ, I thought that was the word the Stalinists used when they pushed the anarchists up against a wall in Spain') had asked him whether he stood up or sat down in the cinemas when they played GOD SAVE THE QUEEN, which was pretty symptomatic of public discussion in Australia, he thought wryly, where the BIG issue among intellectuals was whether Australia should remain a monarchy or not, and he had replied, honestly, that he sat down when he sat down and stood up when he stood up and there was no rationale to seek beyond that. Sufficient unto the instant is the instant thereof.

But the memory of Richard had disrupted his equilibrium, as it always did; had heightened his awareness of his own frailty, the slow daily degeneration of cells which ended in —— what? A labelled urn grinning from somebody's mantelpiece? Johnston swore fervently to himself; that thought, and the fruitless half-hour he had spent at Vadim's waiting for his contact to turn up, combined to sour the taste of the beer in his mouth. He drained his glass, deliberately casting around for some less uncomfortable subject to ponder. His mind flickered back to Paula. Had her glance towards him the other night meant anything, or had he been imagining it? He wouldn't blame her, he thought, for taking to adultery as a way out of the oh-so-padded-and-comfortable cell in which she found herself, stifled with solicitousness and the good life. He had always meant to talk to her about Richard, and just why she had married Graeme anyhow. Abreaction? (*on a bitumen road with soft edges* —— he knew his folk, despite Graeme and his Ornettes and Aylers). And instantly thought: why not now?

He looked around the bar. Graeme and Gina were nowhere to be seen; George had gone long before. 'Where's. Graeme?' he asked Pedro the Pusher, who was standing with his back to the wall, smiling at some private joke. Pedro shrugged. 'Pissed off about quarter of an hour ago.'

'With Gina?'

'I reckon.'

'Where were they going, do y'know?'

'You know Gina.' Pedro jerked his head sideways. 'Her flat's just up the road.'

Johnston turned and strode out of the bar, out into the night air, pushing brusquely through the couples standing around on the footpath, ignoring the cold wind which was beginning to sweep up from Rushcutters Bay and White City and the deep valley which cleft Paddington from Edgecliffe, occasional unseen lightning flashes illuminating the horizon with an eerie, momentary glow as he had always imagined an artillery barrage must have looked during the First World War from miles behind the front. Mud, death and mortality, the Charge of the Light Brigade in his grandfather's house and, over the mantelpiece in the schoolroom, the engraving of straining, wild-eyed horses, toiling tin-helmeted Pommies, cannons poking ugly muzzles skywards as everyone, horses, men, ropes and officers tried to haul them through the mud; Passchendaele, 1917. At least he was alive.

A taxi cruised past. Johnston hailed it with a wave of his

felt hat, hesitated, jumped into the front seat (when in Rome), settled himself down comfortably. The driver, a New Australian with dark Greek eyes and a day-old beard growth above his open-necked blue shirt and a crucifix on a gold chain, looked with neither interest nor disinterest, but simply patiently, at him.

'Pymble,' said Johnston. 'Arcadia Street, Number 19.'

Oh hell how could he? she thought, and put down the telephone. She walked back into the living-room, unconsciously putting a hand to the back of her head as if to draw back her hair, picked up the Vogue again, FALLING IN LOVE, and threw it into a corner of the room. She walked into the kitchen, turned off the gas under the casserole, he can have it cold for breakfast, and stalked back into the living area. It seemed extraordinarily cold and bereft of warmth, as cold as the architect who had designed it, and the anger which had sustained her since her husband's telephone call left her, leaving her drained of emotion and not sure what to do.

She walked upstairs to the nursery and looked in at the children, James with one arm flung back across the outside of the bed just like his father, the baby asleep in her cot, sucking her thumb, in profile a miniature Graeme too; I don't even have them, she thought, and decided: I shall have a bath. Steam rising from the white porcelain, misting over the wall mirror, she undressed slowly and wrote absentmindedly with her forefinger GRAEME IS A SHIT, the words traced like butcher's prices in white against plateglass, turned the taps off, suddenly aware in the eerie silence which followed that rain was splattering against the bathroom window, emptied a cube of Yardley lavender salts (at a dollar a packet, her housekeeping mind calculated) into the water and tested it tentatively, stepping without grace into the bath with her arse in the air because no-one was looking and sliding slowly down, resting her elbows against the cold furled edges, the warm water lapping slowly up her body until she was lying almost full-length staring at the unrippled surface with steam still billowing to the ceiling and the two dull chrome taps and the rain still beating outside.

People tearing each other apart. George and Sonia. Maria and her husband. She and Graeme. Did people really use each other, she wondered? Is that what marriage finally became: an unending struggle, a duel, a steady devouring of each other? Was all that Battle of the Sexes theory right after all? It didn't seem fair: that all that hope and expectation, and in their case all that trying, should come down to two people using each other.

God knows she didn't try to use Graeme. She would have liked to be his —— support, she supposed. He needed it. He devoured people, drew sustenance from them, drained them of energy and emotion to supercharge his own ego. And by continually being replenished he was able to create within the field he had chosen for himself, throwing off ideas and gimmicks and new approaches like a Catherine wheel, sought after by all the publishers and new wave magazine editors, consulted on everything from newspaper layout to the PR graphics for Consolidated Enterprises, written up in all the women's magazines as the 'bright young man of Design' with a capital D, while she stayed at home and looked after the children and propped up Graeme's sagging confidence when he needed it, draining her own energy and life into him like an intravenous drip, until at fifty or so she would be left —— what? a husk, she supposed, an empty and juiceless gourd with the guts ripped out of it by a man who had never hestitated to disembowel others for his own benefit.

But that was unfair; she checked herself and stirred in the bath, shifting her weight from one side of her bottom to the other. Any two people who lived together exploited each other to a certain extent: sisters, brothers, man and wife. Exploit was just a loaded term for relationship. It only became unfair if it was all one-way, all giving and no taking; and she gained much from Graeme. Well, something. Otherwise, why would she feel so annoyed when he failed to come home for dinner? They had something going; or at least she supposed they did. Precisely what, she was not sure.

Once, she realized, she had thought of life as composed of moments of exhilaration; she had lived, really, for those moments of triumph or climax or intensity which suffused her memory of childhood and adolescence, in fact her life until her marriage, with a pleasurable nostalgia. She remembered walking as a young girl of fifteen, of course they started younger now, in her first two-piece along the promenade at Manly on an almost deserted summer morning, the concrete warm under her feet and the sun warmer upon her back, conscious of her tanned body with its long legs and gawky arms and at peace with herself, conscious of the long day which stretched ahead yet, the brief sorties to the yelling surf and the hours spread in a circle with her friends on the beach, heads together and bodies stretched out like the petals of a flower; time seemed to pass slowly in long hours of pleasure then, had not gathered the momentum which dragged her expectantly into her twenties and screaming into her thirties. She remembered dances on the cool back patio of Maria's home at St Ives, the lights turned out and the oldies safely out of the way in the lounge-room, her first kiss, which she recalled with squirming embarrassment because she had insisted on keeping her mouth closed, from 'Liver Lips' Pearce, as the girls at the Presbyterian Ladies' College had so unkindly christened him, and later, not so funny, her first near-orgasm, as she realized it was now, with Jonathan Scott-Thompson, on a tartan rug after midnight at Middle Head with stars shooting overhead and she worried all the time that someone would see them, imagining footsteps working their way closer through the low scrub, Jonathan who was a bastard and had left her cold as soon as he had realized that she was one of the few Women's College freshers who didn't do it and had gone on to seduce someone else in his father's gleaming powder-blue Buick, Jonathan who was something of a prize of whom other girls had boasted 'I won him' after Christmas parties and therefore had left with her a demeaning but lingering regret that she had not carried it through after all. She remembered long drives along the northern beaches to Palm Beach in MGs with the slipstream tearing at her hair and the car radio blaring, beach umbrella and towels and booze stacked in the back of the car and afterwards the continual swopping of places with other Gs as they made it back to the Newport Arms, sunburnt and peeling and glad to be in the shade at last, with all that noise filling her ears, that explosive bonhomie as the North Shore set gathered itself together on Saturday afternoon for an hour or so of drinking, yarning, dirty jokes, arrangements and excitement before separating for dinner and the long-drawn preparations for That Night's Party.

Had it all been as trivial, as ... *tinselly* as it now seemed?

Something had been missing, otherwise she would never have gone overseas. London: a rebirth, like going to Duntroon or changing your name. And she would never have met Richard.

Richard.

By now he had become somewhat vague, blurred at the edges somehow, and yet she remembered his face so well: the graceful blue eyes, hair cut in a fringe which fell straight down across his forehead, the thin and somewhat aristocratic nose, the self-deprecating grin which emphasized his prominent jawbones, a gentle face but without any suggestion of weakness to it except, perhaps, in those lines which drew his mouth down when, shrugging, he withdrew from any course which could bring him into conflict with others; Richard with his old khaki Army shirt and Sam Browne belt and pale jeans, Richard leaning against Rosinante in the one photograph which she still had of him, secreted away in her dressing table drawer despite Graeme's notorious jealousy, Richard and her marching into Ealing Broadway with the banners bobbing and jerking in a long, thin column ahead, the crowds along the side of the street, someone had reached out, an old hand, a man's old and gnarled hand with wrinkles across it and white jutting knuckles, 'good for you girlie'; Richard and her in Rosinante on the way to Greece and that terrible afternoon at the youth hostel in Paris . . . .

It had been raining, a heavy French rain so unlike the English drizzle they had been used to. They had stopped the car in the driveway of the hostel, waiting for it to clear before going inside; even after the rain had eased to the sort of intermittent gusts which, now, blew against the bathroom window, a heavy mist still shrouded the car, rendering the hostel and its surroundings completely invisible. They had decided to wait in the car till it cleared and, almost without meaning to, had begun making gentle love to each other in the front sea (why was it that her memories of Richard were almost invariably sensual, she wondered; was it an indictment of whatever else their relationship had, or had not, contained?); and had not realized, by the time she had allowed her bra to be slipped down to her waist and Richard was mouthing her naked breasts, kalò kalò, with her eyes closed and her elbows raised to keep her sweater stretched above his face, her hands grabbing his hair, that the mist had lifted and that they were clearly visible from the hostel, wherefrom the concierge, beside himself with astonishment and perhaps envy, had sent a trusted female envoy of doddering age, drooping udders and unimpeachable morality to order the perfidious Anglais to desist, and had furthermore ordered them both, or rather Richard, who was more embarrassed than he had ever been in his life, to leave the hostel within half an hour or else the gendarmes and possibly a deep bayou of bloodhounds would be set upon them. AT ONCE! SUBITO! IMMEDIATELY! VITE!

Or the time that, having invested in a motor scooter, Richard had called for her at Earls Court on a bitterly cold night, and wrapped like mummies in coats, scarves,

115

balaclavas and gloves against the English winter with Paula perched uncertainly on the pillion seat they had set out in utter silence for the Academy cinema, so that when, at Oxford Circus, Paula had leant forward and shouted 'Turn here!' in his ear Richard, who by then had forgotten she was on the back, gave a tremendous start, wobbled quite out of control across the middle of London's busiest intersection, and finally fell cursing into the gutter.

Well at least that memory wasn't sensual, she thought, smiling wryly to herself. But Richard had been her first love and —— perhaps the old cliché was right after all, perhaps one never again experienced the intensity of that first involvement, everything afterwards was either a repetition or a variation of something which had been unique. And yet was it right that she should wrap Richard in this haze of remembered sensuality, like a Hemingway heroine, a blank screen for the projection of her own sexual desires, deviations, fantasies? Was it because she had never really experienced that complete sexual fulfilment, or liberation, or richness, or whatever it was, that she felt she should be able to reach? Not a single swift experience, which she had achieved often enough, perhaps more with her husband, wherever he was, the shit, than with anyone else, but a total and satiating sexual exploration, a week or a month of nothing but lovemaking with someone like . . . well, someone like Richard.

But they had never had the time to achieve that.

Which was why, perhaps, at thirty, she still felt unsatisfied; and seized upon memories of Richard to sustain her. It didn't say much for her marriage that she should focus so much of herself upon someone from her past. She had somehow drifted into a relationship with Graeme without really meaning to, and certainly if, beforehand, while she was still going out with Richard, someone had told her she would end up with Graeme she would have been —— well, puzzled, to say the least, in fact quite disbelieving. Richard had introduced her to Graeme and the rest of the expatriate push not long after meeting her on the march, and she had never taken any more notice of him than of Johnston, or George, or any of the others. With his strange, dark, working-class face and thin shoulders and curious intensity about physical things like swimming (he always went for a swim at weekends at the West Kensington Sports Club which he had joined simply so he could use the indoor pool) and off-beat jazz patois he had seemed something of a poseur to her —— or was it simply that, like all the others, he had been overshadowed in her eyes by Richard? And after Richard's death she had been too shocked, too bewildered by what had happened to have been able to even contemplate, let alone begin, any other relationship, and though at the time she had depended so wholly upon those around her, had trusted them and their strength so implicitly, it had been but an automatic response, the reflex action of grief, and she had been no more involved in them than before; less so really, because they were at that time merely props and buttresses, people she could turn to not in any lessening of her independence but in order to preserve it, and she would have been repulsed had any attempt been made to capitalize upon her exposure, had she even recognized it. Graeme had been helpful, had talked to her about Richard or rather had listened, without flinching, whenever she had felt the need to pour out an endless recital of remembered incidents, conversations and arguments about Richard, of new thoughts and theories and questions about his character and his death, her mind reworking the same memories and the same puzzles again and again, trying to fit it all into some comprehensible pattern, trying to pinpoint where she might have noticed something and had had the chance to change the remorseless course of events which, unaltered and unhalted by the intervention of any of his friends or, most blameworthy and least forgivable of all, by herself, had culminated in his dying. She had come to rely on Graeme somewhat, dropping in on him at all hours when she felt low or ringing him at work to ask him to meet her for lunch, she working at Better Books as a

117

lowly-paid shop assistant at that stage and he doing
part-time design for one of the Piccadilly advertising
agencies; actually she had often called around to Oakley
Street to see them all, Johnston, Don, George and Graeme
being the local residents at the time, though the flat had a
sort of floating population of anything from two to twelve
according to who was in town at the moment and who had
just arrived from Australia or who was back from a trip
around the Continent, and whether Sonia was shacked up
with George or was back in the Earls Court bedsitter with
Jackie and herself, and of course Graeme, not either
working full time like Johnston or studying full time like
Don, had been more available than the others; yet
somehow it was usually Graeme she ended up talking
endlessly and almost hysterically to, addressing herself
really, going over and over again all that time past without
regard for time present and certainly not for time future,
yet needing an audience who would at least say yes at the
right time or no or I didn't know that and who would,
finally, take her by the arm down to the Stag and Antler
for a drink, beer and babycham, pintpot and mini-glass,
able to look at the faces around her and at those ghastly
yet so typically and comfortably middle-class English pub
furnishings, the electric light bulbs disguised as candelabra
with red plastic shades over them, the carefully arranged
flowers in old-fashioned Stoke-on-Trent vases, the heavy
floral carpets in some deep burgundy hue which would not
show the cigarette burns and spilt beer too readily, the
rows of exotic bottles against the dimly lit stained-wood
bar centrepiece with its complement of bric-a-brac, glasses,
advertisements, ashtrays and inevitable miniature barrels in
silver or rosewood, the bar counters shining with a discreet
dullness, the ever-so-helpful barmen in their white frilled
shirts and bow ties and tidily brushed, silvering hair; she
had liked those pubs, into which she had seemed to fit so
naturally, they had been so restful and reassuring and yet
not without a certain quiet gaiety when the time came, on
Friday or especially Saturday nights when women in furs

and black cocktail dresses and men in sombre suits came for a drink before the evening's divertissements, and she missed them now that, back at Pymble, she had a choice between the Greengate, with its footballers and GPS types from all over the North Shore, and Buckleys, roaring with bonhomie and beerswilling backslappers and bumfeelers where to get a drink on a Friday afternoon meant fighting the backseat battle all over again.

Only Don, of all people, had acted badly, had buckled under the strain, as no doubt he had every right to —— though she had never really examined the notion in detail, had been content to let it linger unmagnified in the background of her mind, she had sometimes wondered whether there was not the faintest whiff of homosexuality in Richard's and Don's friendship, which had been an extraordinarily close one from the time they had met on board ship on the way over and whose suspect quality (if indeed there was any, and if so it could not fairly be characterized as suspect, which was a loaded term fit only for bigots and poove-persecutors of whom, she hoped, she was certainly not one) would have appertained more to Don, who was something of a sexual recluse and had not, in all the time she had known him in London, had anything to do with a woman, than Richard, who was if not an actual then certainly a potential womanizer, but who nevertheless had about him enough of that uncommon and, as she often thought of it, unAustralian gentleness to attract the camp fraternity to him —— only Don, on that terrible night after Richard had been found, when they had all been sitting around the huge, dismal table in Oakley Street drinking red wine and eating some tortillas which Sonia had fried up for them, not talking much and then mainly about inconsequential things, trips to the Continent, holidays, work and, sometimes, because it would have been false and unbearable and absolutely awful not to have, Richard, only Don had got drunk quickly and silently, spilling some wine on the plastic tablecloth which Sonia wiped up and tearing at the bread

on his plate with distracted intensity, watched a little
fearfully by the others who nevertheless talked on and
tried to maintain some semblance of sanity at this which
was Richard's funeral wake, his Last Supper, these his
friends and disciples clustered around to pay him last
homage and stifle their own grief in their own living,
throwing the combined weight of their years of existence
in the balance against the death of this one of their
number, only Don had played the Judas and suddenly,
quite by accident, had knocked over the claret bottle and
then, as he watched the watery wine skid over the oilcloth,
dropped his forehead to the plate in front of him and
blurted out:

'Why did he have to do it?'

'For Christ's sake, Don!' said Graeme, jumping to his
feet, shooting a glance across to Paula —— 'for Christ's
sake, Don, we all feel like that! Don't let it get you down!'
and had walked around to where Don was slumped over
the table, butter smeared across his forehead and strangled
noises coming from his throat, and tried to shake some
selfcontrol back into him. 'He's bloody drunk,' he said,
and shook Don again, and glanced anxiously back at the
rest of them still sitting around the table, Johnston with
his fork in the air, George not knowing where to look,
Sonia staring at Don and then back at her.

But by then it was too late, because the grief which she
had felt when she had first found out that Richard was
dead and which she had been trying to hold in check all
day, which had broken through from time to time but
which she had doused with words and words and words
and then more words, grew and grew within that yellow
rain-stained and wallpapered room with its funeral table
and mourning accomplices and broken disciple, grew and
grew until she could bear it no more, until she felt the
whole room and her grief would swell and shatter and she
had at last begun to cry, sitting there staring at the table
with the tears scouring down her face; unable to move
until Sonia had come over and freed her and hurried her

off to another room, Richard, who was dead dead dead dead dead you fool Don dead

It was Graeme who took her home that night, though the others had asked her to stay with them, she refusing because she feared she would be sleeping in what had been Richard's bed, or that one of the others would be forced to. And after that it was Graeme who kept an eye on her, took her out every now and then, tried not too heartily to get her to enjoy herself by taking her to hear the Modern Jazz Quartet at the Festival Hall and Jesse Fuller at the Blues and Barrelhouse and, once, to La Bretagne, one of the more expensive restaurants in Chelsea, or at least expensive for them, who like most expatriates existed just above the breadline and tried to save up enough for regular excursions to the Continent, what with Don trying to get by on one meal a day (and that curried beans in a tin) and Sonia buying all her gear at the disposals stores in the Strand and along Portobello Road before it became too fashionable, Johnston being the only one who was comparatively well-off what with his fat freelance cheques and the Melbourne Herald to fall back on, whereas Graeme's income seemed to go up and down like a yo-yo, she never had worked out whether he was paid regularly each week or merely for each design schedule he carried out. Anyhow it was Graeme who looked after her, though Sonia had been marvellous too, and it must have been only two or three months, or was it longer? after Richard's death that she began to realize she had grown quite fond of him, though until then she had never really taken him seriously or indeed taken much notice of him except to like his rather bizarre, directionless irreverence about everything, ricocheting about the flat like some tightly compressed core of energy not sure where it was going to explode next, full of ideas and yet not really seeming to get anywhere, unlike Johnston, who was driving straight for the top and would, no doubt, eventually get there; and besides he was so much younger than she was, well, a couple of years at least, which at that age meant a lot ——

less, she was sure, than it did now, remembering nevertheless how her body looked to her critical eye against the striped sheets they slept in at night. (Would some plain colour, a pale pink, be more flattering?) She found herself looking forward to Graeme's telephone calls, to their hasty lunches in Wimpy bars or, if the weather allowed it, in Soho Square, walking past the strip clubs and concupiscent noticeboards plastered with ads for masseuses and French instructresses and windows decorated with collages of nudes advertising some specialist in 'trick and interesting poses', or their nighttime excursions to pubs or concerts or, more often, simply back to the flat, where over jugs of cheap and too-sweet cider which, if she drank too much of it, made her feel like throwing up, she and Graeme and the others would sit listening to Johnston the Oracle lay down the law about politics, art, aesthetics and the perfidy of womankind. Johnston was the acknowledged leader of the push, though whether from sheer impressive bulk and/or from the violence of his intellectual stances she had never really worked out, and it was he who finally decided when blow-ins and bo's who had overstayed their welcome in the menage were to be thrown out and, if necessary, though it usually wasn't, did the throwing, though one hapless Englishman who had the bad judgment to launch into a rather drunken paean of praise for 'what they did at Sharpeville' found himself bouncing backwards down the stairs from plaster wall to banister, which might have been dangerous had not the luck of the drunks stayed with him and he had survived the first flight to limp down the rest. Graeme had felt rather guilty about that, which was the first time she discovered in him that dislike of physical violence which amounted almost to cowardice, and which made him no match for the Oracle or indeed any of the others, with the possible exception of Don, whom one could as well imagine trying to exert violence from behind those benevolent, bespectacled eyes as of —— well, as of going to bed with someone like Sonia. She had entered the group in a typically spectacular way. George had met her on a train journey through France on his way to Barcelona and attracted by both her plump and pulchritudinous bum and her ready libertarianism, had promptly knocked her off behind the communal toilet of God knows what unlikely provincial railway station in the dead cold of a frosty night and had given her the address of Gunn's Gully so she could look him up when she got back to England. Sonia, however, had returned to London well before George and, having sized up the situation at the flat, had angled herself with blatant and laughable ulterior motive at Johnston, who, so far from being loth, was actually in bed with Sonia one calm and serene Sunday morning when George bounced back from Barcelona and found his bird-to-be warming the toastcrumbs in Johnston's foul and semen-stained bed. Sonia had handled the situation so well, however —— first by brushing the toastcrumbs, and then Johnston, from his, Johnston's, bed, and secondly by explaining to George that she had not expected him to arrive until that night and had been trying to keep their reunion bed undefiled for the night's entertainments, and thirdly by inviting him, George, to fill the gap, as it were, left by Johnston's hasty withdrawal, explaining the while that Johnston was, after all, but one of those people who on the surface were terribly deep but deep down were utterly shallow —— that she had been accepted into the menagerie forthwith and bounced backwards and forwards between the Oakley Street flat and Paula's bedsitter according to whether she and George were in fact 'on' or whether she or George was at that moment experimenting with some other sexual diversion who had blundered unknowingly into their voracious lives.

It was after a particularly late night at Oakley Street that it all, quite coolly, started. She had stayed on till late, drinking and arguing and dreading the thought of work the following morning, which was a Friday, until at last Graeme had said he would drive her home and together they had walked down the winding staircase with its grease-stained wallpaper and missing carpet holders and out, quietly, for the ground floor was the landlady's who had, as did all her race, a strict regard for formalities which were visible to the daylight world of appearances, though she was not so strict about those night-time ones which were invisible, out into the damp night air with the lamp-posts stained a deep black by rain and pools of water reflecting back the streetlamps' eerily orange light. But for once, Rosinante, faithful chariot, had failed to start, despite Graeme's increasingly futile efforts with the crankhandle, and so back upstairs they had crept to find the others already turned in, bodies lying darkly on the divans in the main room; so there had been nothing for it but to go up the half-flight to Graeme's room and, primly undressing to her black bra and pants only and turning her back to gaze at the Michelangelo nude while Graeme, who had insisted on stripping completely, crawled into bed and drew the blankets over him, had joined him there, kissed him gently on the mouth goodnight and then firmly turned her back to him, feeling him lie there tense at first but then slowly unwind and she herself drifting off to sleep, thinking thank heavens that's one crisis surmounted, she could not have borne it had he insisted on trying to sleep with her, so soon after Richard . . . .

But somehow, during the night, they had grown closer together, whether from sheer physical contact or what she knew not; so that when she woke, drowsily, in what must still have been before dawn, listening to the hoots of boats on the grey river and the jangling sound of the milkcart slowly working its lonely way up Oakley Street, and found Graeme, too, half-awake, one arm flung around her, his head apparently lower than hers because his mouth was resting against her freckled arm, it seemed not only natural but almost inevitable that they should, gently and sleepily and not even seeing each other, reaching for each other through the dark, begin to make love, until she had at last unlatched her bra and slid her pants down, wriggling uncomfortably beneath the blankets and using the toes of her left foot to hook them off, and had lain there on her back and let Graeme roll upon her, trying not to think of Richard and lazily looping her arms around Graeme's back, wondering vaguely when she had last had the curse and how ironic it would be if this sleepy coupling should result in what she had always feared, an unwanted pregnancy; but yet had found herself, despite everything, drawn to him and aware of his passion, which she did not share but which did homage to her, and though she had not been roused, really, and later had drifted off to sleep again with Graeme's comforting arms still around her, yet that had been the beginning of everything, a sleepy lovemaking on a cold November morning, warmth amid London's wintry fall, fall, all, all, all, or

She woke to hear the doorbell ringing. The water in the bath was lukewarm, almost cold. She got out, shivering, dried herself and hurried downstairs, wrapping a dressing gown about her as she went.

It was Johnston, grinning, with a jaunty felt hat perched on top of windblown hair and clutching a flagon of white wine. 'G'd evening,' he said.

'Johnston!' she said, genuinely surprised. 'What are you doing here?'

'Enter the ready-made party! Come round to swig a few wines with Graeme, I did. Are you going to invite me in or not?'

'Of course,' she said, stepping back so that Johnston could enter. 'But Graeme isn't here,' shutting the door behind him and leading him into the living-room. 'He rang me from the Windsor Castle about an hour ago and said he wasn't coming home to dinner —— what time is it, by the way?'

Johnston reached into his shirt pocket, pulled out a much-worn and old-fashioned timepiece with a winder on the top, clicked it open and shut and announced: 'Half past nine.'

'Good heavens! I've been asleep for hours. I had no idea it was so late. Look, help yourself to a glass from over there while I go and slip something on. Oh, and there's some beer in the fridge if you want it.'

Johnston! But hadn't Graeme been drinking with him at the Castle? Questions began rising in her mind; had Graeme been lying to her? She had a sudden vision of him ringing from some —— some motel, like the Astor at Woolloomooloo, with its pink-fur Bunny Girl symbol in the foyer and some sleazy bint from the advertising world waiting for him in the bar, what a liar he was! —— and decided, after all, against the high-neck shift which she had reached for in the walk-up wardrobe and wriggled instead into an op-art minidress which definitely needed stockings to look at all decent. She took her time dressing, deftly lined her eyes with Mary Quant and, after a brief glance in the full-length mirror, strolled casually downstairs feeling not so much like Greta Garbo as perhaps Vanessa Redgrave about to meet her Petruchio.

'Good God!' said Johnston as she entered the room, looking up over a tumbler of white wine and an airmail copy of the New Statesman, 'talk about the conversion of the species! You look marvellous.'

'I don't feel it,' she said, flopping down in an armchair. 'The kids have been dreadful all day. I don't know what's got into them. James has been running around grizzling all the time, doesn't want to play with this, doesn't want to play with that, and the baby's just learned to crawl into simply *everything* in the house, I've quite had them today, I really have . . . .'

'Still playing the role of the deprived housewife?' said Johnston.

'You know me too well,' she replied, laughing. 'Am I as awful as all that?'

'Not really. I'm kidding you. Besides, you have my sympathy —— even if you have brought it on yourself.' Johnston's eyes seemed kind beneath their bushy overhangs. 'Can I get you a drink?'

'What's that in the flagon?'

'Hock.'

'Yes, thank you.'

Johnston rose to get a glass for her. She found herself about to ask whether he had met Graeme for a drink or not, but didn't.

'What do you mean I brought it on myself, anyhow?' she asked when they were both sitting down again.

'Well, no one made you get married,' said Johnston. 'Unless you were up the duff at the time, which I didn't think you were. You could've stayed single —— like me. There are bachelor girls as well as bachelors these days, you know.'

'That's just another name for spinster.'

'Well, what's wrong with spinsters, for Christ's sake? I've known some pretty raging spinsters in my time, I can tell you. They wore even shorter dresses than you do!'

Paula felt herself beginning to flush, but restrained an impulse to cross her legs; what did it matter if he could see up past her suspenders? 'That's just the trouble; they're terrified of growing old. Do you think a single life is any sort of life for a woman —— I mean, after a while, after she's, say, thirty or thirty-five?'

'Or a man?'

'Oh, for a man it's different. You've got a career, ambition, success to sustain you. And you can still be attractive to women at sixty, at the age when most women have to buy their sex. The world revolves around men: if you're a bachelor you've got clubs, and sport, and lots of mates to turn to. But can you imagine a club for spinsters?'

'Well then, you've made your decision, haven't you? What are you complaining about?'

'Honestly, Johnno, you make me so mad!' replied Paula, and did cross her legs, and pulled her dress down as well, though it didn't really make much difference. 'Just because you make a decision one way instead of another, that doesn't make everything perfect. I only wish it did.

127

But it doesn't of course; how could it? You plump for one way of life because it seems preferable to the only alternative you have, but it's still —— flawed. It's still got all sorts of discontents built into it. I tell you, women have got the shitty end of the stick in this world.'

Johnston raised his eyebrows in mock horror. 'Well, your language has changed since I first met you, even if you haven't.'

'It's all your doing —— yours and Graeme's,' she replied, restored somewhat to good humour. 'I'd have never talked like that once. You see, I've become emancipated. And a lot of good it's done me ... it's just made me more dissatisfied with my life than I'd have been otherwise! Oh good heavens, I really must stop grizzling; I must be quite unbearable . . . .'

'Quite the opposite,' said Johnston fondly; perhaps a mite too fondly. Then, quite suddenly: 'Do you think you got married on the rebound?'

The unexpectedness of the question brought her up short. She sipped her wine slowly.

'I don't know; I don't think so,' she said. Johnston had cast the New Statesman aside and was leaning back in his chair in a way which suggested he was thoroughly at home, in a way which was both familiar and, somehow, possessive. 'I used to think about that a lot, but I don't any more. I might have started living with Graeme on the rebound; you know, for comfort and that sort of thing. I'd got used to having someone around, to having someone to rely on. But I don't think I married him for that reason. In fact I'm certain of it' —— remembering, quite vividly, the terrible argument they'd had in the flat at Elizabeth Bay, when she had decided to force the issue one way or the other: had she been as cold as that? She hoped not. But certainly it had not been just a rebound. She had made up her mind by then —— 'I'd made up my mind by then that I wanted to get married to Graeme. Simply because he was Graeme. I think that's how it was' —— she corrected herself —— 'I'm sure that's how it was.'

But Johnston, as observant as ever, had picked it up. 'A Freudian slip?'

'No.'

'You're sure?'

'Yes.' She finished what remained of her wine. 'Why do you ask?'

'Perhaps I'm imagining it. I seem to have sensed some sort of —— *strain* between you and Graeme lately. I've even wondered whether your marriage was breaking up, and whether that was the reason. If I wasn't going back to London I wouldn't have asked you.'

You've got a damned impertinence, Paula thought. Because if there was one sure way of creating a rift between two people it was to suggest that there was one, or to be solicitous about it. What was Johnston up to? She looked at him but his face, impassive, gave nothing away. 'That's too simple, Johnno,' she replied, laughing and, by her laugh, giving him the benefit of the doubt. 'It's not between Graeme and me, it's me; the situation I find myself in. I don't like it much and I can't see a way out at the moment. But I'm sure it'll work out.'

'She'll be right, mate,' said Johnston mockingly. He got suddenly to his feet, yawned, and stretched orang-outang arms above his head: 'And tell me, sport, have you got anything for an ole digger to eat? 'Cos I've been on the grog since lunchtime on an empty belly and the quack says it doesn't do my liver any good.'

Paula got to her feet, smiling, quite fond now of Johnston whom she had known now for so many years, since those very early days in London —— how stupid of her to have doubted him! —— and said, walking to the kitchen: 'There certainly is. You can have the casserole I cooked for Graeme. In fact I'll join you; I haven't had any dinner myself yet. Graeme can starve.'

Walking through the door; and feeling, nevertheless, Johnston's eyes upon her.

They had dinner and talked inconsequentially, though once or twice Johnston lashed out in his usual furious manner at the country within which he found himself. 'We're all expatriates here, living an expatriate life in the middle of Alf-land,' he said between mouthfuls of lamb-and-eggplant casserole ('delicious'); 'we used to think we were expatriates in London but actually we were at home. Look how many of us have stayed there! Thompson, and Harry, and John Carrington, bless his heart. That's where we belong, that's why I'm going back. It's *here* that we're the expatriates. Don't you think?' And, without waiting for an answer: 'Don't tell me you feel at home here. Does Graeme? Of course not. Do any of us? George? Sonia? Anyone? Australia doesn't want people like us. They don't want anyone who actually thinks, who tries to stir things up, who's a trouble-maker. Don't disturb me, brother, I'm asleep! A nation of sleepwalkers.' Johnston smiled. 'Not a bad title for a book, is it? Subtitled: How I Married An Alf, Gave Birth To a Victa and Found Heaven in Cabramatta. Or should it be Pymble?' He glanced up, eyes crinkling at the edges, ginger moustache stretching, his face suddenly a Louis Kahan etching of lines. 'That's unfair, isn't it. But you know what I mean. You can't live in this country unless you're an Alf. You've got to be an Alf. Otherwise you couldn't stand it. It's like those signs hung out by London landladies: SORRY, NO ROYS. ALFS ONLY. You can't breathe in this country, it suffocates you, it's like a great stifling blanket pressed ever so solicitously over your face while a tape recorder intones in your ear "conform, conform, conform, conform" AH-H-H-H.'

Johnston gave a hair-raising rendition of someone choking to death, clutched both hands to his throat, eyes watering, cheeks distended . . . . It was so realistic Paula had to laugh at him.

'So that's Australia?' she said.

'No, garlic,' said Johnston, reaching for a fresh glass of wine. 'Good Christ, I must have swallowed a whole clove. Still, very nice, delicious.'

They went back to eating, and Paula thought, for the

second time that evening, how familiar, how *right* somehow, he looked sitting there in what, after all, was Graeme's usual place, and thought, for the first time that evening, how much she would miss him when he went back to London.

'Perhaps that's why I feel so alienated at the moment. Perhaps it's not the married state at all, perhaps it's Australia.'

'Alienation, of course, is a Marxist concept,' Johnston began, 'though like so much else . . . .'

It wasn't until they had finished dinner and Johnston, gallantly, was wiping up that he began his assault upon her, playfully running a hand up her legs as she stood at the sink, up past her suspenders and feeling professionally for her vagina though she, immediately, had thrust his hand away and turned on him brandishing a sloppy dishmop.

'If you do that again, m'lad, I'll slosh you in the face with this,' she threatened, but Johnston merely laughed disarmingly in that jocular, I-don't-mean-anything-it's-only-fun way of his and returned to wiping dishes, though a little later she felt his hand creep around her waist and, before she could do anything about it, insinuate itself down the front of her low minidress which, to do Johnston justice, she had deliberately worn instead of the high-necked one, and brush her right nipple before she seized the offending limb and thrust it, unrepentantly, into the boiling washing-up water.

'Jesus Christ!' Johnston howled, and hopped around the room in contorted agony, holding his scalded hand aloft and trying to look like all three figures in the Laocoon at once. 'Good Christallbloodymighty, you didn't have to do that, did you? What a woman!'

'It'll be worse next time,' said Paula, returning calmly to the washing up; but she had to admit she had been shaken somewhat by his frontal assault, not to say affrontery; and Johnston, sensing his advantage, continued to feel and fondle her throughout the washing up, never allowing it to become serious enough for her to become genuinely annoyed, until, exasperated and flushed and —— and this *did* annoy her —— conscious of the juice beginning to seep between her legs which Johnston, if he succeeded in feeling her up again, would surely discover, she turned on him with as much semblance of anger and disgust as she could genuinely arouse and shouted at him:

'Johnston! For heavens sake *leave me alone,* or you'll have to go home.' She pulled the plug out of the sink, wiped her hands firmly and without a hint of softening on the handtowel next to the sink, and brushed past him out into the living-room. 'What's more,' she added as an afterthought, though she didn't think it had much deterrent value, 'Graeme is likely to be home at any minute.'

'No he isn't,' said Johnston, who had followed her into the living-room.

'What do you mean, he isn't?'

'Your husband' said Johnston choosing his words carefully and enunciating them with elocution-school clarity, 'is at this very minute probably fucking the arse off Gina from the push.'

Paula stopped halfway across the room, turned, and stared at him.

'How do you know?'

'Because,' said Johnston, 'that's what he told me he was going to do when he left the Windsor Castle with her tonight.'

Of course, the party should have warned her.

'Hello, Paula. Graeme! How nice to see you! Do come in.'

It was Millicent's standard greeting, and Paula did not fail to notice how it invariably favoured the husbands over the wives. They followed her in through the vestibule, along the corridor past the racks of upstanding wine bottles and subtly illuminated King George crystal glasses, through the living-room where two or three couples were standing in front of some unframed hard-edge abstracts and out into the enclosed courtyard. It was immediately cooler, one of those quiet Sydney nights when the east wind was blowing in from the sea, loud with the noise of crickets, leaf rustle and the occasional basso-profondo frog. It prickled the skin across her shoulders, bare beneath the straps of her orange shift. Paula linked her fingers through Graeme's. 'Don't you dare desert me tonight,' she said. 'I can't stand these things.'

Graeme grinned at her. 'It's the other way around: with you in that outfit I'm going to have to spend the night fighting men off.' He detached his hand and ran it with husbandly brazenness over her bottom.

'Yoo-hoo, Don! Graeme and Paula are here.' Millicent waved, displaying an immaculately groomed armpit, across the top of the equally immaculate wigs, hairdos and balding pates which at that moment graced the Don and Millicent Woodfall's sunken courtyard. A few faces turned inquiringly around. You don't know me, Paula thought, and I don't know you, so get back to your chit-chat. Did everyone loathe such things as much as she did? Why did she and Graeme come, for that matter? It wasn't their world. Stop the martini wheel, I want to get off. She looked around for a familiar face and was relieved to see, in a corner overwhelmed by bamboo and an unflowering jacaranda, Maria, though not her husband. She smiled and mouthed *we-will-be-over-in-a-second* in exaggerated deaf-and-dumb mime, and then Don's smiling face was hovering above them.

'Hullo, hullo, hullo, I'm glad you made it,' he said. 'Good to see you, Graeme. How are you Paula?'

'Is that a serious question?' Paula asked.

'Well, I suppose it is.'

'I am very well thank you Donald Woodfall, and I'm very sorry we haven't seen you for such a long time, especially as I thought you were the only one of that dreadful London crowd who was at all nice, and I'd like a martini but not too dry thank you very much.'

Don disappeared. Graeme gave her a strange look. 'Have you been drinking?' he said.

'No,' she said. 'But I've decided to enjoy myself tonight. You men have it your own way too often.'

Millicent reappeared with a rather embarrassed couple in tow. 'Darling, I'd like you to meet Barry Engelbert and his wife, Christina. He's a scientist, absolutely brilliant, over from the States for a year or two, I'm sure you'll adore him. Barry, this is Graeme Turner. Oh, and this is Paula.'

They all smiled. Barry Engelbert cast a regretful eye over his shoulder at the group from which he had, no doubt, been dragged unwillingly, but decided to make the best of it and, raising his glass, enunciated: 'Well, here's cheers, as you folk say in Aussicland.'

'I can't cheer because I haven't a drink yet,' Paula said.

Barry-the-Brilliant-Scientist lowered his glass quickly. 'Sorry about that. Can I get you one?' Paula shook her head. 'No, it's all right . . . .'

'Of course, we're not really newcomers, we've been here

a year already,' said Barry's-Wife-Christina.

'Oh,' said Graeme. 'And how are you finding it?'

'Fine, it's just fine,' said Barry. 'I think Australia's just about to take off. Don't you honey? You know, it's right there on the launching pad, and I find it a damned exciting experience to be here just as the blast-off occurs.'

'Oh certainly, and also it's such a *young* country, so many young people, I'm sure they're going to make a difference eventually —— I mean, we *love* Australia as it is, but it's rather backward in *some* ways, isn't it, rather slow, really, but I'm sure all those bright young men coming up are going to change that.'

'We know one of them,' continued Barry. 'Nice young chap, he's interested in Bev, our daughter. In fact he wants to get engaged to her. Of course, when he asked me about that I said, well now, Mart, that's his name, Martin, I said, well now Mart that's fine, I like you very much, I want you to know that; but what about your job prospects? You're not going to university, you're not doing a night course; you're not going to get far just as a shipping clerk, are you? I said to him, I've got to consider my daughter's interests. Now you go away and think about it. And do you know what?' Barry drained his drink. 'He's joined a broker's office, and he's studying accountancy at night, and I'm pretty sure he's going to make it right up there one day. He's going to be in a command position. There's a lot of youngsters like him coming up, they're going to be moving into command positions over the next decade, and they're going to make a difference to this country.'

'And what,' said Paula, 'about all the people who just get commanded?'

'What's that you say?'

Don came back with a martini for Paula and a beer for Graeme. Barry and Barry's-Wife-Christina took the opportunity to excuse themselves. Paula sipped her drink. 'What strange people, Don,' she said.

'What's that wife of yours been doing now?' Don asked Graeme.

'Insulting your guests, baby, that's all. She's in a dangerous mood tonight. Don't ask me why; I just sleep with her, that's all.'

'Perhaps you don't sleep with me enough.'

'My heavens, you have become emancipated. That's not the Paula I knew in London,' said Don patronizingly. 'You were as quiet as a church-mouse in those days.'

'And you are not the irreverent Donald I knew in London either,' replied Paula. 'Do you ever see any of the push these days?'

'Johnston's supposed to be coming around later on.'

'All these people —— are they your friends?'

'Of course not,' Don whispered conspiratorially, 'they're *contacts*. Very necessary when you're at the bar . . . .'

'You're really conforming to the rules, aren't you?' said Graeme.

For the first time since they'd arrived Don looked slightly discomfited. 'Certainly not. It makes no difference: I'm still the same here,' he said, pointing at his narrow pigeon-chest; and then, gesturing dismissively at the house: 'All this is so much camouflage.'

'The difficulty is distinguishing you from the camouflage,' Paula said sweetly. 'That was delicious, Don. Can I have another?'

Don took her glass and Paula walked with him back to the built-in bar which, flanked with rubber plants, looked out through the pushed-back sliding glass doors onto the courtyard. A man in a white waiter's jacket with red velveteen lapels stood behind it.

'Martini —— not too dry,' said Don. 'Do you really think I've changed, Paula?'

Paula smiled up at him. His eyes, behind their spectacles, seemed actually worried. Perhaps, despite all the bank accounts and that newly-acquired sense of authority which she had not failed to notice, he was the same old Don. 'We've all changed,' she said. 'I've changed —— for the worse. I've become a nagger, a worrier, and a bitch. As long as you're aware of it I don't suppose it

136

matters too much.'

'And if you're not?'

Paula thought for a moment. 'Well, perhaps that doesn't matter either. We all grow nastier as we grow older. We begin to take position for granted, and money, and —— all the things we didn't have before. It's absurd to think you're still the same here' —— pointing, in Don-parody, to her could-be-tanner bosom —— 'I've got flatter, for a start. Can't poke young men's eyes out like I used to, though I still try in buses sometimes.' Impulsively she reached up and touched with her lips Don's sallow, well-shaven, slightly lined, once-familiar cheek. 'Only don't change too much. There aren't many Dons around. Thank you.'

She accepted her martini and went off in search of Maria. Don, watching her go, short dark hair thrust impatiently back behind boyish ears, a mature woman's body jammed into a coolly brief dress, walking with the carelessness of someone who knew she didn't have to swing her hips to emphasize her sexuality, thought, and not for the first time: what a woman. Graeme was a lucky bastard; he hoped he appreciated her.

His wife, all spray-set and elegant, drifted towards him. 'Darling,' she said, 'the Scott-Thompsons are here.'

'Tell them,' he said succinctly, 'to get rooted.' He turned to the barman. 'A double Scotch, if you don't mind. Lots of ice, no water. It's for me.' There was as much authority as ever in his voice.

'Hello,' said Maria.

'Hullo. How's everything?'

'Sssh. I'm concentrating. I've got my eye on that rather dark, mysterious-looking American over there. He's been giving me my-wife's-a-dog-and-I-know-it looks all night . . . .'

'Not him! He's not just a leader of men, he's a Commander. Where's Scott?'

'Probably blind already. He went drinking with a few

cronies down at the Schools Club after work, though he knew we were coming here. He's worse than ever . . . .' Paula nodded. Scott, who sold IBM machines, was an occupational hazard casualty of too many soft-sell luncheons and over-the-bar clinchers about whom people always ended by saying 'and he's such a nice guy, too'. 'How's Graeme?'

Paula shrugged. 'He's still Graeme. I think he always will be.'

'And the children?'

'Absolutely wonderful, like hell. One moment they're lovely, the next you wish you never had them. I don't think I could bear to have any more. Though James was funny the other day: he was grizzling "WHERE'S MOI FORK" when it was staring him straight in the face on the breakfast table in front of him, and when I pointed to it the best he could manage was to pick it up and say "that's not a fork, is it?" ' Paula laughed. 'He's a scream. Can't stand to lose face. Like me, now I come to think of it . . . .'

'Have you heard about Buzzy?'

'No. What's happened?'

'She's left Gary.'

'Really?'

'For good.'

'Why?'

'Oh, he was running about with other women. Picked up with some secretary, used to sleep with her on the floor of her boss's office and in every motel in town. It all came to an end when they accidentally set the burglar alarm off in her office; the first thing Buzzy knew about it was a call from the Metropolitan Security Service asking her to identify her husband! Quite a scandal, really, because the Security Service had to notify the firm as well. Buzzy just walked out. It wasn't the first time, of course. Gary's carrying on, I mean.'

'I always rather liked Gary.'

'I still do.'

'You haven't taken up with *him?*'

'Of course not, it wouldn't be fair to Buzzy. Though in my weaker moments I'm tempted . . .' Maria-of-the-Jacaranda-Lourdes smiled her enigmatic smile. Have a weak moment with my husband, thought Paula with unChristian primitiveness, and I'll scratch your eyes out. 'Of course' Maria continued 'Buzzy's been suffering from the housewife syndrome —— as who wouldn't, with four children to look after? And no household help at all. Gary taking up with another woman was the proverbial last straw.'

'I knew she felt tied down by the children. But you know Buzzy, I always imagined she'd be able to think it all out, you know, intellectualize the situation.'

'She did. But it doesn't seem to help much.'

'No,' said Paula thoughtfully. 'It doesn't.'

Graeme materialized from amidst an amorphous group of ankle-length Parisian originals, swept-up hairdos and swept-down decolletages. He was carrying a frothing beer glass from which he drank, grimacing, then held up to the light. 'This horse,' he announced, 'is unfit to race.'

'Graeme!' said Maria. 'Good heavens, you're getting quite thin. Isn't Paula feeding you?'

'Thin? I had to buy him size 36 underpants for his birthday last week.'

'It's a virility precaution,' said Graeme.

'He keeps reading those articles about the dangers of tight trousers,' Paula explained. 'So I bought him some size 36's and put a little label on them —— *"THE TROCADERO: more ballroom than you ever thought possible."*'

Maria reached out an overcompassionate arm and stroked Graeme gently on the shoulder. 'You wouldn't have to worry about virility would you, darling?'

'Put that man down. He's mine!' Paula ordered. 'Besides, you're married.'

'I might as well be married to a brewery for all the good it does me,' Maria said. 'Or a cork-screw.' She smiled

139

brightly. 'Hey, that's a pun. Laugh, everybody!'

Maria's husband chose precisely that moment to descend the steps into the courtyard and veer towards them. He was a once-handsome, well-proportioned man with carefully brushed hair, an immaculate suit, hand-enamelled cufflinks and a suntanned face which, at that moment, was wearing a fixed grin. It was the only sign that he was drunk; Scott, after many years of practice, held his liquor well.

'Hello, look who's here. The Little Wife, the Graeme, and the Adorable Paula. Having a lovely time, are you?' He slid a lecherously sober arm around Paula's waist and peered from face to face: Maria's registered Disgust, Graeme's registered Good Fellowship, and Paula was still trying to compose hers into a blend of Affection and Hands Off when Scott interrupted:

'Paula! Your glass is empty! That's quite criminal —— what will you have?'

'I think I'll switch to whisky, thanks, Scott.'

'With ice?'

'Yes please.'

'And water?'

'What do you think I am, an extremist?'

Scott veered off in the direction of the bar, followed quickly by a Maria who was only too obviously about to give her husband a Piece of her Mind. Paula sighed.

'Poor Scott! I think he's going to get an earful,' she said. 'Sometimes I don't know whose side I'm on —— the husband's or the wife's.'

'I don't think you'll get your whisky,' said Graeme.

'Neither do I —— perhaps I'd better go and get it myself.'

She and Graeme wandered across the courtyard, to be met halfway with a blast of music from Don Woodfall's stereogram. The decibelage was in the jet-engine class, blotting out all conversation instantaneously. After a couple of seconds someone rushed forward and throttled the amp, but not before Graeme recognized what he

140

thought was the soundtrack of *Kismet*. 'Hold my hand while this strange German parrot dies,' he warbled.

The barman drifted into their field of vision with a tray of drinks. Graeme, after a variety of winks, twitches, tics and head jerks which would have done credit to an epileptic, managed to catch his eye. Paula selected a whisky, Graeme chanced another beer. The whisky was nearly all Scotch and no water, and on top of the two martinis it made Paula feel distinctly lightheaded. Graeme was not so lucky. 'This horse,' he began . . . .

'Don,' Paula interrupted, 'is supposed to be a friend of yours.'

'He is — — but I don't have to like his music, do I?'

'Why don't you see more of him these days?'

Graeme shrugged. 'The old group has fallen apart, hasn't it? What do we have in common now — — except London? To try and trade on that would be to falsify the whole thing. It's got to happen naturally, baby, or not at all.' They climbed out of the courtyard into a swirl of bright chatter, background strings (Don had got the stereo caged at last) and plates of North Shore Catering Service supper-food. Paula opted for sauté of chicken, balancing the plate on one knee while talking to some barrister's wife about Colour Visuals, whatever they were, and swapping instant smiles with Millicent as she wafted hostessily by, while Graeme chose spaghetti and attacked it with more verve than politesse.

'Spaghetti, like children, should be seen and not heard,' she hissed in his ear when the Colour Visuals had faded momentarily. Graeme attempted to grin with a mouthful of spaghetti and succeeded only in splattering his dark purple shirt and yellow suede tie with tomato sauce and Parmesan cheese. He swore loudly — — a little too loudly for the couple sitting on his right, who got up and walked away. 'When we get home,' he said, 'I'm going to strip you off and dunk you in an ice-bath. You're drunk already.'

The idea of being stripped naked appealed to her but the cold bath, Paula decided, was distinctly de Sadeish.

'And then what?' she said.

'And then,' said Graeme, less de Sade than Roger the Lodger, 'I shall roll you round the bed till your face turns cherry red.'

That, certainly, did not appeal at all. A phrase from the past tried to dislodge itself and fall into her memory. What was it she had said to Graeme that night in London when, having slept with him drowsily and not really meaning to the night before, the night Rosinante broke down, Graeme had peremptorily assumed she was going to repeat the performance the following night and so on ad infinitum as though he had some God-granted male right to copulation with whomsoever he wished at whatsoever time he wished and in particular, at that moment, with Paula? And he had been terribly angry, heavens he certainly had been, and had shouted something at her about how very Graeme he was and had been and was going to be ... she giggled, remembering what she had said, and leaned across to her outrageously primate-faced and hairy-eared husband, forbearing not to wipe her Mary Quant Orange Meringue mouth upon the back of her hand first, and repeated: 'I want to be loved, not fucked.'

Which was about, when she first enunciated it in London, the most shocking thing she had said in her life.

The party wore on. As parties go it was a reasonable success, Paula decided; nobody enjoyed themselves but nobody chucked up. Then about midnight, when a sizeable percentage of the guests had gone and the remainder were defining themselves down to a hard core of drinkers, stayers and would-be fornicators, who should arrive but a contingent from the push: Johnston, who had been invited; George, who hadn't but should have been, towing not wife Sonia but Gina, one of the Windsor Castle birds; Pedro the Pusher, Eljay, and three or four others Paula didn't know. They burst in through the front door like a phalanx of camp followers, brandishing flagons of Red Ned and bottles of Corio whisky, fracturing the black coffee conversation and spilling themselves untidily around

142

the living-room. Don and Millicent put as good a face on it as possible, though Millicent's bore a distinct resemblance to a lemon.

'Don!'

'Johnno! Good to see you!'

'. . . picked these up at the Windsor Castle, thought you wouldn't mind . . . .'

'. . . of course not. George! Being trying to contact . . . .'

'. . . is Gina, Long John Zarinka, you remember Eljay?'

'. . . and Sonia?'

'. . . couldn't make it.'

'. . . make yourselves at home, I'll get some grog, the barman's gone home.'

An hour later the push had virtually taken over the party. Don's muzak had been replaced by Eljay's portable collection of Muddy Waters and Bob Dylan, and bizarre couples were sprawled lasciviously over the settees; only a few curious voyeurs from the ankle-length Nova-reading ski-holiday Wahroonga-and-Thredbo set remained to watch the goings on and Don looked, for the first time that evening, as though he were actually enjoying himself, a large and goonish grin spread across his white mummer's face, his stoop more vulture-like than ever, a ready flow of reminiscences uncorked by some stray mention of Oakley Street:

'. . . and what about that time in Ravenna when we hadn't eaten for two days, two whole bloody days? So we ordered a huge bowl of minestrone each in some pizzeria and when it arrived you looked at yours, George, and said in a very tight-lipped fashion "there's a fly in my soup". And so there was, doing a little softshoe shuffle across the minestrone singing Who Were You With Last Night, and you couldn't eat it!'

Don chortled, George slightly less so, and Johnston, lurking large behind a pint glass of Don's best Cellar Hermitage '65, did not refrain from grinning.

'And that hostel in Brindisi, wasn't it,' said George, 'with the fearful squat-down dyke where every time you flushed it the whole place sank a foot in water and you had to swim for the door . . . .'

'Après moi le déluge', said Johnston.

'I had an even worse urinary experience at Perugia,' said Don. 'The toilets were downstairs in some ghastly hole with no lights so one night I blundered down there and groped my way from cubicle to cubicle in pitch darkness till I came to one with the door open and let fly in the general direction of the toilet. Whereupon there was a frantic scuffle of feet, and the sound of someone leaping up on the cistern, and a very angry Scottish voice bellowed out: "FOR CHRIST'S SAKE, MON!" '

Johnston, slapping his side with one hand, spilt some claret on the white floor-rug with the other. Millicent rushed for the Wettex in the kitchen. 'Don't worry, I've been wanting to do that for a long time,' said Don, and gaily poured a little whisky-and-water onto the claret, whether to dilute it or to create an Instant Art Happening it was not quite clear. Eljay appeared from rifling what must have been Don's Holiest of Inner Sanctums with an autographed cricket bat tucked under his arm like a guitar, muttering 'Where's the strings, man?'. Pedro the Pusher put an uptempo Chicago blues on the stereo, towed some lank-haired woman in scarlet hipsters, yellow striped singlet, pastryflour face and a mouth which resembled nothing so much as the anal vent of a domesticated fowl into the courtyard, shouting: 'Doesn't anybody know how to dance here?' The party was warming up.

George, running a hand over his balding pate and slicking down both eyebrows with moistened fingers, invited Paula to a Gay Fantastic. She complied, though not before noticing Gina of the Push seemed to have fastened herself onto Graeme. It was windier in the courtyard. She felt pleasantly inebriated —— she never could hold whisky, she decided —— and began dancing and shaking with cool abandon, avoiding any gesture that seemed too professional and trying to let the movements of her body spurt up from her subconscious, improvising like a jazz

musician *you've got to keep moving, baby* which was one
of Graeme's phrases surely, trying to synchronize her
dancing to the music's breaks, crescendos and stop-time
choruses until finally, for a few brief seconds as the song
reached a screaming electronic climax, she felt as though
she were the music, the sound ripping through her body
and exploding like a short-circuit from her fingertips in
rapid-fire eruptions of sound, her whole body caught up in
a complex shimmer of rhythms and sound patterns which
flashed orange, white, green-gold-vermilion whorls and
swirls in bursting abstract expressionist fantasies upon the
white screen of her mind and lit up like lightning like
fireworks like spark-showering blowtorch like blueglare of
oxyweld the white creeper-covered walls of Donald
ex-London Woodfall's right-side-of-the-tracks Wahroonga
courtyard. When, abruptly, the music stopped she found,
surprised, she was earthbound still.

'Where's Sonia tonight?' she asked George when she had
regained her breath.

'At home,' he replied briefly.

'Something wrong?'

'No more than usual.' He shrugged. 'You know how it
is. We've come to an arrangement. I brought Gina here
tonight.'

Paula, from the comparative dark of the courtyard
looked through the flung-back sliding doors of the house
to the living area where, against a background of hard-edge
paintings and Scandinavian light hangings, Johnston, Don,
Maria, Scott and half a dozen others were transfixed as if
within an aluminium picture frame. Graeme was talking to
Gina. She suddenly felt sweaty and a little bad-tempered.
Was she due for the curse? Or was it just the whisky?

'Thanks, George, that was terrific —— but I'm getting
too old for it,' she said, and walked inside.

Gina, as she approached, gave an unfriendly smile and
disappeared into the courtyard with George. Paula sat
down beside Graeme and listened to the talk shuttle back
and forth, thinking: there goes another marriage. On top

of Maria and Scott's little charade earlier in the evening, and the news about Buzzy, it was all too dispiriting. She felt herself plunging from whisky-elation to whisky-depression. Was their own marriage destined to break up too? She glanced at her husband. He was sitting crosslegged, intent upon the conversation, dark unsmiling face beneath the narrow forehead and encroaching hair. There was a quality of seriousness about Graeme which seemed incongruous to those who did not know him well; it was that, as much as anything, which had sustained their relationship for so long. But how serious was he about marriage? How *really* serious? And was he strong enough to endure any crisis in it? 'I'm back,' she said to him suddenly. Graeme frowned in mock annoyance, squeezed her ample thigh, and returned to the conversation.

Johnston, as usual, was holding the floor. 'The act itself is the only important thing. Everything else is secondary. Guilt, remorse, nostalgia, penitence, desire for absolution —— they are all secondary. The act itself is the primary fact, the primary reality.'

'Like criticism and creation,' agreed Don. 'Criticism can only exist because the artist has created something for the critic to criticize. It is a secondary act, parasitical, which exists only because of the initial act of creation.'

'Precisely.'

'That's too easy,' said Graeme. 'Criticism can be more creative than the work of art itself. Look at Johnson —— Sammy, not this bloody pipe-smoking poseur here on my right. A critic might provide more insight into his age than the artists —— especially if the artists are no good.'

'But the critic depends upon the artist,' said Johnston, speaking between pipeclenching teeth. 'The artist comes first. If there were no artists there'd be no critics.'

'So what? That doesn't mean one is more important than the other.'

'But it does mean the one is primary and the other is secondary. The act itself, be it the creative act or any other sort of act, is the basic unit. It is the finite, definite,

146

definitive entity. Once the act is enacted, it is accomplished. Everything else is just so much moralizing after the event, so much talk and horseshit . . . .'

'It all sounds like horseshit to me,' muttered Eljay, from the corner.

'There,' said Johnston, pointing an accusing finger at Eljay, 'sounds the voice of the philistine.' He stopped to retamp his pipe, blew smoke contentedly, settled back.

'Take any act at all. Take adultery. That never worries me for a minute. Why should it? The act exists in itself, the rest is so much . . . .' He waved his hand. 'I don't feel remorse, or guilt, or any such reaction. That won't change the nature of the act itself. Guilt is a social creation, an after-effect forced upon us by the society we live in. It's the involuntary spasm reaction to all those crazy demands, taboos, rules, threats, punishments and mental castrations which are imposed upon us by everyone from our very own father to His Son, Which Art In Heaven . . . . Freed from society we are most truly ourselves, we live and exist through acts which are utterly pure. A fuck is a fuck is a fuck, an essence of purity; it's only the Alfs who defile it as adulterous.'

'I don't agree with that either,' said Graeme.

The discussion drifted on and, as usual, got nowhere. When it seemed to have reached a natural hiatus Paula reached across and touched her husband's neck, running a forefinger around the curve of his ear and down through the black, wiry hair. 'The babysitter, remember?' she said.

'Christ,' said Graeme, 'I'd been thinking it was your mother —— we'd better go.' He downed his drink and turned to where Johnston had added a scattering of pipe scourings to the claret and whisky-and-water which decorated Millicent's handwoven rug. 'Hey Johnno, how about coming around for a drink one night this week?'

'There's not much left of this week,' said Johnston. 'Tonight's Wednesday.'

'What about tomorrow night, then? We haven't got anything on have we, Paula?'

147

Paula shook her head. 'Okay,' said Johnston.

'Beaut. See you, baby.'

In the car it was warmer than outside. Graeme wound the windows down, the light from Don and Millicent's flickering oil beacon casting garish reflections across his face, and set out for Pymble.

'Pretty damned funny party.'

'Yes,' said Paula.

'Millicent's face just about dropped a foot when Johnston and the push arrived! I thought for a moment she would try to throw them out.'

'She wouldn't have dared.'

'No. The most daring thing she's ever done is go to the lavatory without her slippers on.' Graeme negotiated a series of Wahroonga Esses at approaching 5,700 rpm in third gear, unwound his Laocoon hands, slipped into top, relaxed again. 'That bloody Johnston, he's got some strange ideas. Acts without consequences —— it's Hume's causality all over again. No wonder he's never got married. I suppose he's afraid to commit himself. Pretty immature for someone his age.'

'He's only a few years older than you,' Paula reminded him.

'Right. But at least I'm married.'

'I seem to remember a time when you weren't so keen on marriage.'

He smiled at her. 'Touché'. Adding: 'Johnston wants to protect himself against ever feeling guilty about anything: so hey presto, a metaphysics which excludes guilt. Of course, it excludes nearly every other human feeling as well —— like compassion. Johnston is one of the most inordinately selfish people I know. Apart from myself.'

He drove on. Patches of bush drifted past, black pubic tangles like an Arthur Boyd drawing. 'It was good to see Eljay and the rest of that crowd again.'

'With reservations.'

'I know you don't like the push that much . . . .'

'I've got reservations about some of them. Gina, for

instance,' replied Paula, roused at last, remembering what George had told her. 'She's a neurotic. And I'm not being bitchy when I say that; I've seen her in action. She bounces from man to man like a tennis ball, clinging to her libertarian philosophy, making sure she never develops a serious attachment to any of them. She's probably incapable of sustaining any sort of long-term relationship. It's dispiriting, somehow; because as she grows older she's going to become less and less attractive to men, and more and more desperate, and more and more frenetic in her search for . . . bed fodder. Until she finally ends up like, heaven knows, Bea Miles: tearing off taxi doors, reciting Shakespeare on a street corner for sixpence, in and out of Long Bay like a yo-yo. Bea used to be the toast of the libertarians in her younger days; the Queen of the Norman Lindsay push. Now look at her! What use is her past to her now?'

'I once knew a girl in London,' said Graeme, 'who said she was going to spend the first half of her life making mistakes and the second half regretting them. Maybe that's not such a bad way to live.'

Paula, feet braced against the Mazda floor in case of a head-on smash, in which case she, being in the death-seat, would have the chance for neither mistakes nor regrets, wondered why she felt so hostile towards Gina. Envy? Surely not. Though she felt confined, put upon by her marriage it wasn't *that* sort of freedom she wanted. Perhaps it was simply because George had brought her to the party instead of Sonia. 'It seems so unfair,' she said aloud. 'To Sonia, I mean. George makes her life bloody, an absolute hell. I don't know why she stands for it — I wouldn't.'

'That' said Graeme 'is fairly obvious.'

'Well, why should anyone? George puts her in an impossible position. I don't know what he thinks he is achieving by it, but it will kill their marriage eventually. I wouldn't like that to happen to us. I don't know, I really don't; it makes me sad whenever I think of it. How can

149

men be so short-sighted! Perhaps Sonia thought she could change George after they got married.'

'As you,' said Graeme, 'have tried to change me.'

Paula was quiet for a moment. Was it true? Or wasn't it? Oh hell —— she turned back to her husband.

'What are we talking about such dispiriting things for? I've enjoyed tonight, I really have. It was good to see Don again, and Johnston, and George —— I like him, I really do, despite what he does to Sonia.'

'You should've enjoyed yourself,' said Graeme, grinning.

'Why?'

'That whisky really set you off.'

'Unfair!' said Paula. 'I was just feeling in a good mood.'

'Don't have too many good moods —— my metabolism couldn't stand it.'

'Actually it was all your talk about stripping me naked and throwing me in a bathtub of icecubes that got me excited . . . .'

'Would you still like me to do that?'

Paula smiled at her purple-tomato-sauce-and-Parmesan-clad husband, intent over the steering wheel, and wondered what he would do if she stripped off there and then. Hello, constable. It's all right, we're married. 'Let's leave out the ice-cubes: it's too cold,' she said; and shivered. 'It's as bad as Wales. Remember that funny old man who rented us the cottage, the landlord in Beddgelert? What did he say when we left? "Goodbye, my dears. That's right! Happy times! The nights are longer in December, aren't they —— not that I mean any harm by it." '

Paula began to laugh, but it ended as a yawn. She leant over and rested her head in her husband's lap as they set out on the last stage of the trip home to Pymble. The wood-rimmed steering wheel was only an inch or so from her face; she felt Graeme, slowing down, rest a protective hand against her forehead. Lights zoomed by and threw fast-moving, irregular designs against the instrument panel and the interior of the cabin, like those shredded clouds which had eddied and swirled across the sky in —— yes, it was Wales. She remembered snowed-in fields looking like vast saltpans with their stone wall surrounds, and wild rhododendrons strung across the valley slopes like clots of blood, Moel Mairc mountain almost airborne, frozen above the cottage with not even the sound of running water to disturb the silence . . . and once, when they were climbing Merlin's Mound, a shower of sparrows skimmed low over their heads, whistling like a flight of arrows. She turned her head slightly and bestowed a chaste kiss upon Graeme's corduroyed and zippered genitals. 'I love you, darling,' she said sleepily.

Two days later, not so certain, Paula found herself with Johnston's lascivious fingers nibbling at her throat and her mind repeating Gina not Gina of all people surely not Gina

the wave the wave lifting the board abruptly so that he was
on his feet to take the drop falling free falling almost down
the face and then a radical bottom turn throwing his
weight to the right feeling the tail whip around like a lead
weight at the end of a tight string and then forward
already to the nose as the wave bunched behind like a
green fist the board striving for speed and then he was in
trim sliding across the face as fast as the sun's glint stooped
low with trail hand pushing the wave back locked in that
looping curl with the cylinder of light beckoning and then
out! explode out with the waveface steepening back to the
tail crank left as the white water caught him at last and
there was nothing left to do but ride it in till the fin
scratched sand and he was out with board under his arm
and the froth around his ankles, up the beach slowly with
his left leg which always felt the strain of too long in the
water cramping slightly, pushing on across the sand which
felt hot on the top of his feet only to the familiar beach
umbrella and George and Sonia with a transistor and an
Esky beside them in the wilderness is enow and the
children's scattered litter

'Where's Paula?'

'Gone up to buy the kids an ice cream,' said George. He
was stretched out on his back, head resting upon a garishly
striped towel, thin shanks poking out beneath a brief
men's bikini, quite overpowered by Sonia's voluptuous
body clad in genteel one-piece flopped prone in the sand
beside him. She definitely looks better, Graeme thought,

out of a swimming costume than in one. Which was no
doubt why, judging by the paleness of her skin on this
midsummer afternoon, she didn't come to the beach often;
whereas George sported quite a respectable tan. 'Was that
you out there?'

'When?'

'Just then.'

'I suppose so.'

'Not bad, not bad at all. You're getting on top of that
thing,' said George, for whom anything more strenuous
than chess was hardly to be contemplated, but who did
not forbear to dip himself in the saltseasurf when the
occasion warranted. Then, stretching luxuriously: 'Ah, this
is the life.'

'We, the lotus-caters . . . .'

'Don't! That phrase has been demeaned forever. I forbid
it, banish it, Index Prohibitorum it. Besides, I never liked
Tennyson.'

'You're beginning to sound like Johnston; watch
yourself, baby,' said Graeme.

'That phone! When did you see him last?'

'Couple of weeks ago. He's thinking of going overseas
again.'

'Really!' George allowed himself to be sufficiently
surprised to warrant propping himself up on his elbows.
'That's an upset, as the footy writers say.'

'He's been talking about it for some time.'

'Yes, but you know Johnston. Talk is a substitute for
action with him. Once he's thought a thing out, talked it
out to its conclusion, he thinks he's accomplished it. I'll
have to see him on the ship before I believe he's going.'

'Maybe,' replied Graeme, annoyed by George's remark,
though for what reason he could not have said — because
it reflected upon Johnston's capacity for action, or upon
his own gullibility?

'Where's he thinking of going?' Sonia asked, her voice
muffled beneath her arms.

'What?'

'That broadbeamed, broadbacked, broadarsed turd you see there, sometimes known as my wife, asks where The Oracle is likely to go,' said George.

'I don't know,' said Graeme. 'I think he's more fed up with Australia than anything; just wants to get out of the place again. Might end up in Hong Kong or South America . . . .'

'Very strange,' said George, lying back down again, gingerly, on his spine, as though afraid a grain of sand might snap it in two. 'Why did he ever come back, then?'

'Well, he was the last of the group to come back, wasn't he? —— after Don.'

'Have you seen anything of Donald lately?' Sonia asked, raising her head a little so she could be heard this time.

'My wife, she who slumps here beside me like some felled Canadian lumber, or lumber-with-the-jack, which is more likely considering the types with whom she associated, asks . . . .'

'I heard her,' said Graeme. 'No, I haven't seen him for ages. He's been swallowed up by The Law. Holds fey little parties every now and then, which gives his wife a chance to display her latest Marimekko. There's one on this week; Wednesday, I think it is . . . .'

'When's Don going to divorce that bitch?' interposed Sonia.

'There speaks the bitch herself,' said George. He deftly avoided a swing from Sonia's muscular arm. 'Of course, Sonia and Don's wife don't get on that well; it's a sort of disguised lesbian relationship which reveals itself in hostility.'

'Have you been invited?'

'Where?'

'To the party.'

'No,' said George briefly.

'Why don't you crash?'

'And let the Bitch Wife get her claws into Sonia again?'

'Don'd be pleased to see you.'

'Yes, I'd like to see Don again. He's all right, Don is.'

George settled himself back on the sand and closed his eyes. 'And the Oracle —— or the Orifice, as I prefer to think of him. We need buggers like him around to stir things up, don't you think? Even if they are, to any normal man like myself, rather distasteful.'

'That's what I've tried to tell him,' said Graeme.

'You have?' said George. 'Christ, that sounds out of character. Since when have you become the apostle of commitment?'

'I haven't,' said Graeme. 'Not much use being committed in a country where everyone thinks it means being sent up for trial. But I suspect Johnston feels a bit guilty about it all.'

'Johnston's taking the easy way out,' said George firmly. 'What's he done since coming back? He hasn't joined the Labor Party, hasn't become involved in any political movements. I haven't even seen him at Vietnam Action. Did he ever go on any of those protest marches? I doubt it. Johnston wants to change the world without getting his hands dirty.'

With what bright hopes, Graeme thought, we came back. And now? Don, swallowed up in whiterug affluence somewhere out there at Wahroonga; Johnston, thinking of going back to London; himself, still trying to work out his relations with his wife and two children . . . only George seemed to have survived the toll of years, his radicalism still intact, pushing political motions onto the agenda of the Staff Association at the University, giving talks to the Humanist Society on Commitment and the Left, getting himself drafted onto the ALP's advisory committee on education. But did it ever do any good?

'Maybe he's right.'

'Who, Johnston? Nonsense. You're as bad as he is.'

'I just want to stay alive, baby.'

'There it is, the ole Greta Garbo syndrome again —— *I just vant to be alone.* There's going to come a time, *baby,* when the world won't leave you alone. You can't opt out of the twentieth century.' George levered himself irately

155

onto his elbows again. 'You buggers really get me down. You want everything to fall into your laps. Change has to be worked for, Charlie. You don't change anything by turning your back on it and running fast in the opposite direction.'

He paused for a moment, then added regretfully: 'The group is breaking up, father. I'm beginning to feel isolated. You know? A small man with a flag, and no one to look at it.'

'Maybe it's time the push did break up,' said Sonia. 'It had to happen sooner or later.'

'Well, I know you women can't wait to get us by ourselves. You've done all you can to hasten the process, I must say.'

George lay back in the sun again, but Graeme could almost hear his mind ticking over. There was no stopping George once he got started; he had a concentrated, unswerving intellectual energy which had already carried him through to a Senior Lectureship in Political Science and would, no doubt, eventually push him on to a professorial chair. George was prematurely balding ('barometer of cerebral activity, father') with two wispy tufts of hair which stood up on each side of his cranium like a pension-age Dagwood and a nervous tic which made him jiggle his legs in subconscious frenzy whenever he sat down and made him pace ceaselessly around and around whenever he stood up (Eljay had once composed a mock-folk song to him titled 'Restless Legs,' after a new medical syndrome discovered by a country GP in Wagga; it was sung to Hawaiian guitar accompaniment and a certain Elvis Presley slushiness of intonation); only when, as now, he was lying flat on his back did he seem to be able to control the tension which was compacted within that small, lithe frame.

'Come to think of it, haven't seen you around at any demos lately,' said George. 'Where've you been?'

'Ah, you know what it's like. I've got the family and a car to look after.'

Silence. The sun shone blankly.

'How are you and Paula getting on now?'

'Okay. At least I think we are.'

More silence, interrupted only when a larger than usual wave flopped over on the sand with a muffled explosion, the sound rolling up over the Skol-oiled bodies, beach umbrellas, wigwams, windbreaks, surfoplanes, Joseph's Coat beachtowels, bikinis, baggies, boys with sandbuckets and sticky-out ears, girls with ruffled elasticized costumes demurely covering bosomless chests, Dads and Mums in Casbens and florals, to lose itself in a shiny torture-maze of parked cars, gleaming bonnets, arid acres of sizzling white concrete, rusting promenade rails and melting tarmac. Australia, stunned bullock-like in the sun; who, who, I ask, will be the first to raise his arm?

George was at least prepared to raise his voice.

'Are you going to this demo next Friday?'

'Which one is that?'

'Vietnam Action. Martin Place. Starts about five. Sonia and I and one or two others from the faculty are going —— plus all the Labor Club students.'

'I doubt it.'

'Why not, you Pymble-pink radical? Lost your nerve or something? Good Christ, give an honest man a car and a nice home in the suburbs and he suddenly switches sides, joins the bourgeoisie. No wonder Johnston wants to get out of Australia! Too many blokes with cars and telly sets here; if you want idealism you've got to go where people still know what it's like to be poor.'

'It's not that,' replied Graeme, feeling the sun beating down onto his back and arms, drying the salt which his one wipeout had deposited there in snail's tracks of loops and circles and which, later, would be prickly and uncomfortable under his denim shirt. What a man needs, he thought, is not idealism but a portable shower-hose. 'At least I hope not. I don't know. I think I'm changing.'

'You certainly are.'

'Well, politics doesn't seem so important to me now. I'm

not so interested as I used to be in changing the world; I want to experience it as it is. You know? I'm trying to live it now, baby.'

'That's rather extreme,' said Sonia of the armpit-muffled voice.

'What's that?'

'I said that's very extreme, isn't it?'

'I don't think so. Look, there's a lot more to life than politics, isn't there? Politics is a power thing; if you're attracted by power, fine. I'm not. I'm more interested in —— Jesus, I don't know, the whole bit, life, experience, all that jazz. It's like sex, or love, or anything like that: what you're trying to do is experience something very intensely at that moment, understand it —— even become it. What kicks me on is sensation; you know? Maybe I'm a sensationalist. A beautifully designed page layout gives me a tremendous kick; so does getting locked up in the slot of a fast wave; or going to a disco. Sensation, baby. You might die tomorrow.'

'And if you don't,' said George, 'You're left with the debris of what you wrecked yesterday. That's a crazy way of looking at it. You can't live each day as though it's your last, because usually it isn't. If I thought this was my last day on earth I might jump up and try to rape every nubile wench on this beach, but as I'm reasonably sure it isn't I'll make do with Sonia.'

'Thank you, darling.'

Graeme, reflecting, admitted George was right. But he had failed to communicate, what he, himself, still only half-understood, a truth which he grasped only in fleeting moments of exhilaration and perception. He tried again:

'Well, that's not the main thing anyhow. It's more a question of focusing down on the immediate experience. You know, when Paula and I and the kids went up to the North Coast on our last holiday I was walking along the beach one day, just walking along by myself in bare feet with the water looping up in great swirls of foam and the wind blowing in hard from across the bay and those funny little sand crabs whipping sideways on their bent legs and I suddenly thought: this is what really counts. I've grasped the actual quality of this moment, it's precise shape, what it feels like, the unique texture of this instant. The universe in a sandgrain, baby. That's what counts. Not ambition, nor political idealism, nor the power game, nor living for the future, nor living for your kids, nor anything else —— simply life as it is, right now.'

George thought for a moment. 'MY LIFE AS A HEDONIST, PART ONE', he declaimed in the voice of a Royal Easter Show spruiker.

'We're all hedonists.'

'But none quite so unabashedly and unapologetically as you,' replied George. 'Besides, you've got the metaphysics of it cocked up, as usual.'

'I'm listening.'

'Well, I'm very glad you asked me that question,' said George. 'Er . . . what was it again?'

'The metaphysics.'

'Ah yes. Well, father, it's like this. Even if —— something which I don't admit for a moment, mind you —— even if our lives were limited primarily to immediate sensations, that would not exclude activities such as, for instance, politics. Political activity is just as valid an activity as hopping up and down on a surfboard or tramping poor little sandcrabs to death on whatever Godforsaken beach it is you take Paula to for your dirty holidays. And, one would have thought, infinitely more rewarding; because, in the final analysis, infinitely more significant. You pursue the fleeting instant; I pursue the whole world. Politics embraces all of life. Every activity is, in some sense, political.'

'You've dragged morality into it again.'

'Ah ah, not so easy. I haven't. I've merely pointed out that the scope of politics, or social involvement, or whathaveyou, is much broader than, say, shaking all over at a disco; and therefore the scope for diverse and fulfilling experience is much greater too. But of course you can't

159

leave the morality out of it. One of the reasons why political activity is preferable to doing the Frug, as I believe the Youngies call it, is that it is so much more important. It can change the world's destiny. It determines whether the Youngies ever get the chance to do the Frug or not. It's creative, not just narcissistic. And it's worth doing. *That's* what counts, father.'

Graeme, feeling rather out-manoeuvred, retreated to compromise. 'Maybe they're not mutually exclusive, anyhow.'

'What aren't?'

'Politics and —— oh, I don't know, a life of sensation.'

George clapped two sandy hands together, once, then slapped with one his beloved Sonia's broadbeamed bum. 'Hooray, hooray! Murph the Surph has seen the light. One of these days I'll enrol you, free, in my first-year class.'

But Graeme, lying face down with the sun working its balming chemistry upon his body, still doubted. What counted, he thought stubbornly, was the individual's own mystical salvation, his sense of lifefulness. If George got that from politics, fair enough. But he knew his own came from subtler, more tenuous, less easily definable experiences . . .

A scuffle of feet. 'Do you know what, daddy?' asked James. Paula and baby brought up the flank. 'What?' adopting Fond Father tone. 'When the world, when the world end, the sky fall down in the sea, and the mountains get all washed away, and the sun goes out, and you can't see nothing!'

George startled, levered himself onto elbows. 'Good Lord Above! A Jehovah's Witness in the family already.'

'I don't know where he gets that from,' said Paula.

'Did you bring me a Paddle Pop, Paula?' George asked. Paula handed a chocolate one to George, Horne's icecreamlicking Lucky Bastard, and an orange one to Graeme, Zennist in search of the Perfect Wave, and a hideously melted Snow Cream to Sonia, Gae-Tellus Bloom jounced on bulbous waterwing tits. They sat up and ate intently while James, assured of nonfalling sky, shaped Jehovah mountains of sand. Above the sun shone brazenly on bronzeSkol bodies. The time: eternity. The place: Bondibrontecurlcurlcoogeecollaroydeewhywarriewoodwyework. The day:

What day was it? Whatman was working then? Not them. Sunday? Saturday?

Certainly his pursuit of sensation had landed him in some bizarre situations, not least of all this now, lying on this Toledo-rugged and ragtailed gypsy bed, waiting for Gina to emerge from the bathroom where she was carrying out whatever nameless and obnoxiously obstetric obscenities were necessary to prevent conception after copulation —— between the desire and the spasm, between the potency and the existence, between the conception and the creation, falls the Pill. But if it were the Pill it should not have taken her so long hereafter; maybe she was just having a crap. Got a beer bottle in my fist, baby not so sure I got the stopper in my hand. He looked around Gina's room which, despite its fervour and hurricane untidiness, betrayed her immaculate taste and North Shore parentage. Gina was trying hard to live down her background, but Cabana slipcases on her cushions and an original Ian Fairweather on the wall betrayed her; what use, then, the empty banana boxes of emptier Guido gut-rot red flagons stashed like a freestanding Andy Warhol Brillobox construct beneath the window?

He still felt somewhat drunk, but not drunk enough to blot out all consciousness of Paula, waiting alone at home believing, no doubt, that he was still out drinking with Johnston or, worse, not believing. Was he being fair to her? The thought had slipped through his guard before he could stop it; usually he was able to compartamentalize his mind, even his life, so that the truth or implications of what he was doing in one situation did not force their way through the barriers and impinge upon what he was doing in another. It was uncomfortably close, he realized, to Johnston's philosophy; how much had he been influenced by his friend? But it was different, of that he was sure, because he had never believed for a moment that in fact his life, anyone's life, was a bees' hive of watertight compartments with no interconnection, or, with whatever sect of Buddhists it was, that the self had no continuity, that existence was the flame from a row of candles in which each was lit as the last was extinguished, so that each self was *self*-contained and only the contiguity of each successive flame gave rise to the illusion of continuity. For he was aware, only too well, of the carbon line which linked each instant to instant like the wavering pencil linked the numbered spots in a child's puzzle to create, finally, the complete figure, being, person, the last connection (No. 50) being Death. And how, anyhow, even any illusion of guilt, morality, remembrance, consciousness of self-continuity if each freestanding self bore no relation to the previous and subsequent one, how even this, not to put too fine a point upon it, *uneasiness* which he felt in Gina's bed at sometime after pubclose waiting for Gina of the Push, or, as she was sometimes unkindly called, VaGina of a Horse, to emerge in all her naked splendour from this pinkdoored bathroom whence, with a fanfare of Flushed Cisterns upon Bums Argent and a Flourish of Strumpets, she, Gina of the Sky with Diamonds, surrounded by Pink Gypsy Rose Lee fanfeathers, would dance a gay fandango to this his heaving childbirth bed, heaving like the topheavy converted aircraft carrier of which the deckhands said she would roll in the Suez if a wog jumped in and which, heaving herself, had carried him heaving across the Great Australian Bight to Blighty, heaving

Steady, he thought, steadying the bed, which had begun to roll too much for safety, and deciding it might be better if, after all, he sat upright propped against the wall with a pillow behind his spinningtop head, which was George's patent cure for drunkenness, so much so that George spent

162

entire nights, nay entire weeks, sleeping upright at right angles to his luxurious Sonia, waking, which was hardly to be unexpected, to find his back apparently broken at the sixth vertebra from the bottom, that is Sonia's bottom, which was pinchable, plump but hardly pulchritudinous, but had usually straightened itself by midday, when George would manage to struggle from the university down to the South Sydney Leagues Club once again, he George being a great footballer, though he had never played a game in his life, and was indeed loth even to watch except fully six feet safe from the tellyset, though he did not refuse to bend a matey elbow at the South Sydney when his back was straight. And so Graeme né George sat serendipitously against Vagina's puke-pink bedroom and fastened plaster geese against the opposite wall, which at least it did not have, though if the PM had his way there'd be a gnome in every garden, plus A Light in Every Country Window, which was certainly the Worst of Henderson, as mock-Guthrie as St Mary's mock-Gothic, better a cunt in every lighted window, and wondered whether perhaps he would not be better to be on the way home, for what we need is love, baby, IT'S CATHARTIC, BABY, an Angry New Novel by George Formby, come to think of it George did look a bit Formby, minus the buckteeth and ladder, *SHE WAS ONLY BRUSHING HER TEETH,* new improved PEPSODENT with ORTHO-GYNAL, does both jobs at once, and slid out of her like Hope's wet worm

and, sliding, thought

Christ that Gina is certainly taking a long time, why the hell should he sleep with her anyhow, she has bad teeth, and besides it's not the compartmentalize thing it's the thing about loyalty, not morality baby which is something the priests invented to scare shit out of sinners and three coins into a cough-up plate which was why they had to hose down the confession boxes like they hosed out the tail-gunners in the last war but Won or was it Two and Three of course would be better still because they would

have the Bomb, The Lord's Bomb, which had the Pope's
Good Housekeeping seal of approval (think of all those
just wars, baby) and had been consumer-tested by God
Himself, who created man in His Own Image, and also
created evil as a sort of joking afterthought, and who
intervened conveniently enough in the affairs of men if the
Apostles and those red-faced, thick-jowled Bush Brothers
who Paula said came to lecture the Senior Girls at PLC
were to be believed, but had somehow stayed his hand at
Passchendaele, Auschwitz, Hiroshima, Nagasaki, and no
doubt would also fastidiously fail to intervene when the
Rand Corporation and Presidium strategists engineered the
Final Solution, for He, of course, could only be reached,
finally, by the prayers of those guilt-contorted Lesbian
nuns who prayed their lives, wombs, fallopian tubes,
ovaries and rusty vaginas away locked up in castellated
monasteries where self-flagellation had been refined and
sophisticated to a never-ending, insistent and eternal
dribble of blood —— no not morality but loyalty, no not
even loyalty because what price an enforced faithfulness a
sheltered virtue but rather the knowledge that one
dishonest act changed, changed utterly that which you
shared with someone you loved, inserted like some
murderous New Guinea native one thin but fatal sliver of
falsity which working its secretive and tapeworm way
beneath the skin and along the bloodstream speared at last
the heart this sacred covenant of the bleeding heart

but propped himself up again

which would mean WIPEOUT you know like sticking a
coin in the slot of the Wipeout Machine but you *PRIVATE
TURNER!* the scabbard scab if it had hairs around it you'd
find it fast enough the bayonet would find it the bayonet
the bayonet WIPEOUT and you there, lad! you there
where's your matinee passout PASSOUT I said if you've
lost that you can't come in here there the slot or anywhere
the wave the wave where's your passout lad passout I said
passout *PASSOUT*

And did

though not before the storm which had been threatening all evening broke at last with a swift blast of southerly wind, a slamming of doors through the terrace house and the first dust-heavy splats of rain which left fragmented snowflake patterns upon the windowpane

Cold, dark, a slight drizzle falling: typical London weather. He hunched into his duffle jacket and clattered over the concrete pavement, listening to his footfalls and feeling the rain drift into his face. A bus swished noisily past. The wall on his right gleamed dully where the mortar cemented brick upon brick. He was extraordinarily conscious of every sound, every slight movement around him. He wondered if Paula would be in. What to do?

He crossed over Old Brompton Road; there was little traffic at this time of night. Neon light and wrapped Walls sausages in the grocer's window; dull red glow of the corner pub sign; two girls and a man pyramided around the bus stop. His feet fell one after the other in hypnotic monotony ahead of him, the toes of his suede shoes turning black from the rain. Further back speckled brown, then dry brown, two-hole tie. Second bus stop.

This is the house.

He stopped, the wind blowing rain into his face, hesitant at the bottom of the three stone steps which led up to 153 Finborough Road, Earls Court. He felt strangely drained of emotion and energy, as though it were all over now, the questions resolved, the violence surmounted. Yet he knew it wasn't.

He pushed open the front door and climbed, breathing unevenly, up the stairs. Telephone, brass flowerpot with decaying reeds, the first landing; the flowered carpet climbing still upward, dirty brass rails anchoring each step, musty smell of raindamp on nap, bathroom, second landing, the carpet still upward, vomit-green wall, paper patterning, porcelain basin in the corner spotted with tealeaves, the top landing.

Her door.

He waited to get his breath. There was a thin sliver of light under the door. He raised his hand to knock and watched it fall, slowly, light flickering on wrinkles, criss-cross of netlines. The sound seemed to roll muffled through the room on the other side.

Was she coming?

They had been at the Down Under Club since early in the evening: Johnston, George, Sonia, Don and himself. Richard had decided not to go, maintaining that he had had enough booze for one day down at the Stag and Antler that afternoon —— though he hadn't really, sipping his beer with his usual quiet abstraction.

'Why the hell not?' Johnston had demanded in his imperious manner, stalking through the flat in search of a pipe. 'You're letting the side down, sport. Besides, we haven't been to the Brown Chunder for months —— what about it?'

But Richard had been adamant; so, doused in duffle coats and thick corduroys, the three of them —— Johnston, barrelround and jaunty; Don, stooped and bespectacled; Graeme, thin and wiry-haired —— set out through the acrid night air for Fulham. Lamp-posts loomed up out of the smog which swaddled London town that night; buses ground past like illuminated battleships. They strode on untalking, scarves wrapped around their mouths, three hooded monks with but one thought between them: beer.

Half an hour later they were filing down the stairs into the cellar of the Down Under Club. It was low and dark, stifling with cigarette smoke and people and noise. Men and women were crammed three-deep around the makeshift wooden bar with its varnished boomerangs, Bondi Surf Bathers Life Saving Club pennants, mulga-wood ornaments, souvenirs of touring Test teams and empty bottles of Swan and Foster's lager; others were standing around in jostling, rowdy groups, clasping bottles of beer and shouting to make themselves heard above the

166

din. At the far end of the cellar, clustered at the foot of an upraised dais, another group was listening to Rolf Harris singing dinki-di Aussie songs. Nearby three naked aboriginal women with stick-like legs and bun-breasts chased each other across a huge mural of Australia; beneath the map two white women with fence-post legs and what might, upon closer inspection, have proved to be jumbuck udders waited for men to buy them a drink.

'God, what's this?' Johnston said, looking lecherously around, hair sticking up at the back, the beginnings of a ginger moustache sprouting from his upper lip.

'Walpurgis night in foggy Fulham,' said Don.

'What night?'

'Joyce —— the scene in the brothel. Remember?'

Graeme pushed his way over to the bar to order some beers. A harsh Australian voice grated in his ear: ' . . . so I takes this sheila home to Earls Court and whips a few grogs into her and then I puts the hard word on her. Do you think she'll come at it? No fear, not her. She reckons she's got her rags on, see . . . ' Christ, he thought, its a long time since I've been down here.

The bottles came out of a laundry vat of iced water, sopping wet and cold to the touch. He worked his way back to Johnston and Tom and they drank straight from them. The unfamiliar beer tasted almost as sweet as cider.

'By God, that's marvellous,' said Johnston. 'Good to get that into your black gut again, isn't it?'

Graeme nodded. It was too noisy to say much.

'When were you down here last?' Johnston asked him.

'Must be two or three months ago now. It was still summer. Goes quickly, doesn't it?'

'What does?'

'Time, baby.'

'And you're getting older,' said Don.

'And I'm getting older,' said Graeme. But not quite so quickly, apparently, as Johnston, who was running an instinctive hand over his thinning hair. Was his newly acquired moustache a scalp compensation?

Johnston, oblivious of Graeme's speculations on time, falling hair and the mortality of man, waved a Caesarian hand at the crowd in the cellar. 'You'd wonder why they ever come overseas —— they'd be happier in the swill on Flemington race day.'

'At least there's plenty of women.'

'And all of them promiscuous,' said Johnston. 'Fresh off the latest liner: poor lonely little Aussie girls looking for someone to buy them a drink. Go and befriend a few, Donald.'

'I came here to drink, not lech,' Don said primly.

'Ah, but what's wrong with a little stinkyfinger as well? By the way, did I ever tell you about the time I took this sheila to a dance at Goulburn? No? Well' —— Johnston took a long pull from his bottle ——'it was one of those marquee do's, you know, with lots of goodies laid out on trestle tables and sandwiches on limp lettuce and a bloody band with a violin and all that crap. Anyhow, I had this bird I was pretty keen on and before supper I took her out to the old ute and felt her up a bit, you know? Didn't knock her off, just had her wriggling around like a rattlesnake on the front seat . . . Anyhow, back we go inside, the band's packed up for a spell and everyone's hoeing into the supper. Only sandwiches left, so I pick one up, smell it, hmmn, fish; take two bites, Christ! egg and tomato!' Johnston chortled, waved his bottle deliriously. 'And if there's one thing I can't stand it's egg and tomato!'

Don broke in. 'Here's George and Sonia.'

As indeed it was, George edging his way through the thickening crowd, Sonia trundling along behind like a mod Venus de Milo in stretch pants, sneakers and pinkly distended sweater. Don departed to buy them all beers. The cellar was becoming gloomier and gloomier as cigarette smoke and human fug dimmed the chianti-flask lights. Empty bottles had begun to mount the cellar walls and rolled around the floor beneath the feet of the drinkers. People were still pushing in from the stairs and the din of voices was getting louder. Most of those in the cellar seemed to be Australians, the men in back-and-sides haircuts and baggy trousers, the women in slacks and sweaters or ski jackets; a few had kangaroo emblems sewn to the shoulders.

'Might as well have an Australian flag and be done with it,' Johnston said sourly. 'Or stick it up their arses, warbling Waltzing Matilda the while.' He regarded all Australian expatriates, except himself, with unflinching detestation. 'Give 'em another hundred years —— then Australia might be worth living in. Not before.'

'Where's Richard?' George asked.

'Refused to come,' said Graeme. 'Reckoned he'd had enough booze for one day.'

'Is he all right?'

'I think so.'

'He's taken his mother's death hard.'

'Understandably.'

'What's he going to do?'

'Go back,' said Johnston. 'Or so he says. Seems to have made up his mind. For my money it would be better if he stayed. Going back to Australia won't solve anything. And he's pretty depressed about the whole thing.'

They drank on steadily. After the fourth or fifth bottle Graeme began to feel the old warmth spreading out through his loins and drifting by some mysterious chemistry up to the front of his head. A group of drunken Aussies who looked as though they could be footballers started up a raucous sing-song; at the other end of the cellar Rolf Harris had put away his accordion and was telling jokes, the women clotted around him laughing madly at each sally. Other women were standing with both arms clasped around their boyfriends, thrust hard up against them, or talking shrilly to friends. The whole room, Graeme thought, was like a beer bottle which had been shaken too hard and was about to explode; it was hard to say whether it would end in a brawl or bed.

As it turned out it was a brawl. George and Sonia had wandered off to listen to Rolf Harris and Graeme was

169

standing with Don and Johnston over near the wall, where they had been gradually squeezed by the pressure of bodies, when suddenly he felt himself hit in the small of the back and lurched forward, spilling beer down the front of his shirt. He turned to find the man who had cannoned into him still trying to keep his balance, while one of the barmen in a white T-shirt and tattoed seaman's arms grabbed at his shirt.

'You dirty-mouthed Pom,' said the barman, bunching the man's shirt in his fist and dragging him up the wall. The man seemed drunk, his eyes wandering around the room. 'I told you twice we don't have that sorta language here in front of women.' The barman's face twisted into an ugly parody of fury. He freed one hand, leaned back and slapped the Englishman hard across the mouth. The face with its receding hair jerked sideways, and a bit of blood dribbled out of the corner of his mouth. The man put a hand to his lips, brought it away and looked at the blood on his knuckles. He stared at the barman, but made no move to fight.

'What'd he do?' said someone in the crowd.

The bouncer looked around. 'He's been swearing in front of women all night,' he said in a slightly higher and louder voice than was necessary. 'Dirtiest words I ever heard. I warned him, I did. I warned him.'

Johnston eased himself forward. The man in the suit and tie was still up against the wall, looking from side to side. 'Pretty damned funny thing to hit a man for,' Johnston said.

The bouncer looked around; Graeme wasn't sure if he'd heard the words or not. The crowd shuffled restlessly; was there a threat to it? The bouncer glared at the man, his yellow kiss-curl of hair falling forward over his tanned, Irish face. 'Beat it,' he ordered, and turned back for the bar.

Johnston swung around to Graeme and Don, his frame seemingly bigger than ever in the low cellar. 'Let's get out of here,' he said. 'It's too much like bloody Australia.'

170

Outside in the still smog-thick air George and Sonia decided to catch up on an Ingmar Bergman revival, and at the last moment Don joined them. Johnston and Graeme set out on the walk back to Chelsea. They strode along in silence, each thinking about the brawl and the Down Under Club.

'That shithead barman was just looking for an excuse for a fight,' Johnston said at last.

'Pretty weak excuse.'

'Ah, that's the dinkum Aussie for you. He probably meant it. No foul language in front of the girls; treat 'em like sluts, say what you like about 'em behind their backs —— but we must preserve their honour to their faces. A nation of fucking hypocrites. Who wants to go back?'

It took them half an hour to walk to Chelsea. They stopped at an off-licence which was still open and bought some bottles of bitter from the smiling, parchment-faced shopkeeper in a black waistcoat who had three strands of hair plastered stiffly across his bald pate like the prongs of a toasting fork. In Oakley Street, down towards the river, the smog seemed heavier and more acrid. Graeme put a handkerchief to his mouth as they stopped outside Gunn's Gully. Johnston fumbled for his key, then glanced up towards the top storey.

'That's funny, the light's not on,' he said. 'Richard doesn't usually turn in this early.'

'Might have gone out after all,' said Graeme.

They walked upstairs and let themselves into the flat. Johnston turned the light on. It was in a state of typical disarray: empty beer bottles cluttering the table and windowsills; ashtrays, saucers and typewriter ribbon cases overflowing with stinking cigarette butts; lopsided piles of papers and magazines stacked up against the wall; the two divans where George and Johnston were sleeping unmade from the night before, blankets pulled hurriedly over sheets to give the illusion of tidiness, dirty pillows doubling as cushions.

'This place stinks,' said Johnston, and opened one of the

main windows half an inch. 'Mustn't let the smog in.' He stood one of the quart bottles on the centre table. 'I'll stick the others in the fridge.'

The kitchen door, however, was locked. He tried the handle a couple of times. 'Did you lock this?'

'No,' said Graeme. He came over and tried the handle himself. It seemed to be locked from the inside. Johnston deposited his two bottles of beer on the floor outside the door, straightened up, then suddenly bent down again as though he was listening to some sound on the other side.

'Can you smell something?'

Graeme bent down, sniffed, and stood up frowning. 'What is it?'

'I don't know.'

Johnston turned and slapped on the door with his open hand. There was no reply. He slapped again, twice, and waited. There was still no reply.

'Richard!' he called out, mouth hard up against the door.

It wasn't, in fact, until Johnston called out, had actually given concrete form to what, until then, must have been a vague and unformulated thought swimming up from his subconscious, striving for the surface and coherent expression, that Graeme remembered with instantaneous clarity the conversation in the club. Richard?

He backed off and suddenly lashed out at the door with his foot, kicking high towards the lock. The door refused to budge. He kicked again, ineffectually. By this time, however, Johnston had caught his purpose and with an agility surprising in such a bulky man hurled his shoulder at the door. The wood panel splintered, but the lock held as firm as ever. They tried again, both together this time. Still the lock held, but Johnston's shoulder burst through the panel. He reached an arm through and, fumbling in the darkness, slipped the latch from the inside.

The door swung open and a repulsive smell of gas struck them full in the face. Johnston flicked on the light.

'Good Christ!'

He shambled across the room like a great bear, swung mightily. The heavy castiron frying pan smashed through the window, splintering glass and wood.

It was too late.

Richard, lying face down on the floor with his arms cradled around a pillow he had taken care to bring from the lounge room, towels and teacloths stuffed along the inside of the door and against the bottom edge of the now exploded window, the curtains drawn and drawers shut and the gas meter butterfly cock turned as far as it would go, stuffed with shillings, everything as it should be but for the open oven door and the terrible, stomach-retching odour of coal gas, was already, though not obviously, for Johnston bent down and put a head to his mouth, and then a mouth to his mouth, trying to force beery breath, oxygen and a will to live into lungs which had given up the will to do anything, trying at first with a frantic desperation so that his breathing was hoarse and unearthly in that gas-sick and coldly entombing room as wind blew in through the smashed window, and then more slowly as he realized the futility of it, and then not at all as he stood up and ordered Graeme, who had at least turned the stove off, to help move him into the lounge room, grabbing the arms while Graeme, unbelieving that he was actually doing it, seized the slim jean-clad legs and stumbled backwards under the weight and under the fierceness of Johnston's assault which was almost though not quite yet grief, Richard, whom they knew so well and yet now apparently not at all, with whom they had argued, fought, shouted, talked, drank, sworn, despaired of, maligned, cursed, envied, pitied, touched, lost touch with, laughed with, laughed at, loved, Richard of the pale hair and wool-edged fawn windjacket and silver buckled belt and airman's boots, of the slow self-satirizing smile and careless shrug and country-bred defensiveness and too vulnerable soul, Richard was already, and now more obviously, with his head flung brokenly back so that Johnston had to grab him by the hair as they lumbered him into the lounge room, Richard, already, and now quite obviously, without chance of change, recall or rescue, obviously now, oblivious to all, beyond anything, oblivious, was dead

In Gina's Brillobox terrace flat, Graeme Turner, four years older, four years colder and four years nearer death, flung himself over the side of the bed and was sick again and again and again on the floor.

In the bedroom it was dark, dark as the raindriven night outside, dark as sin, dark as adultery. Of course, the party should have warned her —— not about Graeme, but about Johnston. She turned uneasily away from him, remorse seeping through her already, not the discontent of unsatisfied desire because he was, of course, an accomplished sexual performer, as so he should be after —— how many years? thirty-five, thirty-six? —— of libertarian bachelorhood, but the first wounds of self-driven and self-flagellating remorse, her insatiable hunger for self-examination already forcing her to ask herself why tonight, of all nights, she had chosen at last to betray Graeme, whether he deserved it or not and whether he was, in fact, at that moment betraying her with Gina . . . .

Gina! Who was a bitch if ever there was one, a twenty-one-carat fully-guaranteed right-down-to-the-bone one hundred per cent bitch, with her fat and flabby body jammed into too-tight black jersey dresses —— at least she had more sense than to try and wear jeans —— and her too, too obvious suggestions and suggestiveness, come-ons and comeuppances, the quickly lowered lids, the knife-edge intellect used first to score off men and then, apologetically and slyly, to suggest that she wounded them only because they *interested* her, they had something to them, they had *ideas*, no cabbages they, tied down with backlawn wives and barbecue responsibilities and swings on the frangipanni, but rather original and therefore rather frightfully attractive *intellectuals*, when all she was really interested in was the size of the bulge behind the zip fastener; Left and Right were not political terms to Gina but indications of which way, as the tailors so gallantly put it, men dressed. Gina! Gina whose bulging breast and ample hock, uncorseted, gave promise of pneumatic bliss — how had Graeme described her once? yes, as a typical Norman Lindsay nude, with tits like saucepan lids and bum like a Clydesdale horse, Gina of the spirits, though she hadn't realized at the time that Graeme probably knew already from firsthand experience what Gina uncorseted looked like — what a foul and filthy dissembler she had married! Well, Graeme could have a long cool on-the-sofa think before he came near her again, he would probably have to be scrubbed for a week to make sure he didn't pass on VD to her, or to the children for that matter.

Graeme, how could you?

As for Johnston — well, that was but a moment of pique, it didn't mean anything, had no significance, and besides it served Graeme right if she did, though it was rather hard to convince herself of that, lying there with the accusing and unforgiving dark of their marriage bed around her, what would she do with the sheets? because they were sure to be wet still unless Graeme came home with the cock, his cock no doubt powdered Henrymillerwise from Ginabusage, Heavens she would have to change the sheets, which would mean lumping that heavyweight Johnston off the bed, what if he refused? well then leave him there, let him snore on until Graeme came home: there you are, Graeme, your friend and my lover, Humphrey Stearns Johnston, in all his glory, with a mole on his bum and ginger moustache to match his pubic hair, your mate, my mate, the People's Friend, Everybody's Alley, Back-to-Tors, Backdoors and Upyours Johnston — wadderyergonna do, get your rifle and shoot him? here, I'll load it, you just pull the trigger and fire, about fourth bump down on the backbone I'd say, just there, see, where I bit him in my ecstasy, on his back? well, Johnston knows some mighty cute positions, I can tell you; file my petition? why, I can't even touch it with a powderpuff . . . .

But it wasn't so funny, really, not funny at all. Oh God, Graeme, where are you

She got up from the armchair and walked across to the record player, woken from her reverie by the sound of Johnston flushing the toilet at the end of the corridor upstairs, put a record on with automatic hand; *that*, no doubt, was how it would have been had she accepted Johnston's only too obvious invitation to retaliate in kind against her husband's infidelity; there was a moment, perhaps, when she might have weakened, might have been prompted by the sudden sense of shock she had experienced (which no doubt Johnston had calculated to a nicety) when he first told her about Graeme and Gina to have, out of sheer spite and distaste, taken Johnston up; when she said:

'You're not serious?'

'Yes.'

'With *Gina*?'

'I can't say I like his taste in women either; but then he's not my husband.'

'What do you mean by that?'

'I've always envied Graeme marrying you, girl; it's the one sensible thing the lad's done in his whole life. But since then his women have deteriorated rather. He's not so fastidious now.'

'Women?'

'Surely you realized that?' said Johnston, advancing a little closer, but still as bluff and hale-hearty and carefully uncompromised, though eagerly compromising, as ever. 'You can't be so stupid as to think he's been faithful to you all these years? He's had three or four women since I've been back, for a start.'

'I don't believe you' —— though, scarifyingly, in her heart, she did.

'Graeme doesn't deserve you, Paula.' Johnston reached out a hand and ran it delicately across her throat and down over her plump breast till it came to rest on her hip; she was surprised at how quickly her senses responded, the nervous tingle of anticipation which she thought she had left behind with her girlhood. 'He's a shit. Why don't you do something about it?'

Which was where Johnston, though he didn't know it, made his mistake; for the phrase suddenly reminded her of what, in a fit of pique, she had scrawled across the steamy bathroom mirror earlier in the evening, and that, by some curious reflex of her memory, brought back to her momentarily Rosinante refusing to start (or had Graeme just *pretended* it wouldn't start, the bugger, she had never thought of that before, she would ask him tonight) and her arms around him lazily on that sleepy morning; and the moment passed, the uncertain scales tilting the other way, the anger draining out of her and replaced by a curious and lonely sense of loss; so that without saying a word she simply brushed Johnston's questioning hand from her hip and walked distractedly away and looked out through the mosquito-blinded ceiling-to-floor window through bars of trees and sickle-shapes of gumleaves visible even in this storm-and-rain-blown night down past swollen thunder-scapes of air to where, invisible, the clay-yellow creek caught fern-cool raindrops from the branching overhangs and thick bottlebrush where in summer the children played, or rather would play when the baby was old enough to join James, and found herself cooled and reassured somehow by this, this so familiar and uncommunicative hillscape hung about with the ambience of their lives, and had thought instead or had half-thought, the question hardly formulating itself but the syllables which had been at the back of her mind for some time now, for how many days or weeks or even years she would not like to say but for quite some time now, at last jiggling themselves into proper order: what is happening to us?

So the moment had passed, or she assumed it had; realizing now it was the Modern Jazz Quartet, something melancholy and almost nostalgic, was it 'Odds Against

Tomorrow'? which she put on the record player, the gentle and insistent piano arpeggios reminding her of *Moderato Cantabile* as Johnston, no Belmondo, descended the stairs and effected the sort of re-entry Bob McTavish or, perhaps, Cary Grant might have been proud of. She was needled by his composure and, flumping down in the chair, said:

'Tell me, Johnston, did you think telling me about Graeme would make me sleep with you?'

Johnston smiled expansively, reached for his flagon of hock. 'Anything's worth a try —— I thought it might have worked.' He looked unsuccessfully around the room. 'Glass?'

'Get it yourself ... in the kitchen,' she said; and immediately regretted sounding so petulant. 'Oh, and you can bring my glass of wine from the table, if you wouldn't mind.'

Johnston came back with her glass, handed it to her gallantly and poured her some hock. 'Why —— did you object?'

'Yes,' she said. 'Do you always go around trying to seduce your friends' wives?'

'I wouldn't have quite called it seduction —— I didn't get very far, did I?'

'That's not the point.'

'Friends' wives, anybody's wife —— it's not my fault if they're stupid enough to get married. Marriage is just a priest-inspired confidence trick; women are women, whether they're married or not. It takes two to copulate; nobody *has* to sleep with me. If a woman can resist anything but temptation she should have been Oscar Wilde. I'm not to blame for the neuroses of other men's wives.'

'That's an easy let-out for you.'

'It's not just a let-out —— I've believed it all my life. That's why I've never got married. I'd only be unfaithful to my principles if I did.'

'But Graeme——'

'Graeme's a nice bloke, I shouldn't have called him a shit. But he does some stupid things sometimes, and one of them is racing off other women when he should be at home sleeping with his wife.'

Paula sipped her wine, feeling uncomfortably that Johnston was getting the better of the argument when right was clearly on her side.

'Don't tell me you came all the way out here just out of sympathy for me.'

'That,' said Johnston, his eyes crinkling again and his smile splitting across his face, 'would be asking too much. But I felt like talking to you, whether I succeeded in lugging you off to bed or not. Well I didn't so let's forget it.' He got up. 'Here, have another wine.'

But she would not be mollified so easily, and held her glass away. So Johnston shrugged, and walked around the room inspecting the paintings, studying each one in almost overcareful detail, flagon clenched by the neck in one meaty hand and bulky shoulders stretching his sports coat tight —— she knew the sight so well, from years and years back in London when he had not been quite so, not quite so *moulded*, so absolutely certain of the correctness of his ways and might have allowed a wayward fringe of doubt to creep into his thinking —— or was it just the music making her sentimental? —— whereas now he had become, virtually, what he had always pretended to be, the hard wisecracking shell which had been adopted to protect what must have been, well back in Johnston's history, right back in his schooldays perhaps, a too exposed and too easily lacerated nakedness of response (he had probably been an intellectual, a misfit, a 'swot' even then), become not just a shell any longer but the person, just as one of those coral reef sea-creatures whose names she had forgotten gave their lives over to creating the superstructure which, fossilized and preserved in saltbrine, they died to become.

But perhaps Johnston was right about marriage. Though she had been defending it to him earlier, she now found herself wondering why. Was there anything, except myth and social convention, to sustain the idea that everyone needed a partner in life? Why should they? Surely independence, utter individuality, was the natural state, and perhaps the best one; a woman's need of other people might best be satisfied by a series of affairs, not just random tomcat things but deeply involving, deeply enriching affairs of the sort —— well, of the sort Francoise Sagan's women seemed to have. If it could work in France it could surely work in Alf-land too —— smiling inwardly, thinking: we are all influenced by each other, we are all involved in each other at some level, I have even begun thinking in Johnston's phrases. Marriage? Everything she had seen of it had merely demonstrated that men and women were not destined to live out their lives with each other, that every woman needed more than one man to satisfy her needs and, she presumed, every man needed more than one woman. Which was why Graeme was out with some other woman, with Gina of all people, at this moment, right now, and, if Johnston was to be believed, had been unfaithful to her again and again since they had married.

Or —— she clutched at the hope quickly, looking up, jerked from her thoughts to find the music stopped, the record player clicking and Johnston, his Sothebys calculation of the paintings' worth completed, apparently immersed in the New Statesman once more —— was he lying to her?

'Johnston,' she said. 'Are you lying to me?'

'No,' said Johnston instantly —— had he been pretending to read? —— 'why should I?'

'What about the other times?'

'I'm not sure about those; I didn't follow him into the bedchamber' —— shrugging —— 'but I know he left the Castle tonight with Gina.'

'Are you sure?'

'Of course I'm sure, I was there drinking with him.'

At least Graeme had not lied about that. 'Maybe he was just taking her home.'

'Maybe.'

'Why isn't he here now, then?'

'Are you asking me?'

'Yes, I am.'

'Well, I'd say it was because it wasn't maybe.' Johnston closed the New Statesman, threw it on the table and jumped to his feet.

'Look, enough of this Graham Greene talk,' he said, walking over towards her chair. 'It's making everything too complicated. Are you going to sleep with me or not?'

Sleep with him? Well, perhaps that was the way adultery should be committed after all, she thought. Not in passion, or some raging sexual desire, or accidentally, against one's will almost at some drunken party or on some promiscuously crowded ski holiday, a Thredbo fling, but quite coldly and calculatingly, as part of a pattern of freedom which ranged beyond marriage because that obviously was how Graeme felt, as confirmation of woman's equality and the unfairness of the marriage relationship —— unfairness? did she say unfairness? she meant, she had meant something like imperfection . . . .

But her mind had not lied, and she felt all the grievances of the day, the endless injustices and disappointments and the sheer debilitating boring unending imprisoning suffocating routine of housewifeliness and motherhood which she had tolerated all day, had suffered and borne simply for Graeme's sake, Graeme who was now whatever it was Johnston had said he was doing to Gina, churn through her being, a righteous sense of injustice laced with self-pity (the unfairness of it!) spurring her to act, do something, make one definitive and uncompromising act of renunciation; so that when Johnston, cautiously good-humoured and playful still, which would allow him to retreat with pride, independence and self-regard intact should he be rebuffed, but with a fine edge of seriousness lurking behind it, reached out and in that authoritative, possessive way of his lay a hand backed with fine, ever so fine wisps, moths' antennae, of red hair upon her neck, bending down, kissed her, as, of course, he had done so many companionly times before, he found, somewhat to his surprise after his earlier rebuff, but not to his unpreparedness, and certainly not to the detriment of his ability to take advantage of the situation, that

It was at that instant, she knew, on that smog-dark night in Earls Court, Graeme standing helpless on the carpet with his duffle jacket black with rain, it was at that instant she lost the island. Or perhaps, really, she had lost it earlier on that other day when Richard and she, the pine needles and those damned cicadas, perhaps that was when she lost that precious sense of certainty, of a world comprehended and stabilized, which she had managed to retain intact and which had sustained her throughout her childhood, despite the terrible, endless rows between her mother and father, the shouting and high-pitched, monotonous voices behind closed doors —— despite all that (or perhaps even because of it, for it had forced her to create an island of sanity where everything was insulated against the tides and currents of the emotional stormworld which surrounded her) she had managed to keep intact some belief in a gyroscopic world which never toppled over completely, even after her parents' divorce, in which her mother had gained custody of her because it was Percy, the fool, who had been carrying on with the pert, middle-aged, short-haired and lacquered-nailed personal secretary of the firm's Managing Director, which was hardly any recommendation for the custody of a thin, intense and obviously rather too brooding eleven-year-old girl, because if anything the tension decreased once her mother and father separated, the rows were over, the situation resolved at last —— no matter how unsatisfactorily. She was protected by a child's innocence, enveloped in an unfractured and unfracturable calm as in a transparent plastic bag until the fracture actually occurred.

Which it had, that day at the island.

For she had, unconsciously, banked so much on that moment. Whereas her friends lost their virginity with nonchalance, or by accident, being fuller of brandy-lime-and-sodas than they has realized and faced with a more determined GPS ruck-forward than they had bargained for, or, like Buzzy, with grim determination in the back seat of a car, she had held onto hers, safeguarded it, had even rebuffed Jonathan Scott-Thompson because this was to have been a crucial and symbolic act of freedom, a deliberate vouchsafing of herself, a transference of this, this unity, this individual, this Paula, from family to some other being whose love would protect and support her, sustain her, provide her with the sort of emotional underpinning she needed. And the transfer was to be painless, free from pressure, a voluntary step from the innocence of childhood into the safety of adulthood. For, whoever she lost her virginity to, she knew she would love.

Instead of which she had felt nothing, absolutely nothing, no, nothing, absolutely nothing. She had stepped from innocence into the void . . . .

That night, as they lay in their guilty Greek bed, the night heat outside the whitewashed stone-and-plaster-daub house as oppressive as it had been during the day, the omnipresent threat of the sea drifting in from beyond the breakwater, she tried to safeguard herself still and said:

'Richard, I know you won't like this —— but I don't want you to sleep with me again.'

Which had really stopped him short. He turned towards her, tilting her chin so he could look at her properly.

'Why not?'

'Because for me it's wrong. I mean, not wrong; but I don't want to. I suppose I've always wanted to be a virgin for my husband; it's the least I can give him. Now I won't be, but at least I needn't be —— used. I wouldn't like him to be second best.'

'Doesn't sleeping with me mean anything to you?' he said.

184

'Of course it does, Richard. And I wanted to today, I really did. I told you so. But it's wrong, I just know it is. You're not my husband.'

'Is that a proposal?'

'No.'

'Okay.'

'That's the trouble with you,' she said. 'You agree with me, you say you agree with me, and you don't mean a word of it. You said at the start of this trip you wouldn't try to make me sleep with you. Well, I'm not blaming you, but it's happened, hasn't it? And I don't want it to happen again. I mean it, Richard, I don't want it to.'

'Have it your own way.'

There was an air of petulance to his voice which was justified, perhaps, but at that moment, her cheeks raw with beard rash, feeling she had been through the sort of day which, in that particular version, no woman deserved to experience and which she never wished to experience again, it angered her. She jerked her face away.

'I'm sorry,' he said immediately. 'How do you feel?'

'Awful. I'm frightfully sore. You're too big.'

He laughed, and she had to smile at him. It was as though the tension which had existed between them, unstated, all afternoon, ever since that cicada-pierced moment in the pines, had been broken at last.

'It always hurts the first time,' he said.

'What do you mean, the first time? How many damned virgins have you done this to?'

'What do you want to know for?'

'I just want to know. Don't lie to me, Richard. It doesn't make any difference.'

'Then there's no need to tell you.'

'Yes there is. I want to know.'

'Guess.'

'No.'

'Four.'

'I'm the fourth?'

'No, you're the fifth.'

185

She regarded him quizzically for a few seconds, then laughed quietly. 'You bastard,' she said.

Still, she had kept to her resolve, for the journey back to London at least, which had not improved relations between them; but Richard had been tolerably understanding, and had not tried to dissuade her from her determination too often, though there were times, God knows, when it was hard enough to keep it —— was it merely some sort of crazy puritanism which allowed her to make love with Richard in every way short of actually sleeping with him, or was there some real and significant distinction between love play and (though she hated the word) copulation? Whatever the reason, she had held out until London, and then through a sort of mutual cooling-off period, because both of them felt they had been acting under an artificial intensity of pressure during the Greek journey, thrown together day and night whether they wished it or not, depending upon each other as a protection against loneliness and even for mere physical safety —— as that night on the winding, tortuous road which clung to the side of the rock-strewn mountains between Athens and Delphi, crawling along in Rosinante for mile after mile, hour after hour without ever sighting another car or another person, or indeed any sign of human existence except, if they were that, the cave-like hovels which Greek goatherds had built from raw rock and earth into the mountainside, gloomy caverns of incest and murder which were hardly fit for animals let alone men, where no Pan pipes played but where, no doubt, primitive beings played out a bizarre parody of the hates, loves and savageries of the old Gods; was that, perhaps, where the old myths started, in those sky-high hovels cowering from the brute sun where men, in darkness, dreamt and spun tales about the passions which disfigured their own half-animal lives? They had stopped at last about an hour before midnight, pulling off the side of the road onto a small, stony lay-by so other cars could pass; and though, earlier, they had heard the howling of the wild dogs which they had been told at the Athens youth hostel lived in the high mountains around Delphi they sounded well away in the distance and, spreading their sleeping bags on the ground beside the car, they had tried to sleep.

And had, for perhaps an hour, or even less. When suddenly, disturbed by a rushing and tumbling through the low underbrush, she had woken in time to see a short, mongrel-looking dog burst into the clearing, followed by another, and another, with the sound of others coming fast through the brush like the noise of a waterfall or a current of wind.

Richard saw them too. He picked up the jackhandle beside his sleeping bag and swung wildly at one dog which had cantered at full speed into the clearing and, probably without intending to, had skidded to within an arm's length of them. He missed, and the other dogs slunk back; but by now there were half a dozen of them, snarling and prowling around the edge of the layby like wolves circling a sandy arena, swinging their heads and watching the figures backing off towards the car. Richard paused long enough to throw the sleeping bags into the back seat and then ran around to the driver's side, jumping into the seat and yelling, 'wind up the windows', the jackhandle still in his fist as he yanked at the starter. Rosinante, as ever, was slow to fire, and before they could move the dogs had surrounded the car, yelping and snarling and jumping up at the windows, sure as cowards that their quarry was defenceless; she had a quick, nightmare glimpse of saliva-wet teeth, the cruel short-eared faces, bodies blurring past the window pane, and then Rosinante jerked and kangarooed off into the night, the yelping and howling soon left behind.

It was not that, however, but what happened later which really frightened her; for as Richard explained, perhaps a trifle too calmly, as they drove on through the night, Rosinante's weak headlights swinging from rock face to rock face in the gloom ahead of them as they followed the interminably winding road, it was hardly likely that the dogs would attack anyone who was actually on his feet confronting them, though it might be different if they found a solitary sleeper on the ground; though even then, surely, the animals' inbred fear of man would make them hesitate. They had intended to keep on driving until they reached Delphi. But Richard, who had already been at the wheel for several hours, Rosinante's top autobahn speed being about 30 mph and her average on Greek roads rather closer to 5 mph, began going to sleep at the wheel after a while, waking with a start as they approached a corner and Paula shouted at him. So they stopped again, driving right off the road till they were hidden by bushes; but stayed in the car this time, the back seat piled with luggage (Rosinante lacking anything as grandiose as a boot) and they both trying to sleep in the front, propping themselves against the inside stanchions.

Richard was soon asleep, exhausted; but Paula, remembering the dogs, found it impossible to, try as she might with her head resting against the back of the seat. After perhaps half an hour she heard another car winding its way along the road higher up the mountain, watching its headlights glancing off rocks and low brush as it drew closer. Then the lights went out and the sound of the motor, too, vanished into the still Greek night. The driver, she decided, must have pulled off into the underbrush on the side of the road, and composed herself for sleep again. She dozed fitfully. But was woken, abruptly, by an unearthly screaming carrying across the still air, a high, ghastly, inhuman scream which went on and on and on like an animal in pain, a scream of such terrible and tortured intensity that Richard, too, woke with a jerk and they stared at each other, listening as the screaming went on and on with the same pitiful, unbearable insistence. It ended as abruptly as it had started; and a little later headlights swept down the road again, the sound of an engine split the night, and within a minute or two a car rushed past where they parked next to but invisible from the road, snarling off to Delphi.

Neither could sleep then; and as soon as the first light began to drift across from the peaks which stretched off to right and left of them Richard started the car again. To their surprise they found they were only a few miles from Delphi. They drove in along the narrow, house-enclosed main street, souvenirs and knitted Greek bags hanging from the doors of the whitewashed houses, old women in black dresses with wrinkled parchment faces sitting on the stone doorsteps, and searched out the youth hostel, where a smiling Greek hostel-controller with a small black moustache and an almost bald head showed them to clean, welcoming though separate bunks and assured them, with a slightly patronizing but still polite air for the cowardly Anglos, that the so-called wild dogs which lived in the mountains behind Delphi and which were, anyhow, but village dogs which had run off into the bush and lived on dead goats and each other, had never been known to attack a man yet. It wasn't until three days later, back in Athens, that they discovered from a newspaper that the Greek police were searching for a motorist who had picked up a hitch-hiker, a young English boy of seventeen, on the road to Delphi and had sawn his head off with a penknife while the boy was still alive, leaving his mutilated body in the dusty olive-green undergrowth only a few miles on the Athens side of the City of the Oracle, where the road began to sweep down from the mountains and a car's headlights could be seen for miles.

Greece. Its Mediterranean cruelty seemed a reflection of their own unease.

But then, after they returned to London, and after a fortnight of deliberately avoiding each other, everything changed between herself and Richard. Whereas in Europe they had been thrust together without choice, forced into a close emotional conjunction no matter what tensions and currents were running between them, and therefore felt obliged to strive to be free, now it was different; now, voluntarily, they sought each other out. The grey city by the Thames gave them a closeness they had not felt even on the road to Dephi. In a way the Greek trip had been like one of Heracles' tasks, an ordeal of character —— and they had survived.

Which was why, on that cold and winter-doomed night months later, when Greece seemed aeons away, part of some pre-transubstantiative existence, and Richard lived, comfortably, but a few blocks away; which was why, on that cold and winter-doomed night, wearing her tatty old dressing gown and her hair all over the place, she had answered to that urgent rap on the door, wondering who on earth it could be dropping in at that late hour unless it were Sonia angry and swearing from a late-night argument with George, or just possibly Richard himself, drunk and depressed, and had found instead Graeme.

Graeme! Graeme black with rain and death and not even enough sense to say what he had to say slowly

which was why, on that cold and winter-doomed night, she realized she had lost then and forever, if she had not lost it before with Richard on that sun-crazed afternoon, had certainly lost then, on that smoking, smog-stupid midnight in another country, the island.

that her mouth opened and for the first time that evening she allowed Johnston's tongue to explore her

Driving home, with Gina left behind him like a bad taste in the mouth, the white Mazda coupé cruising past the wharves with the wide-rim radials making a steady thump-thump-thump on the uneven bitumen road and the windscreen wipers hissing through synchronized arcs to clear the light rain which had begun falling over Sydney town, over the grey white-numbered Woolloomooloo wharves and Observatory Hill where weather bureau boffins plotted thunderstorms in the squat convict-built tower and Pinchgut awash in a sea of rainspotted topsoil like some landlocked submarine and the tops of brutalist city skyscrapers where washing lines, geraniums in sandboxes, pot plants and rusty kiddies' trikes defied the architects' penchant for formalism, rain across Broadway and the concentric neon rings atop the Car Sales Emporium and Grace Brothers' mock-Turkish spires and the University with its larger mock-Gothic ones, rain falling across Leichhardt and Balmain and Johnston Street, Taverners Hill and Burwood and Beecroft, slicing through the TV towers at Gore Hill and blotting out the traffic beacons at French's Forest as, heavier now, it swept on up towards Como, Mount Ku-ring-gai and Berowra Waters, out over that desolate Hawkesbury sandstone country where bare crumbling rock shrugged the water from its back and gave struggling sustenance to those weird, contorted, soil-stunted scrubs and grotesque gums which disfigured Arthur Boyd's nightmare imagination, rain over dirty old Sydney, convict Sydney, Sydney whose wooden

three-masters and rotting cargoes and harbourfront Bond
Stores traced in grey etchings by Rum Corps draughtsmen
still caught at the guilty heart of this vaster city with its
proliferating suburbs sweeping out to the west, old Sydney
laid on its back like a prostitute burdened by this oyster
sky and abused by these scuds of rain which blew sudden
gusts of darkness across the tiers of lights which, ahead,
signalled the entrance to the expressway.

I am now, he thought, I am now making a righthand
turn in my little white coupé which I have earned by the
expenditure of God knows what precious reservoir of
imagination and talent and I am going home. I am Marcello
Mastroianni and I am going home to Mastroianni's wife
Anouk Aimée with the camera picking out the cats' eyes
set into the central concrete strip of the expressway, grey
blur of the safety rail, the Mazda picking up speed in third
and the lights whipping past on either side, the engine
ticking over like an electric clock and the thump-thump of
the radials changed to a steady hiss as they knifed over the
rain-drenched bitumen. Droplets of rain quivered and
shook outside the range of his wipers, then precipitated
themselves downwards and were swept aside like flies to
the gods; I have entered, he thought, that nirvana which
the automobile has created for everyman, that sense of
absolute power and absolute security which maketh the
hero, I am the hero, I am modern man, I am hurrying to
whatever destination this moment or this scenario is
leading me but whatever the consequence or if Hume is
right whatever the subsequence this instant remains
inviolate, this is, is, is.

He reached down, fingered the 2UW button on his car
radio:

'I'd love to turn —— you —— on —— ' one of the good
old oldies, LEGALIZE CANNABIS, cannabis? I thought
that was a form of sexual intercourse, baby, like fellatio.
Fellatio? The music chopped out violently as the car swept
into the tunnel beneath the Domain, the rain suddenly
gone, the cars, his own and the others, caught in a white

stasis of illumination, soundless and almost motionless, and then slam, out into the darkness again, the rain the quivering droplets

who was it, was it Johnston? of course, it was Johnston who most firmly and obstinately believed in the inviolate independence of each instant and who, moreover, tried to live up to it despite the havoc it caused his friends lovers brothers others just as he too had once tried to live out his metaphysics with Paula before they were married and had merely succeeded in almost sundering each from the other Christ! Years later, remorse forced his foot down on the accelerator and the car drifted a little as it wound through the tunnel and onto the bridge, the tolls lined up like sentry boxes designed in Austerican Baroque and lit up like ship's beacons, through the tollgate zz-ch-li-i-ing as the automatic counter scraped the underside and then cutting across lanes to the fast chute on the right and over the great humpbacked whale of the bridge itself, girders now as well as lights swinging up towards the car windscreen and then flipping over the top like horses' hooves over a ground level camera. It was a wonder their affair had not broken up altogether after that.

What had rescued it?

'The BRIGHTER 2UW, eleven-ten on your trannie, the beat sound that's right on the MINUTE, you can't BEAT the new UW . . . '

Well, he had never stopped to work it out. Perhaps he should have, instead of working by instinct, as always, letting things take their own course, blow over, allow one minute to follow the next until they added up to hours, days, weeks and life by then had resumed normality. Were there crossroads in one's life, he wondered? Were there really crucial moments of decision, utterly irredeemable crises where a move one way or another affected what happened to you for the rest of your life, moulded it in shape A instead of B, made the other course forever foreign and out of reach?

He doubted it. That was too close to Johnston's

minute-by-minute thing, the separation of each instant from the other, so that it was possible for some to be gratuitously loaded with huge burdens of significance and others to have none whatsoever. Whereas in reality each moment evolved imperceptibly into the next, Zeno's arrow was never motionless but always moving, oneself, one's life, was always moving, moving forward, flowing inexorably from one instant to the next, each instant *becoming* the next so that it was impossible to separate them; one's life was an arrow, an arrow in flight. Which meant that no single instant determined it, no single event broke the chain of causation; everything we did had a million causes, was inextricably entwined with what we had been and what we were about to be, and decisions evolved out of a million past occurrences, and so perhaps there were no decisions really but only happenings.

Happenings? Maybe the Flower People were right after all. And Johnston. What counted was the inviolate instant.

But that could not be. It was too final, for a start; and too simple. Relationships persisted, traditions burgeoned and grew strong, each event was part of the Heraclitan stream. History was not composed of crucial instants but immense social movements and forces, moving as irresistibly as the lava stream; each individual's life was as broadly determined, each instant but part of the chain. What seemed to be crucial instants were but climaxes to past series of instants; there were no crossroads, only fulfilments.

Of course, it was a safe philosophy. It kept our metaphysics warm. It guarded one against climactic errors, and climactic decisions. Determinism? Well, perhaps it was; *there's a dumb deluge driven across night's chasms, hard in upon us, unresisted, beating our lives to patterns imposed past all defeating by our poor wills; we are storm-carried storm-shed, battered by streaming multitudes* . . . Rain over the world, even as the rain slashed across the windscreen of his car now and drove dumb deluges down the curved glass, arc glass, rainbow glass, another of God's promises broken. God? God is alive and well in Mexico City. But you see, even if your life were determined, it made no difference because you still had to act as if it weren't, you still had to live, move, act, decide, like you couldn't just sit around and wait to be *determined*, man. So it was not determinism but the instant-by-instant existentialism which Johnston propounded and the push lived by which distorted man's vision like God's untrustworthy arc and covenant because life was motion, the arrow, the arrow, the arrow in flight, the arrow moving as this car was moving, swinging left inside another with rainblurred indicator flashing, everything was dynamic, movement, our lives, people, relationships everything, everything moving, no certainty, only movement, a closing and opening of distances, beings in tension.

Oh Christ Paula.

He had a sudden memory of her as he had first seen her: cool and self-assured at one of the parties which, mysteriously, seemed to materialize from nothing at Oakley Street. She had come into the kitchen from dancing in the other room, her hair disarrayed, a glass of whisky in one hand, and he remembered being surprised at how low-keyed and unimpressive, almost, she was, when he had expected her to conform to the brittle intensity of Richard's other women; instead of which she had smiled her uninvolved, rather diffident smile and talked briefly to him about music while he wondered just what sort of a woman she was and what lay behind that clear oval face free from make-up and the cool brown eyes with which she met him, Richard, as usual, had told him her name and little else. What's in a name?

What indeed? Innocence? Strength?

It was a blend of both, he thought, a calm acceptance of her own being and a quite instinctive readiness to pare away complexity and reduce living to essentials which was Paula's particular gift to the world. It had taken him a long time to realize it; at first he had been inclined to dismiss her as naive, and certainly while she had been going out with Richard he had not bothered to get to know her any better. It was only after Richard's death, when she had been flung into their lives much more deeply than she had ever been while Richard was alive, that he had found himself moving imperceptibly closer to her, had found himself caught up in that peculiar calm ambience which Paula Sinclair seemed to distill and had begun to understand how precious and unique her simplicity was. It had been a slow process, something which had begun as friendship or, more truthfully, out of mere sympathy for Paula after what had happened with Richard and had slowly developed into something else. He had fought against it somewhat; not against sleeping with her, which he had been determined to do from the very start, Paula having a certain sexual consciousness about her which, admixed with the selfcontainment with which she seemed to approach life, acted as a challenge to most men, and certainly to himself, so that he had finally had to fake Rosinante's not starting late one night at Oakley Street to persuade her to sleep in the same bed with him, and even then she had held out —— for a while. But, as reluctant as ever to commit himself too deeply to anything or anyone or to face up to any sort of decision, he had tried for some time to keep their relationship at a purely sexual level, even on that holiday in Wales —— though it was there, really, that he first realized how involved he had become in her; and besides, he had been suspicious of Paula's upper-class manners and morality, that pervasive Killara-and-PLC background which could still annoy him and laced her dislike of the push, and that primness which had consigned them to just about an anti-sex life on the P & O liner which brought them back to Australia, a voyage which he had fondly imagined beforehand would be some sort of extended experiment in sexuality (despite the separate cabins) and which, to his astonishment, Paula had decided was a suitable occasion for a calm rethinking of everything between them, despite an occasional piece of revanchism in the D-deck shower room with the door

196

locked, steam whirling and clouding around their water-drenched bodies and the shower turned on full blast to drown the sound of their crude and soapsudsy lovemaking. It was not really until they had both come back to Australia, and he had managed to persuade Paula (despite her fear of that blue-haired mongrel heeler of a mother whose husband, no wonder, had long since divorced her) to live with him that they had begun to learn to love each other.

Though, in a way, it all went back to Wales. When he and Paula descended to the smoke-grimed kitchen that morning a new fall of snow lay across the countryside, broken only by the cat's tracks meandering across the slope and, on the road winding up the mountainside, the twin knuckleduster imprints left by the chains on the farmers' lorries. Later they climbed up the road towards Cnicht, noticing where the longtailed Welsh sheep had huddled against the walls for shelter at night: eight or ten oval shapes in the snow, each oval littered with sheep droppings. Four white snowgeese flew overhead in an imperfect arrowhead as they climbed, one leader, two on his left flank, one on his right; when they wheeled, honking, towards the frozen lake which lay in the valley below another goose took the lead, the others reforming themselves into an arrowhead. On that cold and frozen day, the snow crunching beneath their boots, the fields unmarked but for the cat's tracks and, beneath the cottage, the lines left like ski trails by Evan Jones and his dog, fine white clouds drifting northwards across the mountain range like snow blowing from the high peaks, on that day, with a week already spent together in that decrepit crofter's cottage, seeking out each other's bodies beneath piles of blankets in that embarrassingly noisy bedstead which reflected faithfully, with an awe-inspiring repertoire of creaks, groans, rasps, screeches, sighs and detonations every movement they made upon it, and another week to go yet before the gut-wrenching return to London, Chelsea, work, the daily tube, apartness, on that day he had been sure that here, at last, with Paula, he had stumbled across what, he supposed, years of aimless drifting from continent to continent and person to person and relationship to relationship had, unknowingly, been leading to.

And so they had married.

Which had surprised a lot of people. Like George, who still believed that living together was the correct state and that marriage was but a flawed and bourgeois institution, which of course gave him a certain immunity against guilt for his extramarital adventures. But George, he thought — he decided it there and then, fingering the radio button, one stringbacked glove on the wheel, ole reliable 2UW cutting in with a sudden blast of frantic rhythm-and-blues

ya gotta do right, baby
ya gotta do right
ya gotta move right, baby
ya gotta move right

George, he decided, was wrong. A man and a woman living together had to move somewhere *ya gotta move right baby* either towards marriage, which institutionalized their relationship, or towards separation, which destroyed it. It had to move somewhere. Though marriage, of course, was fluid too, despite the forms it had evolved for perpetuating itself —— forms which he had in fact somewhat damaged that night and which made him force the Mazda coupé a little faster than usual through Artarmon Chatswood Lindfield Killara the commuter stations of the Cross. Which was why he was wrong ever to take Paula's love for granted, to assume that it at least was free from the world's flux, a constant; to think that no matter what came between them and what crises they endured, what brought their flesh together and what ripped them apart, always the arrow's momentum would carry them on. Marriages were not destroyed by instants; thus, somehow, he had come to assume the continuity of her love, which had been and therefore, moving through the past and the present into the future, would be. But that was absurd.

For what if Paula, without warning, should simply stop loving him? Through no fault of her own, perhaps, nor his, nor for any reason, even unwillingly, but nevertheless should irrevocably and quite finally discover she did not love him? For love, like anything else, changed, wore away, grew fierce, grew mild, suffered death but not rebirth, was part of the flux. And how easy it would be to snap the invisible conjunction, like snow geese in Wales, beings in tension, which held him and Paula together

He turned off the highway and climbed left into Arcadia Street. No longer the hero, Marcello Mastroianni, but Graeme Turner, mortal and vulnerable, he parked the car and ran, braving the rain, down the first series of steps which descended to No. 19. The concrete was slippery and he slowed to a half-hop, half-walk past the terraced flowerbeds which Paula had built from rocks on sultry Saturday afternoons and down onto the patio which fronted the house. He paused for a moment, wondering suddenly what to tell Paula should she be awake, and noticed that though the bedroom light was off so was the one in the living-room, which she usually left on when he was home late. A vague uneasiness stirred in him, fuming from gut to mind like alcohol (of which he had certainly had too much that night); it was strangely familiar, yet he found it impossible to identify. He dismissed it as guilt and pushed the front door key into the lock.

As he did so a slight sound from inside the house halted him. It had sounded almost like footsteps; surely there was no one prowling around inside the house in the dark? It certainly wouldn't be Paula, who left a trail of blazing lights wherever she went, expecting as she opened each door that THE OGRE, dread relic of countless children's tales and Norse sagas and half-remembered trolls on frightening islands, would leap out at her. A prowler then? There had been a scare further up the street a couple of months before; if it was some bugger in rubber-soled shoes and a macintosh he had better work out how to tackle him. The rifle, he knew, was in the kitchen where he always kept it next to the broom cupboard; perhaps the best thing would be to go straight for it, hoping to Christ he didn't bump into whoever it was on the way. Or perhaps there was no one there anyhow.

He put his briefcase down on the stone patio, tensed himself, then turned the key and half-ran in through the door. The rifle, he thought, the rifle . . . .

He was halfway to the kitchen, muscles bunched, ready to chop a clenched hand at the throat of any figure which should block his way, when the light suddenly went on in the living-room. A moment later Johnston, bulky and coatless, appeared in the doorway.

'Johnston! What the hell are you doing here?'

'Waiting for you.'

'Waiting for me?' Graeme looked at him, too surprised to even begin thinking. 'In the dark?'

Johnston said nothing. The man's face was shut, brooding; his eyes, beneath closeknit eyebrows, suddenly looked as white and distant as some suppli-cating quattrocento saint in an Italian mural.

Then Paula's voice came from the living-room, impeccably casual but with a ragged edge of strain to it so that it came out higher pitched than normal: 'Is that you Graeme?'

Graeme looked at Johnston's morose, unyielding face, then turned abruptly to shut the front door. A cold gust of rainsmelling wind blew into his face. Time! I need time, he thought, and reached down for his briefcase. Time! What the hell had been happening? Surely not Paula . . . and Johnston? Johnston, who had been drinking with him a brief couple of hours before? Johnston, who knew he was at the Windsor Castle —— Christ! Had he come straight out here? He picked up his briefcase, walked back inside, shutting the door and regarding its tanned and stupid back longer than was necessary. Briefcase? He threw it onto the floor, shouldered his way past Johnston and walked into the living-room. Paula, who avoided his eyes, was busily

200

rearranging chairs in the room; but on the floor still, staring and accusing him, were the two guilty cushions.

'What the hell has been going on here?'

Paula looked up from her unnatural business, her face flushed, her eyes never ceasing to move, and bent over to pick up the two cushions.

'I know what it looks like, but it hasn't,' she said.

'What do you mean it hasn't?'

Anger began to swell inside him, a senseless and unfeigned anger such as he had not felt for years, such as he thought he had long since left behind.

'What do you mean it hasn't? FOR CHRIST'S SAKE, stand still and answer me!'

Paula looked up at him, her face clenched as though she were on the point of breaking down, and glanced helplessly across at Johnston.

'What she means,' said Johnston, who had ambled back into the room, 'is that I have been unsuccessfully trying to — — race her off. The emphasis is on unsuccessful.' Graeme swung around to face him, and Johnston essayed a joke. 'I must be losing my touch.'

Graeme, the cuckold, stared at him, realizing he must behave with dignity, that nothing so unbecame a man whose wife had been unfaithful to him as blind, unreasoning anger, that the only way to salvage any dignity, any respect at all from such a hopelessly undignified situation was to play it cool, play it cool, man; that he should do a Boyer, stroll across the room, reach for a cigarette, except he didn't smoke, contemplate the two of them, think of some sufficiently vicious and final thing to say, a mallet-blunt and irrevocable forever decision which would restore the advantage to him — — but instead felt all his anger and resentment, which he realized he could not fairly vent upon Paula when he had been out until midnight with some other woman, veer around towards Johnston who, as stolid and unforthcoming as before, was standing a few feet inside the doorway. He stared at Johnston, traitor, seducer, wife-fucker.

201

'You bastard! You utter, corrupt bastard!'

'Look who's talking,' said Johnston coolly.

'What do you mean?'

'Paula knows where you've been tonight, sport.'

'So?'

'So she knows you've been knocking Gina off.'

'Did you tell her that?'

'Of course I did. It's true, isn't it? You're a bloody beaut; come storming in here accusing everyone of everything when you've been stirring the porridge of the biggest lay in town.'

For perhaps the first time in his life, and he was soon to regret it, Graeme Turner performed an action without thinking about it first. He half-walked, half-ran the few paces which separated him from Johnston and swung wildly at the shut, heavily creased face. He missed as Johnston, shuffling quickly out of the way, thrust out a protective elbow. It caught Graeme in the stomach and he fell, heavily, to the floor. Johnston moved warily backwards, fists held up in front of him like a prizefighter.

Graeme looked up at him, retching for breath, wondering what to do next. Johnston had a reputation for violence: he stood no chance against him in a brawl. He got up on one knee, his mind racing around stupidly like a headless fowl, vaguely aware of Paula somewhere in the background. What a fool he must look. He hung his head down for several more seconds, waiting for his stomach to stop heaving.

The rifle? The rifle. Onto his feet, along the passageway: in the kitchen corner, .22 calibre muzzle gaping at the ceiling, was the J. G. Anschluss single-shot he had bought for rabbit shooting up the coast. He reached out for it, feeling the German steel of the barrel in his left hand, surprised as always that it should be so heavy for such a small gun. Cradling it under his right arm, he walked back towards the living-room and worked the bolt-action breech, steel slamming against steel.

Johnston was walking almost diagonally away from him

towards where Paula was standing in the corner when he caught sight of the rifle. He stopped short, staring at its obscenely open prick-mouth. Graeme had the idea that Paula was screaming at him, but it seemed to be in the distance somewhere. He raised the rifle to his waist, holding it with both hands, swinging the muzzle around so that it was pointing at Johnston's fat gut. Then, with the habitual movement of years of rabbit and kangaroo shooting, he took up the pressure of the trigger . . . .

The rifle?

That was absurd. Man gutshoots best friend. Twenty years. So much for pacifism. Or cowardice. Cowardice? Paula had weaned him from violence. Who, who are the violent ones? Not us. So that, lifting himself to his feet, he found himself confronted, rifleless, with nothing resolved.

'Johnston,' he said. He was surprised to find that the anger he had felt before, propelling him unthinking at Johnston, had drained away; now he was dissembling it. 'Johnston,' he said, 'get out.'

A long moment of silence hung between them; was Johnston deceived? He gave no indication of moving. Then, with extreme deliberation, the big man walked across to the settee, picked up his houndstooth jacket and strolled along the passageway to the door. Wind and a smell of rain, blackness blowing in from outside: he was gone.

Graeme suddenly felt very tired. He walked listlessly across the room towards where Paula was sitting, unsteady elbows resting on drawn-up knees, and sat down at the other end of the settee. He was utterly exhausted.

Paula stared at him with bright, accusing eyes.

'I hate you!' she said venomously. 'You're everything Johnston says you are. Don't ever touch me again.'

Graeme clasped both hands behind his head and wearily closed his eyes. It was going to be a long night. Some reply, however, was obviously expected of him.

'I don't think I want to,' he said. 'Johnston's been there before, anyhow.'

'That's a dirty thing to say!'

'It's true, isn't it?'

'No, it isn't. Though I'm sorry now I didn't let Johnston sleep with me . . . .'

'What were you doing then?'

'Nothing.'

'I don't believe you.'

'I don't care what you think; you can believe what you like.'

'What were you doing on the floor then?'

Paula didn't reply. Graeme, opening his eyes to watch her reaction, pressed home his advantage.

'Well?'

'That was nothing. I'd already rebuffed him. He was persisting, that's all.'

'And you?'

'I was persisting in saying no.'

'Flat on your back, with the lights out?'

Paula's head swung around abruptly, her face taut. 'I wasn't flat on my back, as you so delicately put it. Johnston turned the light out against my will. I told you, I didn't sleep with him. You can believe it or not, just as you wish. I don't give a damn.'

'How far did you let him go, then?'

'What right have you got to know?'

'What do you mean, what right?' his voice rising to a shout. 'I'm your husband, aren't I?'

Paula gazed unflinchingly at him. 'Sometimes I wonder. Where have you been tonight?'

'I thought,' Graeme said, getting to his feet, walking over to the Parker sideboard, feeling in his coat pocket, emptying car keys, small change, good luck charm, ink pencil and three peppermint Lifesavers into the ornamental teak bowl with mannered ritualism. 'I thought Johnston had already told you all about that.'

'Yes, he did. It wasn't very nice to hear.'

'What wasn't?'

'To find out that you had been sleeping with that Gina

woman —— and that you lied to me when you rang up tonight.'

'Did Johnston tell you that?'

'Yes.'

'He's a liar.'

'And so, darling, are you.'

'Paula, I wasn't lying when I rang up. I'd been going to drink on with Johnston.'

'And?'

'He shot through. Reckoned he had to meet someone at Vadims. I suppose he came straight out here. Were you expecting him?'

'Of course not.'

'Anyhow, I waited on at the pub for him. I got talking to Gina by sheer accident. When the pub closed I took her home. That's all there is to it.'

'Then what were you doing from when you took Gina home till you got here?'

Graeme, pinioned at last, turned back from the sideboard and walked over to the settee. He sat down heavily. He felt as though he had a hangover already —— how many middies had he downed at the Windsor Castle?

'Do you want to know the truth?'

'Yes.'

'I passed out. On her bed. After that I was sick on the floor. Gina was not pleased. I had no intention of sleeping with her anyhow. I was just drunk.'

'That is not a very likely story.'

'Perhaps not —— but it's true. It's so unlikely I wouldn't tell you if it weren't true.'

'I'd like to believe you, Graeme; but you're such a liar. I'll never trust you again —— never, ever.'

'I tell you, I didn't touch Gina. I didn't lay a bloody finger on her. I'm not interested in Gina or any other woman in the push. She's got a good mind and that's all. She attracts me about as much as a visit to the dentist —— which she needs badly anyhow. There's absolutely nothing between Gina and me, Paula. Which is more than I can say for you and Johnston.'

'Graeme, it won't do —— it just won't do. It's no use your trying to shift the guilt onto me, like you always do. I won't stand for it. Johnston came out here simply to take advantage of the fact that you were getting off with Gina, which he was careful to tell me about. And it still didn't do him any good. You're being quite unfair —— which is another thing I should expect from you by now.'

'Besides,' she added after a while, 'that was a stupid, absolutely stupid thing to do, to try to hit Johnston. You know what he's like.'

'What's he like?'

'He could have hurt you.'

Graeme felt that, at long last, his wife was thawing. He reached out an arm along the back of the settee towards her but she shrank away from him as though he had the plague.

'Would you like a drink?'

'No.'

'Paula, I'm sorry about tonight. It was just one of those things. I don't give a stuff for Gina. As for Johnston —— well, I still don't know whether you slept with him or not, but I don't really care. Not any longer.'

'Why don't you?'

'Well —— once I would have died of shame if I found my wife had gone to bed with another man. My pride was terribly important to me then.'

'It seemed pretty important to you tonight . . . .'

'That was just for a moment. I lost my temper. I haven't done that for years. But now I don't care, really. The morality of it doesn't seem to matter any longer. It doesn't make any difference to the way I feel about you; I accept you as you are.'

'Are you being serious?'

'Yes,' he said.

'Graeme . . . .'

'Mind you, that isn't an invitation for you to sleep with anything in trousers that takes your fancy,' he said. 'I

206

don't know: if you feel the need to sleep with someone like Johnston something's wrong with our marriage. That's what really worries me. I don't really care about my pride much any more; but I care about us.'

It was a speech such as might have softened the heart of the veriest termagant, and it did not fail to have its effect upon Paula. 'You're a sloppy old sentimentalist,' she said. 'I care about us too. That's why I didn't sleep with Johnston. I told you I didn't.'

'You're not lying?'

'I'm not lying.'

Her oval face, washed of make-up, the thin, cropped crown of hair, the intent and serious eyes, reassured him.

'I don't know about you, I could do with a drink,' he said.

He returned with a glass of beer in one hand and a gin-and-tonic in the other. Paula accepted the gin. Graeme sat down beside her. The house was absolutely still, silent, as if immersed in sleep. With nothing to measure it by, time ceased to exist; the universe had stopped revolving. This, he thought, must be what this house is like when I am out at night, when Paula is waiting for me to come home. The stillness seemed to swell to unbearable proportions, stifling, suffocating; he felt an irrational desire to get up and smash something, to swing a pick-axe at the jeering plateglass windows, anything to shatter this oppressive and surrealist silence. Instead he sat absolutely still, listening to it swell and swirl around him.

He acted; but his lips had formed the words, and a stream of air had hissed out, before the sound began:

'I tore up those graphics I've been doing for Cassidy today.'

'Tore them up?'

'That's right. Ripped them up and threw them into the harbour. I haven't even got any copies, thank God. They made a nice pattern.'

'Why on earth did you do that? You've been working on them for months.'

207

'I know.' He shrugged. 'I suddenly got disgusted with myself. Here I am churning out crap for bastards like Cassidy when what I should be doing is —— I don't know, something else anyhow. Not graphics for Consolidated. I've never got around to making that film we used to talk about on the boat —— remember? I've still got the script outline in my briefcase; haven't looked at it for years. Haven't even tried to make that documentary on Ocean Street. I walked along it again tonight on the way to the Castle. Fantastic. I'm sure I could work it up into something good.'

'And so?'

'So I've decided to give Cassidy the bypass. It means a couple of thousand dollars down the drain. No holiday for a while, baby. But it'll leave me free for two or three months. I'll ring the ABC tomorrow and put the idea up to them.'

'You've said that before.'

'I know. This time I'm going to.'

'I wish I could believe you.'

The silence returned. It penetrated every corner of the room, veered towards them, threatened to envelop them. Graeme attempted to stave it off.

'We're a fine pair. We've spent the night trying to be faithful to each other. And succeeded. Maybe we've got something going after all.'

'It's not much.'

He peered morosely into his glass. 'If it's all such an effort, maybe we should stop trying.'

'Speak for yourself.'

'You know what I mean. Something must be wrong with our marriage if it takes so much —— sustaining.'

'Any relationship needs a lot of sustaining,' she said. 'It's so corny —— it's just like the agony columns. You have to work at it.'

'It shouldn't be so hard.'

'You expect everything to come easy, Graeme. I sometimes wonder how I could not have realized it earlier on.'

'Why did you marry me, then?'

'I thought I loved you.'

'And now?'

'At times like this, I'm not so sure.'

'You can always leave me, you know.'

'I know that.'

'Do you want to?'

'I'm not sure. Sometimes I think I should —— for your own sake as much as for mine and the children's. You ask too much of everyone, you know: you use them, quite shamelessly. Even your children.'

'You're free; you can do as you like,' he repeated.

'Oh Graeme, you're being stupid. Nobody's free. We all have responsibilities, loyalties —— it's only the push that believes you really can be free, that you owe nobody nothing. And look what it does to them!'

'What does it do to them?'

'I know you admire them. That's why you spend so much time with George and Sonia and all that crowd —— and Gina, I suppose. . . .'

'That's not right.'

'Well, whether it's right about Gina, or not, you spend a lot of your time with them. I sit at home here night after night while you go out drinking with Johnston, or George, or someone else, and then you ring me and tell me that you're not coming home to dinner —— do you know how many times you do that? At least once a week. Sometimes two or three times.'

It was, Graeme felt, time to defend himself. 'You've never really accepted me as I am, have you?' he said.

'What do you mean?'

'It's like I said on the way home from Don's the other night,' he said slowly. 'You know? You set out to change me from the day we got married.'

'I don't think I try to do that.'

'Of course you do. You don't like me spending so much time with the push. You try and clip a man to the shape you'd like, lop off a bit here, a bit there, turn him into a

209

nice little domesticated —— cuckold.'

'Now who's being bitchy? I told you Johnston didn't
. . . .'

'All right, all right. So he didn't. But you know what I
mean. You start off loving someone for the man he is, and
then one morning you wake up and find you've destroyed
all the things you loved about him in the first place.'

'I suppose I should just sit back and let you fool around
with Gina —— which is what you were doing, no matter
what you say —— and never utter a word of protest
because, after all, that's the way you are.'

Graeme shrugged. 'You know I've always been a
womanizer . . .'

'That's lovely, that is! A man's a womanizer, but if
you're a woman you're a nymphomaniac!'

' . . . and I don't take it any further than that. I'm
interested in women; I always have been. But I don't go to
bed with them.'

'But you'd like to?'

'No.'

'You're lying again.'

'Paula, shut up! What's the use of telling you anything if
you're not going to believe it?'

'Well, I have to square what you tell me with what you
do. When your husband comes home at midnight after
spending the night with another woman . . . .'

'We're not going back to that again!'

'No, we're not. All right; so you don't go to bed with
other women. What stops you?'

'Loyalty to you, I suppose.'

'Loyalty. And that's all?'

'Oh no, more than that. Sometimes, just sometimes,
after we've had a row or something . . . .'

'Which occurs so rarely . . . .'

'Which occurs so rarely, sometimes I feel like sleeping
with someone else but, unlike George, I don't. Partly it's
because I know you wouldn't like it. But more . . . well,
even if you didn't know about it, it would change me. It

would make me feel different, make our love quite spurious.'

Paula grimaced. 'Don't talk to me about love.'

'No, I know that's not much use. You spent the first year of our marriage telling me you didn't know what love was.'

'I thought you would bring that up,' she said.

'And why shouldn't I? That bloody motel on the North Coast, and you not even sure you loved the man you married. What a honeymoon!'

'You've always held that against me, haven't you?'

'I suppose so.'

'It's no use trying to remake the past, Graeme. I was very young in those days. I wasn't sure what love was. And I didn't think the words mattered very much.'

'Yes you did. That's why you would never say you loved me.'

'That was a long time ago.'

'I haven't forgotten.'

'Graeme, you'll have to get over it sooner or later. We can't go on tearing each other to pieces for what we have or haven't done. We're just like the others: all the push crowd, they all seem to want to destroy each other. I haven't seen a marriage that works yet.'

'Not even our own?'

'I'm not sure. Look at tonight; it hasn't been a very marvellous night, has it?'

'We don't have rows every night.'

'I sometimes feel the time between rows is spent getting over the last one or preparing for the next.'

'Well, I suppose any two people are bound to fight some of the time; it's a sign that their relationship is alive.'

'Or dying.'

'Have it your own way.'

'No, I didn't mean that. But if you look at us, and you look at the others . . . it depresses me, it really does. I sit at home here, and stew over all these things, and want to talk to you about them; and then you ring up and say you

211

won't be back till late . . . .'

'I'm sorry about tonight.'

'Oh, it's not just tonight, it's all the other tonights. I'm caged up here all day with the children, and the housework, and the washing . . . . Do you know what I found myself thinking today? That all the really good things that have ever happened to me, all the things that I remember with most pleasure, they all happened before I got married. Honestly, Graeme, sometimes I feel that if I spend another hour, another single hour, in this house I'll got out of my tiny mind, I really do; I feel like screaming the place down, picking up the children and rushing off somewhere. I just can't stand it. Not any longer.'

Graeme was silent. In his empty glass suds of beer drained slowly towards their nadir. Through the quiet of the room he could hear, quite plainly, the remorseless ticking of his wristwatch. Normally it was soundless. Now, fidget wheels marked off his span of life. Eternity. The race, stumbling, to the crematorium.

He stood up, walked out to the kitchen, rinsed his glass under the cold water tap and upended it on the white plastic drying rack. The gesture was so habitual, so automatic, that it suddenly became infused with nostalgia. No good things since they had married? What about . . . what about . . . ?

He walked back into the living-room and slumped down in the armchair, well away from Paula. Outside, the storm had blown itself out. Instead of buffeting the gum trees, which he could see dimly through the window, in great gusts of rain, a grey drizzle was falling over Pymble like a benediction. Swollen globules, tear-shaped and heavy-bottomed, clung to the windowpane.

'We'd better get a divorce,' he said slowly.

Paula took a long time to answer. Her glass was still in her hand; she seemed to be staring, unseeingly, at the clinker-brick wall opposite, which they had carefully left unpainted to create some folksy warmth amid the acres of sterile white.

212

'You think it's come to that, then?' she said at last.

'It would seem so. I haven't given you what you wanted. I thought I could, once; but I haven't. Perhaps Richard would have. It wasn't fair that you should lose him.'

'It's not that.'

'No. But the end result is the same. We've failed.'

'I suppose so.'

'Yes.'

The effort had exhausted him. For the second time that night he felt utterly weary, as though nothing in the world mattered as much as sleep. He had not felt like that for years; not since when, working at the nursery-garden by day and going to the university at night, sleep had come to seem the most desirable and gorgeous prize of all, visiting him in the middle of lectures in the most seductive variety of images: in Second Class railway carriages with No Smoking pasted on the window, his head jolting against the wooden window frame as soot blew past the glass and frosty platform lights lit up the nameplates of Harden, Goulburn, Cootamundra; on the top floor of double-decker buses, knees jammed against the seat in front, felt school hat pulled down over his eyes while Pyrmont, Annandale, Leichhardt, Haberfield slid by to a staccato rattle from the bus cord and he hoped, drowsily, too tired to open his eyes, that the conductor would remember to waken him; in the front seat of his father's utility on their visits to the Hendersons down on the South Coast, jolting over the dirt road to the farm at night with rabbits scurrying ahead in the searchlight glare of the headlamps and bottomless pools of black water studding the road like mines, waiting to waylay the truck in treachery; even, sometimes, in his own car when he was at the wheel, certain his eyes were open, jerked awake only by the buffeting of tyrewalls against the kerb, the rasp of wheelrim on concrete, the frantic and instantaneous straining for consciousness, comprehension, reaction as he realized he had been asleep

Which he had been.

For how long?

He sat up and looked around. Paula had disappeared. He listened hard, conscious of how absurd he must look, sitting there like some querulous turkey, a latterday Bertrand Russell, hair awry, face white and drained of blood, the beginnings of next day's beard sprouting like a harsh fungus from his face, suede coat wrinkled from where he had been asleep, one sock up, one sock down. From upstairs, in the attic room, he could hear, faintly, Paula moving around. No doubt she was preparing to go to bed. Should he follow her up? Perhaps she would prefer he didn't; would prefer no more scenes, no more arguing, no more nothing. Perhaps, even now, was preparing to leave him.

Alone?

Immediately, like a multi-episode trailer from the film which he would never make, snatches of the previous day flashed before his mind, projected upon a blank screen of memory: breakfast, TROOPS FOR VIETNAM, Cassidy, the torn squares of paper floating away on the harbour, book conference, the Windsor Castle, George, and Johnston (whom he would never see again), Richard, the Down Under (what was it doing here?), Richard again, dead this time, Poor Paula, Paula and Queen Jane, Fleet Street, Gina, Gina in the Sky with Diamonds, the rifle, WATCH OUT! IT'S LOADED! how prick-ugly, to die here in Pymble with the lorikeets whistling like larrikins and Dad driving the ute WATCH OUT! THE RUT! turning arched over the rain the rain or was it blood-wet roadway while here Johnston whom he would never see you there lad the slot the wave and George shouting at the demo WATCH OUT! at your back the wipeout machine the wipeout when one fucking stupid mistake could tear the North Coast honeymoon labour ward children when the sun goes out from stringback fingers her too with her childhood flames and closecropped hair the arrow the sunscorched arrow always to move with purity of flight

from loneliness aloneness alone
    which, curled up like foetus in armchair womb of
Paulalessness, at last, he was

Orange bowls on the breakfast table, a clean life and well-ordered, two spoons for the children, two forks, the blue-and-white check tablecloth which her mother had given her as a wedding present —— or had it been for her glory box? —— everything in its place, the last twist of the knife or perhaps of one of those thin slivers of glass from the shampoo bottle which she had knocked to the bathroom floor, an accident of course, though if there were no accidents but only Freudian volitions was the spurt of blood which had disfigured those white tiles as she had vouchsafed to Richard her own bloodstained virginity a symbol of some new sacrifice or some new womanhood? The idea was too fantastical as, confronted by an ordinariness of orange bowls, shower-cleansed of what remained of the night, she waited for the family to awaken and watched the light seep around the edges of the trees beyond the balcony their trunks barring her from the world outside so that even now, as she lay utensils monotonously on the breakfast table and watched the morning yellow begin to trickle down the trunks and across the balcony, they merely emphasized her alienation.

Alienation?

Of course it was typical of Johnston to use both his own philosophic detachment and her own domestic disenchantment to his own ends, to try to capitalize upon them for the sake of a quick fuck, and certainly she should have had more sense than to have been deceived, even fleetingly, by Johnston's labyrinthine blandishments which, she was sure, she would have resisted sooner or later, though just how much later had not Graeme walked in the door before Johnston had had time to exploit the advantage created by her shock at such crude evidence of Graeme's infidelity she did not know; for what would a swift bout of adultery with Johnston have proved, what solved?

And here, caught in the intricate spider's web of orange bowls, barred trees and established affections, she sighed; for she had a sudden vision of her life stretching endlessly before her, as boring and unvaried and predictable as a gibber plain, pegged out by domestic appliances and a demanding husband and the clutching hands of children, hairy male and hairless female hands piling stone on stone to create the ritual mound in which, eventually, the sacrificed body of the wife-mother would lovingly be buried . . . . But that, she thought, shaking her head firmly at the wall calendar on which, with one of her husband's ink pencils, she obliterated yet another day, Friday, that was nonsense, a paperback nightmare bought cheap from a rack of women's magazines and agony columns, a scary chimera conjured up by some sob sister who, witty, pithy and wise, vented upon her careerless sisters her own envious spinster's sexual spleen; for she had, after all, married voluntarily, had borne children voluntarily, certain within herself that that, truly, was what she desired; and had thus created, through her cleaving to what she felt, rather than knew, was right for her a way of life which others envied, or pitied, or opposed, and which Johnston, to whom any challenge unsurmounted was a form of defeat, felt obliged to destroy. But had she gone wrong somewhere? Had her instinct, if that was not too perilously close to the woman's intuition which she had always rejected, unwittingly let her down? And if so, where?

She turned back to the kitchen dresser, reaching with the same instinct which had apparently proved so disastrous in her past life for the table napkins which would match the orange breakfast bowls, conscious that in this, her thirtieth year to heaven, with one day gone, another day to go, the children awake in the room upstairs and a husband talking of divorce, something must have gone wrong somewhere; her mind circling back, searching along the edge of memory like a gull the wind's tide, wondering where the oyster-grain of discontent lay, where, where: her mother, plump and high of voice, love's eunuch? an inturned girlhood, a university of books, not brew-ups? a dearth of Richards, a solace of Graemes? a slow degeneracy into wifeliness, motherhood, incarceration? Where, where? But there seemed no break; try as she could, each phase led as inexorably as the moon's to the next, the flow was uninterrupted, it was the same stream no matter where her memory stepped in and stepped out; she could seize no instant, no decision, crossroads, crucible, crux, crisis, and say here, here it was, here I turned against the grain, splinters began, grew to fragments, fragmented, tore the whole apart; she could not, led by God or by any other deity over her past life, have said here, this I would have changed, this was wrong, here the turnaway, blind, to a different destiny, the present instead of perfect self; the cotton thread which had guided her Theseus-like through the labyrinth was unbroken, unflawed, consistent — and, like Theseus's, led to the wrong conclusion. If there were any fault-line, it was in Richard's death. And yet, though she had turned what they had been together over and over again in her mind in the intervening years she had never been able to persuade herself, despite what she knew to be an execrable capacity for self-delusion, that it could have been any different. Not that Richard need have died; they should all, and she especially, have saved him from that. But though she comforted herself so often by remembering him, reworking and recreating all that had occurred between them, embalming him in a cocoon of remembered sensuality, she knew in her heart, had always known, in fact, that a week before his death their affair had, in its reality if not in its forms, come to an end.

Richard walked across and switched the radio off with an abrupt twist of his hand, choking the BBC announcer in mid-sentence. Paula, sitting on the divan with her legs crossed, tried to look composed.

'So you're going back,' she said.

'Yes,' said Richard. 'I have to.'

'You mean you want to.'

'No, have to. What else can I do? I'll be too late for the funeral. But at least I can be around, wind up her affairs, all that sort of thing. And there's my sister. I can't get out of it.

'Back to the womb.'

Richard shrugged. 'I owe Mother something, even if it is too late.'

'But Richard, she's dead now. I don't want to seem callous, but I can't believe that's the only reason you're going back. There must be something else. Why can't you tell me?'

Richard, ill at ease, walked around the room with both thumbs hooked over the belt of his jeans. He stopped in front of the radio, switched it on and off before any sound could emerge, swung back again. 'I don't know,' he said at last. 'I really don't understand it, even myself. It just seems the time has come. I feel I must return, get back to where I started from. If I stay here any longer, God knows what will happen. I get terribly depressed sometimes. I don't seem to know where I'm going, what I'm trying to do. I feel if I go home I might be able to start all over again. A clean beginning, no history, just like joining the Army. Do you ever feel like this?'

'About Australia?'

'Yes. This need to get back, find yourself again, connect up with the person you were. I feel —— stranded here, isolated, something that's been washed up on Hastings beach. The adventure's over. I don't want to make another trip to the Continent; if I saw the inside of another cathedral, honestly, I'd scream. I need to see my sister again, and my mother's family, see what's happened to

219

them while I've been away. See what's happened to me, too. It's over.'

Paula looked around the oh-so-familiar room: peeling plaster, divans along the wall, dirty coffee cups on the table, an ashtray crammed with cigarette butts, blankets drooping to the unswept floor. For a while, when she first knew Richard, she had tried to keep the flat in some semblance of order, had even cleaned out the main room with a carpet sweeper and hot water a couple of times, but had soon abandoned the attempt. Richard and Don were more fastidious than the others, and the room they shared always had a cared-for look about it (Don even went so far as to buy flowers regularly for the landlady's chipped cream window vase) but the rest of the flat reflected the disarray of their lives.

Richard was standing awkwardly near the table, reaching into his jeans for a packet of cigarettes, as graceful as ever in his faded denim shirt, big-buckled belt, Oxford fringe brushed forward, the gentle but pronounced curvature of his face obscured as he leant forward, hands cupped, to light a cigarette. It was a gesture which she knew so well, which she had observed so many times, that it wrenched at her. The flesh-warmth of us against the world, she thought; for a while, by clinging to each other, we can defy the knife, but soon we'll be torn from each other, our flesh severed, and we'll be alone and bleeding again. What does it mean?

Merely, no doubt, that he doesn't love me.

'And so,' she said, 'is our little affair.'

Richard glanced embarrassedly at her. 'You'll be coming back to Australia soon.'

'I'm not so sure —— I've not been here as long as you. There's still a lot I wish to do. But that's all beside the point. Once you've gone, you've gone.'

Richard came over and put an arm around her, turning his head to blow the cigarette smoke away from her face. She felt the familiar weight of his arm upon her shoulders, smelt the familiar odour of denim and Gauloises which

220

always clung to him, saw the fair hair which laced his wrist like cobwebs — and yet, already, the sudden closeness which she had felt a few seconds before at an equally familiar gesture was fading, retiring to a safe distance. Was she already girding herself for their separation?

'Paula love, I don't want to leave you. You mean a great deal to me, as you know. Why don't you come too?'

Was it an invitation? Or was he just trying to be kind? She hardly bothered to consider it.

'Back to Australia? Just like that?'

'Why not? You're not going to stay over here forever and ever. We could go back on the same ship.'

'And?'

'I love you, Paula.'

She turned her face towards him, withdrawing a little so she could see his quizzical blue eyes, then kissed him lightly on the cheek.

'You don't have to say that,' she said. 'There's no need to.'

'But I do.'

'Richard, you don't love me — not really,' she said quietly. 'You tell me you do and I suppose you want to; but you don't. Inside you're quite cold and ... untouchable, somehow. You've always been beyond reach. I don't think you know how to love; you certainly don't love me.'

'That's not true . . . .'

'Yes it is, and you know it. You say all the right things, and I suppose you mean them in a funny sort of way. I suppose they're as true for you as they ever will be. But really you're quite uninvolved. I'm sorry for you in a way. Someone'll rescue you from your selfishness one day, but it isn't going to be me.'

Richard took his arm from around her, dragging at his cigarette. He blew the smoke towards the ceiling in a long exhalation of breath that was almost a sigh.

'Are you just being bitchy because I'm going?'

'No.'

221

'You've never said anything like this before.'

'Yes I have —— on that first night you tried to sleep with me, and I didn't want to. You like to experience a fashionable sense of love, but that's all it amounts to.'

'Don't, Paula.'

'I'm sorry, Richard. I'm not trying to hurt you. It's just that sometimes your . . . your utter indifference wounds me. Female vanity, I suppose. I give all of myself to you, or try to, and you just take it as your right. I sometimes think you are more involved in your friends than me. All of you, in a way: you, Don, Graeme, even Johnston. Women are just accessories for you; you reserve your real emotions for your mates.'

'That's not true. I love you more than I've ever loved anyone.'

'I suppose so.'

'There's no way I can prove it, Paula; if I could I would.'

All of a sudden she reached out to him, resting her hand lightly on his arm. 'I believe you, Richard. I suppose you do love me in your own way. But it shows something about us both, doesn't it? We neither of us care enough to alter our lives for each other. It's hardly the grand passion.'

'Did you ever think it was?'

'I suppose not,' she lied. 'But I was a virgin, remember? I still haven't gone to bed with anyone else. It's about time I did.'

'Don't,' he repeated.

'What do you mean, don't? You're casting me aside like an old trollop —— why shouldn't I start acting like one? Johnston would like to sleep with me, I know. Why should I keep myself for you?'

Richard looked so ludicrously hurt she didn't know whether to laugh or cry. Why, he's just a baby, she thought, wondering why she hadn't realized it before. She splayed her fingers through his hair. 'I can't come with you, Richard. Much as I'd like to. Whatever you say, this is the end of our little affair. But —— we've plenty of time together before you leave, haven't we?'

'Of course.' He drew back, half-puckish, half-apprehensive. 'It's all right, then?'

'It's all right,' she said, reaching up towards him; adding as an afterthought, addressing herself rather than Richard: 'But one day I hope you get hurt, like you've hurt me.'

How many times since then, writhing, had she wished those words back? For five days later Richard was dead, and she was to blame . . . .

No: she could not, would not, add guilt for Richard's death to her burden of memories which, mumbled over like rosary beads, already weighed too heavily upon her life. She had not meant those spleenful words, an involuntary response uttered in a moment of sorrow. In the days which followed she and Richard had seen almost as much of each other as before, though he had been more withdrawn than usual. No: it must have been the crisis in Richard's life, his mother's death and the prospect of returning to Australia and everything else that had followed, which was comprehensible, surely, only to his very closest friends, such as Don, that had precipitated that final, obliterating depression

Richard Don Richard

Her memory grasped at something, faltered, veered away again

It was so long ago

No: she could not bear the burden of guilt for Richard's death. Nor could she, equally, blame upon that blind and smog-omened night when Graeme, at her doorway, had blurted out what had happened, the shape of her own life. Had she loved Richard? Of course; and yet, she thought, and yet there were varieties of love. Ever since that first, disastrous day on the island she had been hopelessly, inextricably involved in Richard as she could have been only with her first love. Richard had represented everything to her: safety, a refuge, rockfast security in an alien world. But the intensity of her involvement in

Richard had been more a measure of her own compulsions than anything else. Neither of them had ever considered getting married. From the start, somehow, they had thought of what they shared as an affair: not a prelude, but a complete and precious unity in itself. And even before Richard's decision to return home they had both begun to feel the strain of such an unaccustomedly close relationship, she by one of her rare onsets of pimples ('you need sex, dearie, to keep a clear skin' —— which was a lie, not to say clever propaganda, for she and Richard had been sleeping together so regularly it was only by the grace of God and Durex that she had not become pregnant), Richard by bouts of moodiness and sour introspection which had culminated finally in that farcical night of Gromolski's party, which he had gone to by himself while she waited at Earls Court expecting to see him walk in the door at any minute, until at eleven o'clock she had taken off her shoes, stockings, new brown-and-rust check skirt which she had bought only a few days before at C&A's and had flounced, alone, into bed. She had been furious, absolutely furious, with him.

And a few days later . . . .

Richard: the fine gentle hair like rain, the wry and tight-cheeked smile as though at some secretive, ironic joke, the smooth skin which he shaved only every couple of days ('should I grow a beard? a courtier's, perhaps' his face grinning at her in the bathroom mirror), the slender wrists like a ballet dancer's, the Gauloises stuck in his shirt pocket like a badge, the deep creases from the guitar strings in his fingertips so that, when he ran a hand over her bare skin, there was an unexpected and uncharacteristic roughness to his touch . . . Richard: they were all to blame.

Paula Turner reached up to the dresser for wheat germ, Farex and brown sugar, fumbling awkwardly because of the band-aid around her cut finger. She glanced at it briefly, noticing in passing the wrinkles etched ever more deeply into her ageing skin. Yes, certainly it would have been easy enough to discern there, in Richard's suicide, the fault-line in her life —— but dishonest. Whether he had lived or died (and she did not always admit this to herself, least of all when, brought to the brink of neurosis by this her desperate and daily round, she retreated to images of Richard to comfort and assuage her, investing him with all the virtues which she knew only too well her husband did not possess and erasing all those quirks and marks of utter self-concern which, once, she had known only too well marred his manhood), the death of their parting was already upon them. Search as she might, the thread was unbroken. This moment, this insignificant and empty moment of domestic drudgery and household routine, this habitual and unthinking gesture by a housewife alone in a kitchen in Pymble, surrounded by a cathedral of trees and burdened by a sleep of children, seemed the logical outcome of everything that had ever happened to her and everything she had ever been.

The thought made her pause: she finished setting the table and walked over to the balcony window, staring out through the trunks of the gumtrees to the yellow creek which wound through reeds, blackberry bushes, lantana and the occasional stunted willow at the bottom of the slope. It was now quite light and, above her, she could hear the children beginning to waken and chatter to each other. Only James could talk, but the baby did the best she could, lolling nonsense syllables from her tongue and experimenting with new inflections from her cotside. The overnight storm had cleared, though high overhead she could see the scalloped edges of drifting clouds; it seemed to have washed the slope clear of summertime dust and drabness, so that everything, clay, fallen bark, willow branches, clumps of kikuyu grass, crumbling sandstone ledges, took to itself a new and artificial brilliance. As always, the scene both reassured and disturbed her: reassured, because she now knew it so well, knew its moods and vagaries and felt calmed by its incontrovertible beauty; disturbed, because her mind had never quite come to terms with landscape of any sort, had never been able either to rid it completely of anthropomorphism or to graft upon it some completely acceptable emotional texture, so that it, and her reaction to it, was always shifting, unstable, the quick-change correlative of her own moods.

Which, in a way, now she came to think of it, was precisely the way she felt about marriage. Perhaps she had never come to terms with that either. There were times when she felt that her life with Graeme and the children gave her all she could possibly ask of life, having always assumed in an old-fashioned and, she supposed, thoroughly romantic way that the shape of her existence would be taken from the man she loved and the family she created — when she felt compassionate, enriched, multifoliate, the still centre of an infinitely variable world which cherished and sustained her and which she in her turn nourished for what in fact was the reason for having children (would she have more?) if not that it simply gave you more people to love; there were other times when she felt not only that it was excruciatingly demeaning, a death of any woman's spirit (which, somehow, she was prepared to forgive — romantic self-sacrifice again?) but also, as the night before, that it was (and this was not forgivable) a ghastly and nightmarish mistake, because she had, through blindness, accident, rebounce, Fate, self-delusion or sheer stupidity, married the wrong man.

Her memory circled back again, searching over the events of that chaotic yesterday: Johnston, the bath, the shock she felt at Graeme's betrayal (or was it betrayal?), the sound, irrelevantly, of the rain slashing against the kitchen window pane, the children asleep, Johnston's persistence, her own surprising vulnerability — surprising to her, at least — the tedious and only too familiar argument, though this time a new element had entered: divorce.

Did Graeme really think they should get a divorce? Did she think so? What of the children, chattering away like magpies up there (she would have to dress them soon, and also wake Graeme who, when she crept out of bed, was sleeping off what would no doubt be one hell of a hangover) —— or weren't they the deciding factor? After all it was a husband and wife thing, something between a man and a woman. She thought suddenly of her mother, blue-rinsed and selfpossessed, her honour sacrosanct, her chance of happiness shattered . . . . Divorce! To think that it had come to that, that she, of all people, who had sworn never to let what had happened to her mother occur to her, who had always demanded, Buchmanlike, Absolute Safety and Absolute Stability, should now be considering, quite calmly and with no emotion except perhaps a low-temperature resentment that Graeme should have brought her to this, should now be considering the possibility of breaking apart from her husband.

Or was she?

Was she really?

And here, surely, was the crux of the matter. For, despite what had happened last night, the shouting and arguing and the double-headed coin (Gina on one side, Johnston on the other) of deception which they had used against each other, rung in for the service of a deadlier and more potent game than two-up, despite the numbing confirmation of her fears about her husband and the almost equally numbing discovery of doubts about herself, despite the waste of spirit which had afflicted her all day, all week really, and had made of this her sun-shrined and willow-blessed home a barred prison constructed brick by brick from one man's ego, despite this and everything else which had gnawed at her vitals in how many was it? four years, yes four years of marriage; despite this and so much more she still, nevertheless, did not really consider leaving him; did not really, standing there, watching the unwinking sandstone ledges and the slight glance of light upon what, though she could not see it, must have been the creek's mottled surface, listening to the children becoming more impatient and the day's routine looming

227

closer without possibility of defiance or even, unfortunately, radical reshaping, find herself steeling her nerves to walk out as, once, before they were married, she had; did not think about it at all really, but rather found her mind casting aimlessly and without apparent resolution over the surface of what had happened to discern what, what fresh insight, if any, what fresh truth she could wrest from her marriage.

Nor, though she could not be sure, of course, had the disordered sequence of events which still ran through her mind, merging and jumping back and thrusting forward and falsifying, like some badly jumbled and manic movie, nor had that seemed to jolt Graeme out of his unassailable, infuriating, all-assuming certainty about themselves; for when, at long last, he had dragged himself upstairs hours after she had left him fast asleep in the armchair, she, threequarters asleep in the low double bed and yet, with part of her being, at least, waiting for him, had felt his arm go around her waist, not to waken her, nor supplicatingly, nor even as a gesture of reconciliation, but simply the unconscious and inevitable gesture of the man to whom she had been married for so long, as though this were a pattern of habit and affection beyond all chance of alteration or destruction by their poor wills, the sum and irrefrangible total of all their past lives, instants, quarrels, doubts, conversations, actions, involvements, emotions —— love?

Perhaps that, in the end, was all they had in common: a stubborn, unfashionable, quixotic, self-wounding, despairing, death-fated, yet shared, belief in love. Even if they rarely lived up to it.

She turned back from the window. She felt curiously free, as though some burden, some crippling and long-sustained wound of the emotions had at last been cast aside, shed like an outworn skin. What was it? She walked back to the kitchen, hearing the door slam upstairs —— James? Or Graeme? She half-filled a saucepan with hot water from the tap, placed it on the stove, flicked the switch to 'simmer' and reached, automatically, for eggs from the wooden rack along the wall.

Of course: the island. It was as though her consciousness of it, the long years of regret and harking back, the perpetual striving to recreate it, had been washed away without a trace during the rainstorm which had beaten against the windowpane and against their lives during the night. Thoughts raced through her mind, stumbling in their effort to find cohesion, jostling against each other, struggling for formulation; she felt excited, keyed up, as though something terribly important, something quite crucial and explicative was about to materialize here, precisely here, before her in this unlikely kitchen in Pymble. Of course, she thought; of course, there was no island. She had demanded it all her life, striven for it; and perhaps, as a child, she had indeed possessed it. But her childhood had disappeared on that other island in the sun-stricken Aegean with Richard and, strive as she might to resurrect it, the attempt was futile. There was no island. Life was as turmoiled, as current-torn, as beset by unfathomable tide shifts and sea rips as that foam-strewn bowl of ocean, edged about by mountains and adorned by one shining crescent of sand, where she and Graeme had spent their honeymoon and which, ripped this way and that, clutched at by unseen currents, wind-whipped and storm-stirred into one vast, heaving, cyclonic infinity of water, seemed to her now that which she had been journeying across all her years. There was no island. Her vision of safety had been a delusion, the fairytale dream of the child who had thought all that seawaste presupposed a landfall. One outgrew it, like one outgrew God. It had been the temporal in her clutching at — — immortality?

With a rush, a tumble, a gusto of pyjama-clad energy, James exploded into the room. He was clutching at the cord of his trousers with one hand, hitching them up to his waist, hair awry, eyes alight, a smile like Graeme's sprawled across his face. For an instant he stood there, transfixed momentarily in the doorway like a sodium-glare still, happily defying the edict that made the kitchen out of bounds before breakfast; then, with staccato rimshot of feet, was gone. She smiled at where he had been, checked the orange bowls on the table, the simmer switch on the stove, thinking: that, really, is the only immortality.

But even as she turned to the door to dress the children for breakfast the questions started up again. Immortality? Hardly; a child alive was no comfort to the corpse in the grave. Perhaps, in some subtle chemistry which she did not understand, the parents lived on in their children; though, if one could believe what one read, which one couldn't always, of course, it was less her and Graeme's unique arrangement of chromosomes which counted for most but rather the infinite daily round of familial existence; less their blood coursing through their children's veins but rather their uncertainties and philosophies, such as they were, precipitated not in their children's bloodstream but in their — well, hearts, she supposed; which meant . . . ?

She didn't know; it was too hard, too complex a skein to unravel. She began to climb the stairs to where the children and, above them again, her husband awaited her. Already the excitement she had known a few minutes before had disappeared; her day had returned to its familiar and mundane level, the Irish-weave carpet relinquished no mysteries, the white plasterboard ceiling stared back as blankly and unremittingly as ever. From the children's room she could hear James trying to engross the baby in conversation; from the bedroom above, silence. Perhaps she had better leave Graeme to sleep on; time enough later for him to descend with a hangover, remorse and a laughable determination to be, forever after, amen, the Perfect Husband. She reached the landing and turned, briskly, to face for the millionth time the stairs, children, husband and a life of questions.

*Some more Australian Penguins
are described on the
following pages*

Thomas Keneally

A Dutiful Daughter

'It is the duty of a good child to let
his parents know the second they
turn into animals...'

When Barbara Glover reached
puberty, her parents suddenly
assumed bodily forms so unnatural
that they had to be kept from the
world and tended like farm animals.
Uncertain whether she or they caused
the 'accident', she has found herself
bound in dominance over them,
impelled by a fierce love to organize
them and her younger brother
around the family's affliction.
   A Dutiful Daughter is the act of
an exceptional and provocative
imagination, an authentic specimen
of the new fiction which is not content
merely to reproduce realities but
insists on making them up.

Barry Oakley

Let's Hear It for Prendergast

Prendergast is 'the tallest poet in the
world'. A refugee from the dullness
of commerce, he moves in on his
old and unwilling school buddy
Morley, who from then on follows at
a discrete distance inspecting the
wreckage as Prendergast goes from
one fiasco to another.

But the world Prendergast is trying
to inflame is made of asbestos –
rock-solid Melbourne manages to
resist all his guerilla attacks on
conformity, censorship, Moomba and
the Shrine of Remembrance, till he
goes down in an explosive and
spectacular climax.